AFRICA'S EXODUS TO THE PROMISED LAND

THE JOURNEY OF BLACK PEOPLE FROM EDEN LOST TO EDEN RESTORED

SEDNAK KOJO DUFFU ASARE YANKSON

AFRICAN VOICE IN THE AMERICAN WILDERNESS

Pre-Publication GC Edition
Copyright © 2010 Sankofa Heritage Books
Sednak Kojo Duffu Yankson
sedy7@hotmail.com
http://www.africasroots.com
Tel. (516) 486-6385

Printed in the United States
ISBN: 978-0-9770261-1-1

FOREWORD

Dr. Me rvyn A. Warren (Provost a   nd Professor of Preaching Oakwood University)

As if you haven't noticed, the "D ark Continent" is shedding voluminous light these days. What would ancient pundits say, those who pinned the starless label on Africa, if they were privileged to witness today her latest unearthed links to a rich Christian heritage -- one more valuable than her famously pillaged diamonds and gold? Indeed, in recent years, impartial scholars are now calling attention to what might be called the "blow up of the cover up," meaning that which for centuries has been suppressed or unknown about the Motherland is now coming to full view.

Interestingly enough, the special recoverables of Africa have become a trilogy: her lost precious minerals, her lost culture, her lost Christian heritage. Among this trinity of wealth and experience, the latter might be the most contemporary shot heard around the world. Why? It is because the Christian religion in Africa is something we have traditionally traced and dated to those worthy eighteenth, nineteenth, and twentieth century missionary endeavors when, according to what we are coming to know more clearly, Christianity enjoyed a home there long before. If our coming of age and understanding are correct, those invaluable and sacrificial missionaries added priceless ingredients and icing to a cake which had already been on the menu and tasted all along.

Would you like to know more? Then join in this volume the journey by Sednak Yankson who will take you on a salvation safari the likes of which you have not known before or will soon forget. From our college classroom days together (his student inquiries taught me the listening teacher), his seminars at ministerial and instructional conventions, his steady pen-to-paper output together with his pastoral and pulpit work all feed into his passion to get the word out about Africa's ultimate voyage -- the Promised Land! Enjoy the trip and be blessed!

ACKNOWLEDGEMENTS & DEDICATION

Again all glory goes to God for placing on me His call to ministry and for inspiring my mind to accomplish this project. I thank the Great God of Heaven and the Father of our Lord and Savior Jesus for laying the ideas of this book on my heart.

I salute all my friends who have been supportive in the accomplishment of this project. And that goes:

To all the churches that have given me the opportunity to share with them excerpts of this message, especially East New York where I minister at the moment.

To Mr. Oswald Greene for the cover design and other illustrations. It was genius of you to capture a vision in my head and display it on a canvass in such vivid colors.

To Dr. Ermine Leader for her input in the editing and to Pastor Charles Leader for recommending his beloved wife!

To Pastor C. Manie, Pastor I. Lewin, Dr. C. English, and Winnie Benjamin (Yaa Asantewaa) for graciously looking over this project; ensuring that every "t" is crossed and every "i" is dotted. A thousand thanks to the numerous people whose encouragement has helped to make this project a success! Best of all, a million thanks to my family for your gracious understanding in allowing me to write!

I dedicate this book to all the churches I have pastored since I began my ministry. When our journey on earth is over and Jesus comes to claim His own, may we all be accounted worthy to present our gifts unto Him at His Inauguration when He is Crowned King of Kings and Lord of Lords on Mount Zion. See you all there; by the Throne of God, by the Grace of God! To God be the Glory, great things He has done. Amen! And Amen!

TABLE OF CONTENTS

PROLOGUE

THE MOVEMENT OF "YAH" PEOPLE TO THE PROMISED LAND

By the time the fool has learned the game the players have gone home. (African proverb)

We are not there yet! We are on our way to Eden! We have many rivers to cross, oceans to traverse and mountains to climb, but with the assurance that "we as a people will get to the Promised Land."

Meanwhile, they have taken away our names, our history, our culture, our achievements and our heritage and given us falsified view of ourselves and we call it progress. This fallacy is the fundamental malady of the modern black 'man' in America and in all colonized Africa. To restore us to wholeness is to restore the truth about us; our history, identity, spirituality, heritage, culture and destiny.

We must know the truth about our royal noble past, our historic intellectual achievements and our spiritual leadership roles. We must know that our ancestors were the builders of great ancient civilizations, mighty kingdoms and powerful empires. We must know our heritage backwards and forwards; past slavery to Saharan Empires, past Timbuktu to Mesopotamian Empires and past the Flood all the way to the Garden of Eden? We ought to know our African heritage past Slavery to Emancipation/Independence, past Neo-colonialism and poverty to our future vindication and restoration.

We must establish the truth about the identity of our African ancestors; the Egyptians, the Ethiopians, the Sumerians and the Mesopotamians and know where we are coming from so we may know where we are going. We must know we lived in Eden where one river refreshing the Garden flowed out into four parts; to Gihon, Pison, Euphrates and Hiddekel. It was Ethiopia; Africa which was encompassed by Gihon; Pison went through Havilah, Hiddekel (Tigris) flowed towards Assyria and Euphrates covered Mesopotamia; all in the land of Ham (Genesis. 2:10-14). We lived in Eden. Our empires stretched out from Ethiopia to India; from the Nile to the Tigris all the way even to the Ganges. The Nile was our cradle and the Niger took us in. We crossed over the Red Sea and the Dead Sea was in our backyard. We played in the Jordan, Euphrates refreshed our feet and the Tigris and the Ganges were within our reach, and all of these were in our domain.

1

We built empires along the way. The Sumerian, the Acadian, the Assyrian and the Babylonian Empires were all Cushite. After building the Empires of Mesopotamia, we went on to build the Egyptian and the Ethiopian Empires. From there we went on to build the Carthaginian and the Phoenician Empires and then we built the Saharan Empires. We built Ghana and Mali Empires on gold and the Songhai Empire on books producing the most famous University in the world on the Sahara Desert in the Motherland.

From the inception of history, we have been on the move. From Eden, we encamped in Mesopotamia and onward to East Africa, then to North Africa, and through the interior of Africa, and now scattered all over Africa and around the world. We are still moving! We are on our way to the Promised Land: we are going to Eden. Langston Hughes captures our journey in pictures:

> I have known rivers, ancient, dusky rivers. I've known rivers.
> I've known rivers ancient as the world, and older than the flow of
> human blood in human veins.
> My soul has grown deep like the rivers.
> I bathed in the Euphrates when dawns were young.
> I built my hut near the Congo and it lulled me to sleep.
> I looked upon the Nile and raised the pyramids above it.
> I heard the singing of the Mississippi when
> Abe Lincoln went down to New Orleans,
> And I've seen its muddy bosom turn all golden in the sunset.
> I've known rivers: Ancient, dusky rivers.
> My soul has grown deep like the rivers.[1]

Ours has been an impossible journey but God who brought us on our way, has made it possible! Through many dangers, toils and snares we have come. 'Tis Grace that brought us safe thus far and Grace will lead us home. But, we have more rivers to cross and mountains to climb and so we are going to need instructions along the way. Walden Johnson provide from experience:

> Stony the road we trod, bitter the chast'ning rod,
> Felt in the days when hope unborn had died;
> Yet with a steady beat, have not our weary feet
> Come to the place for which our fathers sighed?

> We have come over a way that with tears has been watered,
> We have come, treading our path through the blood of the
> slaughtered, Out from the gloomy past, 'til now we stand at last
> Where the white gleam of our bright star is cast.

> God of our weary years, God of our silent tears,

---

[1] Langston Hughes, http://www.poetryarchive.org.

Thou who has brought us thus far on the way;
Thou who has by Thy might, led us into the light,
Keep us forever in the path, we pray.

Lest our feet stray from the places, our God, where we met Thee,
Lest, our hearts drunk with the wine of the world, we forget Thee;
Shadowed beneath Thy hand, may we forever stand,
True to our God, true to our native land[2]

Hughes and Johnson captured our history poetically. Martin Luther King captured our destiny prophetically! Through him we catch a glimpse of our glorious destination when he prophesied on that last fateful night:

> "I just want to do God's will. And He's allowed me to go up to the mountain. And I've looked over. And I've seen the Promised Land. I may not get there with you. But I want you to know tonight, that we, as a people, will get to the Promised Land. And I'm happy, tonight. I'm not worried about anything. I'm not fearing any man. **Mine eyes have seen the glory of the coming of the Lord.**"[3]

"The Glory of the Coming of the Lord," is our destination and not the American dream! It was about this promise that Dr. King dreamed, "that one day every valley shall be exalted, and every hill and mountain shall be made low, the rough places will be made plain and the crooked places will be made straight and the glory of the Lord shall be revealed and all flesh shall see it together."[4]

It was about this promise that King called us "to speed up that day when all of God's children, black men and white men, Jews and Gentiles, Protestants and Catholics, will be able to join hands and sing in the words of the old Negro spiritual, 'Free at last, free at last. Thank God Almighty, we are free at last.'" That's when the redeemed (Revelation says) will stand on the sea of glass and sing the song of Moses and the song of the Lamb!

"We've got some difficult days ahead. But it doesn't matter with us now because we've been to the mountaintop and our eyes have seen the glory of the coming of the Lord!" We are going to Eden. That's what this book: _Africa's Exodus to the Promised Land: the Journey of Black People from Eden Lost to Eden Restored_ is all about. The journey may be difficult but we have a prophecy that says; "We as a people will get to the Promise Land!" So, Keep On Walking Until We See The Glory Of The LORD!

---

[2] James Weldon Johnson; (1871-1938)
ttp://en.wikipedia.org/wiki/Lift_Every_Voice_and_Sing
[3] Martin Luther King Jr.
http://www.americanrhetoric.com/speeches/mlkihaveadream.htm
[4] http://www.extension.umn.edu/units/diversity/mlk/mlk.html.

3

PART 1

BIBLICAL
HISTORICAL
AFRICA

Brief Historical Narrative Of The Motherland

CHAPTER ONE

AFRICA'S MESOPOTAMIAN ROOTS

If You Refuse To Be Made Straight When You Are Green And Young, You Cannot Be Straightened Up When You Are Dry And Hard. (African proverb)

Who were the Egyptians?

There still exist the nagging questions about the identity of the ancient Egyptians. There has been so much conjecture about the identity of the ancient Egyptians who built the pyramids. Some say they were Black, others say they were White. By the account of an important "eyewitness," Herodotus, the man Western scholarship credits as the father of history, we will look down the corridors of history to see for ourselves the true identity of the Egyptians and Ethiopians. The truth we will have to contend with is the discovery that Egyptian Civilization was a true African Civilization and the pyramids were indeed built by African ingenuity.

So who were the Egyptians? Modern historians do not qualify to speak about the identity of the Ancients without consulting ancient historians. The most credible way of dealing with this question is to find the answer from the ancient historians themselves, rather than relying on modern historians who have to conjecture or relate secondary information to us. We go to ancient sources or eyewitness accounts and then supplement them with other secondary information.

> "The first eyewitness we call to the floor is [the] ancient (white) Greek historian Herodotus. He is recognized by many as the first great historian and the father of History somewhere around 457-450 B.C. He wrote in the Histories that: 'The Colhians, Ethiopians and Egyptians have thick lips, broad nose, woolly hair and they are burnt of skin.' (Can you imagine someone with that description in Mississippi, in the 1940s, demanding to sit in the front of the bus?)[5]

---

[5] Joel A. Freeman Ph.D., and Don B. Griffin, *Return to Glory: The Powerful Stirring of the Black Man* (Woodbury, NJ: Renaissance Productions, 1997), 20.

Whoever confused Herodotus' eyewitness description of thick lips, broad nose, woolly hair and burnt skin to be white folks was misguided and dishonest. Yet that is what whole generations of historians have done to perpetuate the false belief of identifying both ancient Egyptians and Ethiopians as white. The question is: If there were no pyramids; (one of the seven wonders of the world) would there be a controversy over the identity of the Egyptians? Maybe not!

Egyptologist's Testimony

Cheikh Anta Diop, an African Egyptologist and Anthropologist, in his address to the First International Congress of Black Writers and Artists in September 1956 said, "We have come to discover that the ancient Pharaonic Egyptian civilization was undoubtedly a Negro civilization."[6]

The implication of Diop's point, which the West continues to deny, is that if the ancient Egyptians were Negroes, then European civilization is derived from African achievement. Diop's point is succinct. Modern civilization is rooted in African civilization. "The ancient Egyptians were Negroes." And therefore, he laments, "The moral fruit of their civilization is to be counted among the assets of the Black world. Instead of presenting itself to history as an insolvent debtor, that Black world is the very initiator of the "western" civilization flaunted before our eyes today. Pythagorean mathematics; the theory of the four elements of Thales of Miletus, Epicurean Materialism, Platonic idealism, Judaism, and modern science are rooted in Egyptian cosmology and science."[7]

The truth about civilization is that no one nation knows it all. Inter-borrowing among nations occurred throughout history. The problem of history is simply that the West, for whatever reason, refuses to acknowledge the contributions of Black Africans to civilization. Diop sets the record straight: "Roman history is Greek, as well as Roman, and both Greek and Roman history are Egyptian because the entire Mediterranean was civilized by Egypt; Egypt in turn borrowed from other parts of Africa, especially Ethiopia."[8]

Other scholars of ancient history give credit to Ethiopia as a major world centre of learning. Chancellor Williams connects the dots: "Ancient Greek scholars, through Herodotus, referred to the completion of their education in Ethiopia with pride and it appears as a matter of course. So much has been

---

[6]Cheikh Anta Diop, *The African Origin of Civilization Myth or Reality* (Chicago: Lawrence Hill Books, 1974) ix.

[7]Ibid., xiv.

[8]Cheikh Anta Diop *Civilization or Barbarism: An Authentic Anthropology* (Brooklyn New York: Lawrence Hill Books, 1991), xviii.

built up against the black race since those far away times that it will be difficult for many people of today to realize that whites of the ancient world did not seem to regard the question of Ethiopia as the principal center of learning as even debatable."[9]

Diop tackles the Egyptians question directly, he writes:

> The Ethiopians said that Egypt was one of their colonies, which was brought to them by deity Osiris. The Greek writer Herodotus repeatedly referred to the Egyptians as being dark-skinned people with woolly hair. He said they have the same tint of skin as the Ethiopians. The opinion of the ancient writers on the Egyptians is more or less summed up by Gaston Maspero (1846-1916) in the 'Dawn of Civilization', where he says: By the almost unanimous testimony of the ancient historians, they (the Egyptians) belong to an African race which first settled in Ethiopia on the middle Nile, following the course of the river they gradually reached the sea. [10] Going on, he said: For all the writers who preceded the ludicrous and vicious falsifications of modern Egyptology, and the contemporaries of the ancient Egyptians (Herodotus, Aristotle, Diodorus, Strabo, and others), the Black identity of the Egyptian was an evident fact that stood before their eyes, so obvious that it would have been superfluous to try to demonstrate it."[11]

In short, Diop implies that modern historians have not been entirely honest about Africa's history.

Classical Historians' Testimony

Herodotus: Master of History

Eyewitnesses of the ancient world categorically affirmed that the Egyptians and Ethiopians were Black people. Herodotus insisted on that fact and even attributed the dark hue of their skin color to the heat of the sun. "For example, to prove that the flooding of the Nile cannot be caused by melting snow, he cites, among other reasons he deems valid, the following observation: 'It is certain that the natives of the country are black with the

---

[9] Chancellor Williams, *Destruction of Black Civilization.* (Chicago: Third World Press, 1956), 93.
[10] Cheikh Anta Diop *Civilization or Barbarism: An Authentic Anthropology* (Brooklyn New York: Lawrence Hill Books, 1991), xix.
[11] Ibid., 1.

heat."[12] He thought that the same heat that made the Egyptians black also caused the flooding of the Nile by melting the snow. "His statement that Egyptians are black with heat has also been used to describe Ethiopians. In fact, the word Ethiopia means 'black or burnt face' in Greek."[13]

Herodotus was very clear about the physical Negro characteristics of the Egyptians and the Ethiopians. Anta Diop summarizes in the following:

> The Greek writer, Herodotus, may be mistaken, when he reports the customs of a people, but one must grant that he was at least capable of recognizing the skin color of the inhabitants of countries he visited," His descriptions of the Egyptians were the descriptions of a Black People. At this point the reader needs to be reminded of the fact that at the time of Herodotus' visit to Egypt and other parts of Africa (between 484 and 425 B.C.) Egypt's Golden Age was over. Egypt had suffered several invasions, mainly the Cushite invasions from Western Asia Called the Middle East, starting in 671 B.C. If Egypt, after years of invasions by other peoples and nations was a distinct Black African nation at the time of Herodotus, should we not at least assume that it was more so before these invasions occurred?[14]

Diop goes on to add that if Egypt is a dilemma in Western historiography, it is a created dilemma. Ironically, Europeans do not know what to do with ancient Egyptians because they fail to acknowledge their true identity as black. Their dilemma is compounded by the fact that to acknowledge Egyptians as black is to attribute their civilization to Africans whom they have stigmatized as incapable of civilization. To deny the fact of their African identity is to deny the basic historical fact that has been immortalized by European pen and African Sphinx. Diop makes it plain:

> The Western historians, in most cases, have rested the foundation of what is called "Western Civilization" on the false assumption, or claim that ancient Egyptians were white people. To do this they had to ignore great Masterpieces of Egyptian history written by other white historians who did not support this point of view, such as Gerald Massey's great classic, 'Ancient Egypt', 'The Light of the World' (1907), and his subsequent works, 'The Book of the Beginnings and the Natural Genesis'. Other neglected works by white writers are 'Politics, In tercourse, and Trad e o f the

---

[12] Cheikh Anta Diop, *The African Origin of Civilization Myth or Reality* (Chicago: Lawrence Hill Books, 1974), 1.

[13] Freeman, Joel A. Ph.D., and Don B. Griffin, *Return to Glory: The Powerful Stirring of the Black Man* (Woodbury, NJ: Renaissance Productions, 1997), 20.

[14] Diop, xix.

Carthaginians and Ethiopians' by A.H. L. Heeren (1833) and The *Ruins of Empires* by Count C. DeVolney (1787).[15]

Rudolph Windsor sounds convincing. His emphatic conclusion of the identity of the Egyptians is Biblical and powerful. He writes, "The Egyptians are Africans, and descendants of the Hamites. All Hamites are the offspring of their father, Ham. The first Egyptian was called Mizraim according to the Hebrews. This Mizraim was the son of Ham (Genesis. 10:6). Ancient and modern scholars have established the location of Mizraim as Egypt. The word Mizraim is a plural form meaning Upper and Lower Egypt."[16]

John Henrik Clarke chimes in: "The ancient Egyptians were distinctively African people."[17] Therefore, without controversy, we can conclude that the original Egyptians and Ethiopians were black African people whose descendants—The Akans, the Gas, the Ewes, the Yorubas, the Igbos, the Hausas, the Bantus, the Futus, the Dagombas, the Falashas, the Xhosas, the Zulus etc., are still living in Africa, carrying their same ancestral names. Here are examples of ancestral names: Tutu, Dhufu, Duffu, Manfe, Mane, Manie Amena and Summa. These names are still used all over Africa.

Even though Western invaders of Egypt tried to chip off flat noses and thick lips and break off heads that were African features, the images on the pyramids survived to tell African story.

Depiction of the Great Sphinx of Giza

They can chip off our ancestors' features but they can't erase their African names and identities:

[15] Cheikh Anta Diop, *Civilization or Barbarism: An Authentic Anthropology* (Brooklyn, New York: Lawrence Hill Books, 1991), xix.
[16] Windsor, Rudolph R. From Babylon to Timbuktu: A History of Ancient Black Races Including the Black Hebrews (Chicago Illinois: Windsor's Golden Series, 1988), 30.
[17] John Henrik Clarke, *African People in world History* (Baltimore, Maryland: Black Classic Press, 1993), 22.

Here is an African Face Chiseled in Stone

Many of those with all-African faces simply had their heads knocked off. All to no lasting avail. The facts of history could not be completely changed. One troublesome fact was that most of the greatest kings and queens of Egypt were Black Africans; so great, indeed, that their names were richly spread over pages that glorified the Egyptian past-their names not their African Identity. In history these Blacks are simply Egyptians, and not Cushite, Ethiopians, or Nubians.[18]

Great Sphinx of Giza

Black African Face Chiseled In Stone

Chancellor Williams penned these down for posterity:

---

[18] Chancellor Williams, *Destruction of Black Civilization.* (Chicago: Third World Press, 1956), 77.

The Great Sphinx, the portrait statue of the Black Pharaoh Khafre (African identity generally disguised by historians with the name "Cephren"). He was the first ruler to break from the classical tradition of portraying all-important Blacks with pronounced "Caucasoid" features. Acting as though he foresaw what the trend of history would be, Khafre had his racial identity carved in this solid rock for the ages. Note, however, the long and arduous labor that was required for them to chip away that massive flat nose![19]

The ancestral features can be chipped away, but their African names and identity cannot be erased from history. The stones do speak indeed!

Egyptians and Ethiopians' Relationship to Africa

"The first Pharaoh who united the kingdoms of both Upper and Lower Egypt was an Ethiopian leader by the name of Menes[20] or Aha Mena.[21] "In Addition to uniting Egypt, Menes is also credited with founding the ancient city of Memphis, which was located between the two kingdoms. Because of its central location, Memphis was one of Egypt's leading cities and it served as the capital for a considerable period of time. The city was named after Menes, and its ruins lie far from present-day Cairo."[22]

Interestingly, this name Memphis; the capital of ancient Egypt is the same name for a modern city in Ghana. It's pronounced "Manfi" in the Akan language and not as the Europeans call it. That Ethiopia was a dominant part of Africa, and Egypt was part of the Ethiopian Empire in the beginning, has been attested to by Chancellor Williams. He writes: "This book begins where the history of blacks (Africans) began in Egypt (Northern Ethiopia) and the Sudan (Southern Ethiopia)." [23] According to Williams, ancient Ethiopia was Africa and Africa was Ethiopia. "In ancient times "African" and "Ethiopian" meant the same thing: A Black."[24]

Modern Contradiction and Confusion

The blatant contradiction in modern scholarship reflected in renaissance thinking in opposition to the classical scholarship of Herodotus, Aristotle, Diodorus, Strabo, Philo, Josephus, Origen, Augustine, etc. stems from racism

---

[19] Chancellor Williams, *Destruction of Black Civilization*. (Chicago: Third World Press, 1956), 72.
[20] Ibid., 36.
[21] Richard L Green, ed., *A Salute to Historic African Kings and Queens* (Chicago, Illinois: Empak Publishing Company, 1996), 8.
[22] Ibid., 9.
[23] Ibid., 35.
[24] Williams, 30.

and nothing else. The racist historians would try to have their cake and eat it at the same time by advocating "the so called curse of Ham" on all Black people to justify slavery and at the same time deny that ancient Egyptians, the direct descendants of Ham were black. Western historians sought to misrepresent the true physical features of these skilled people of ancient times. For some reason, it was to their advantage to fool the world into believing civilization had its beginnings with white people.

However, the fact cannot be denied anymore that the ancient Egyptians, the Ethiopians, the Babylonians and the Canaanites were all Hamitic, or Black people, and most importantly, initiators of modern civilization via Greece. The Greeks were middlemen and not the originators of civilization as it has been purported and perpetuated in text books by the West, which refuses to give credit to Africa where credit is long overdue.

It must be stated that the Greeks were NOT the originators of civilization. Civilization began in Africa or with African ancestors. It was borrowed by the Greeks and communicated to the West by the Arab traders. Williams writes: "The most important classical manuscripts had disappeared from Europe entirely during the so-called "Dark Ages." The only sources that existed were those copied and preserved by the Arabs, without which scholars generally agree, the great European Renaissance could not have occurred."[25] John Henrik Clarke seemed to know about some other African documents that impacted European civilization. He writes:

> Prince Henry got hold of a cache of maps, which were mostly made by Jewish gold dealers who had been dealing in the Western Sudan and the coast of West Africa. The Western Sudan is comprised of the nations in Inner West Africa as opposed to the coastal nations of West Africa. Europe is beginning to see the shape of certain parts of Africa; they are no longer guessing on all of it. Prince Henry, now with these maps, began to open up a school for chart-making and map-making to let the Europeans know something about other parts of the world.[26]

Clarke suggests that it was by employing the wisdom gleaned from those African maps that Prince Henry trained men to exploit Africa and the rest of the world. "Using the maritime information the Africans and the Arabs had preserved at the University of Salamanca [Spain], Europe would now go back to sea; it had previously forgotten longitude and latitude."[27] "Prince Henry—

---

[25] Chancellor Williams, *Destruction of Black Civilization*. (Chicago: Third World Press, 1956), 206.

[26] John Henrik Clarke, Christopher *Columbus and the African Holocaust* (Brooklyn New York: A & B Publishers Group, 1993), 26.

[27] Clarke, 26.

while called the Navigator—didn't navigate anything and there is no evidence that he ever went to sea."[28]

This raises a question worth pondering. Could it be possible that some of these documents and maps that Prince Henry acquired came from the lost books from the African library at the fall of Timbuktu? Timbuktu was one of the two universities of learning in the world manned by none white Africans during the time of European Dark ages.

The fact is the Greeks were not the originators of Civilization. Civilization began with the sun-kissed dark-hued descendants of Ham in the Fertile Crescent either in Mesopotamia, or in the Valley of the Euphrates, or on the continent of Africa in the Valley of the Nile. "Africa was the cradle of a religious civilization based on the conception of one Supreme God, Creator of the Universe."[29] Cushite civilization was the root of all civilizations and Egyptians were not white.

In light of the forgoing evidence, it is obvious that the time is well overdue for the world to admit to and respect the achievement and contribution of Black Africans to civilization. As a global community, there is a need to acknowledge the fact that we have been duped by historians who have tried to hide the facts of history to their own gain.

Adolph Hitler was reputed to have said, if you tell a lie long enough, or loud enough, people would come to believe it. But we know that "Truth cast to the ground will rise again!" *The time has come for all to admit to the deception and to acknowledge Africa's c ontribution to early civilizations of mankind.*

By these facts, African children of the world demand an overdue check of respect for our achievement and contribution to civilization. We will not take no for an answer until the check is cashed, history is revised and the condition of our people is changed.

---

[28] John Henrik Clarke, Christopher *Columbus and the African Holocaust* (Brooklyn New York: A & B Publishers Group, 1993), 26.

[29] Chancellor Williams, *Destruction of Black Civilization.* (Chicago: Third World Press, 1956), 34.

CHAPTER TWO

CUSHITE EMPIRE

A Tiger does not have to Proclaim his own Tigeritude. (African proverb)

Abraham's Interaction with Africans in the Bible

The descendants of Ham were not limited only to the continent of Africa. They also dwelt in Mesopotamia. The descendants of Cush, the son of Ham, dwelt on both sides of the Nile River in the Western Sudan in Africa and Eastern Sudan in Arabia and all the way to India. Even today, apart from the infusion of African slaves in other lands, remnants of indigenous Africans who emigrated in the ancient times can be traced in many unlikely places as far as India, Arabia, Russia and China, mingling with other ethnic peoples. Historically speaking,

> The Cushites appeared to have spread along tracts extending from the higher Nile to the Euphrates and the Tigris rivers. History affords many connections between Babylon, Arabia, and Ethiopia. There is more than adequate evidence that the ancient nations of Babylon, Akkadia, Sumer, and the Chaldea were inhabited by Cushite tribes (Ethiopians), on all sides of the Tigris and Euphrates rivers.[30]

Nimrod, the father, founder and builder of the Old Babylon or Babel, who also built Nineveh the Ancient Capital of the Assyrian Empire, was a Cushite. He was the son of Cush, son of Ham, the father of black folks. It was among the Cushites, the Egyptians and the Canaanites who were all Hamitic descendants that Abraham lived and moved from place to place.

There is nothing in the Bible that suggests that Nimrod was a bad man. Western theologians often use the phrase that describes Nimrod as "mighty hunter before the Lord" to depict him as evil. However, there is nothing negative about this phrase. In those days you needed a hunter to build a nation because hunters were the ones who could provide, feed and sustain their people to keep the nations growing and thriving. That was why he was the

---

[30] William Smith, Bible Dictionary, 155.

leader of his people. But the most important thing about Nimrod was that he did his job "before the Lord." It could have been referring to any aspect of living before the Lord.

The statement was used in reference to Abraham who walked before the Lord. It is equivalent to "doing everything as unto the Lord." Nimrod's life before the Lord was a positive moral statement. We are told: "Walking uprightly' before the Lord is a common expression in Scripture for moral living"[31] It meant therefore that Nimrod was a man of God and that any caricature of him is Biblically unwarranted and no serious theologian should indulge in it. So Nimrod, like Abraham, lived before the True God.

Ham and Shem Genetically Mixed

Ham and Shem's descendants have been mixed at the biological level since the floodwaters receded. Here, I just have to point the reader's mind to the obvious social intercourse that produced the inevitable genetic bond. Abraham, the father, had Egyptian and Ethiopian wives; Hagar and Keturah respectively. Another high profile marriage was between Moses and Zipporah the Ethiopian. Then there was David and Bathsheba, the Hittite, whose marriage produced King Solomon the Great.

Note what was said about Solomon and his Egyptian wife: "And Solomon brought up the daughter of Pharaoh out of the city of David unto the house that he had built for her: for he said, 'My wife shall not dwell in the house of David king of Israel" (2Chroniclesn. 8:11). What about the relationship that existed between the Queen of Sheba; her Highness the Empress of Ethiopia, of whom Solomon fathered Menilek, out of whose line descended Emperor Haile Sellassie of Ethiopia?

Wallis Budge, referring to <u>Kebra Nagast</u> which deals with the story of the Queen of Sheba and Solomon, says of the scribe that translated it into Ethiopic: "He firmly believed that the lawful kings of Ethiopia were descended from Solomon, King of Israel."[32] What about Solomon's other African wife, the Black Beauty Queen who said in the Song of Solomon, "Look not upon me, because I [am] black, because the sun has darkened my skin: I am black, and comely" (Song of Solomon 1:5). Comely means beautiful. Black is still beautiful!

The relationship between Ham and Shem occur several times in the Bible and it is a shame theologians can't find any. If it wasn't between Judah and Shuah the Canaanite (Genesis. 38:2), it was Rahab of Hamitic descent who

---

[31] Adult Sabbath School Bible Study Guide, Oct., Nov., Dec., 2003 Teachers Edition (Pacific Press 2003), 154.

[32] Joseph John. S.J. Williams, *Hebrewisms of West Africa, from Nile to Niger with the Jews* (New York: Biblo and Tannen, 1967), 164.

15

married Salmon to produce Boaz. Boaz fathered Obed by Ruth and Obed was the father of Jesse, and Jesse was the father of King David, the royal ancestor of Jesus the Son of God, the Lion of the Tribe of Judah (Matthew 1:5,6). So Biblically speaking, Ham and Shem's descendants are mixed biologically.

One historical fact which is overlooked by many is t hat whatever color ancient Ethiopians were, ancient Egyptians were also. The fact is that they were of the same father Ham, whose name means hot or black.

Whatever, color ancient Egyptians were, ancient Israelites were also of the same color. Otherwise, Moses could not have been adopted as the son of Pharaoh's daughter and successfully raised in Pharaoh's palace for forty years without anybody noticing that glaring and obvious face of white Moses, which would have been radically different from that of the black Egyptians. Could a white Moses be in the midst of a sea of black Egyptians faces and nobody including "Egyptian FBI" find out for 40 years?

Rudolph Windsor states emphatically that, "Originally all Hamites and Shemites (or Semites) were black. Abraham was a black Shemite and a descendant of Shem. The name of Abraham was Abram before he was referred to as Abraham. The three Hebrew patriarchs were Abraham, Isaac, and Jacob. This Jacob begot twelve sons, who later fathered the twelve tribes of Israel. Abraham was the father not only of the Hebrew-Israelite nation, but also of the Arab nation."[33] Now, black may not be a politically correct rendition, but dark complexion is theologically sound.

Abraham among Hamitic Black People

Abraham was a son of Terah (Genesis 11:26-27), and husband of Sarah. Their family lived in the land of Ur of the Chaldeans among Hamitic people. He and his father's house moved from Ur intending to go to Canaan, but stopped on the way to settle in Haran in the Northwestern part of Mesopotamia where Terah died.

At seventy-five, Abraham left Haran for Canaan (Hamitic territory) to fulfill the call of God. He settled somewhere between the hills east of Bethel and west of Ai but relocated to Egypt (also Hamitic territory) because of a famine in Canaan. Abraham's family left Egypt and traveled to Bethel and since there was not enough pasture for their sheep, Abram gave his nephew Lot, his choice of the land. Lot chose the plains of Jordan toward Sodom, leaving Abram to live at the terebinth trees of Mamre at Hebron. Abraham dwelt in the land of Gerar and Beersheba and later defeated Kedorlaomer, king of Elam. It was upon his triumphant return from battle that Melchizedek (Hamitic) met him and blessed him (Genesis 14:18-20; Heb 7:1-10).

---

[33] Rudolph R. Windsor, *From Babylon to Timbuktu: A History of Ancient Black Races Including the Black Hebrews* (Chicago Illinois: Windsor's Golden Series, 1988), 33.

Abraham was a pilgrim in the land of Canaan (Hamitic) but he would later own the land through his descendants. Eventually, his descendants mingled with Egyptians, many of whom the Mixed Multitude (Hamitic stock) joined the Israelites in the Exodus to Canaan. Besides mingling with Egyptians, they also mingled with Ethiopians, Canaanites and Babylonians. Many Israelites chose to stay in Babylon instead of going back to Canaan after the Babylonian Captivity.

The Assyrians were a mixture of Shem and Ham because Nimrod the son of Cush (Hamitic) founded Nineveh the capital. It was the Assyrian king that later (around the middle of 700 B.C.) removed the Ten Tribes of Israel into captivity and assimilated them into the Mesopotamian (Hamitic) population.

The fact is that the Ten Tribes were not lost. They mingled with the Mesopotamian people who were essentially Assyrians and Babylonians or Cushites out of which came a series of migrations southward after the fall of the Mesopotamian Empires. Historians report repeated waves of migration from Mesopotamia to Africa.

> But the subsequent scattering of a Jewish presence and influence reaching deep into the African continent is less widely acknowledged. Pressed under sweeping regional conflicts, Jews settled as traders and warriors in Yemen, the Horn of Africa, Egypt, the Kingdom of Cush and Nubia, North African Punic settlements (Carthage and Velubilis), and areas now covered by Mauritania. More emigrants followed these early Jewish settlers to Northern Africa following the Assyrian conquest of the Israelites in the 8th Century B.C., and again 200 years later, when the Babylonians, leading to the destruction of the First Temple, conquered Jerusalem.[34]

Mesopotamians, Cushites, Israelites and Egyptians, all drifted to the continent of Africa as a result of various invasions. G. M. James confirms that, "During the Persian, Greek and Roman invasions, large numbers of Egyptians fled not only to the desert and the mountain regions, but also to adjacent lands in Africa, Arabia, and Asia Minor where they lived."[35] Anta Diop describes this phenomenon when he writes, "Thus combined, these histories would lead to a properly patterned past in which it would be seen that (ancient) Ghana rose in the interior (West Africa) of the continent at the moment of Egyptian decline, just as the western European empires were born with the decline of Rome."[36]

---

34 George E. Lichtblau, *Jewish Roots in Africa* http://www.ubalt.edu/ kulanu/africa.html.
[35] George G. M. James, *Stolen Legacy* (Chicago, Illinois: African American Images, 2002), 39.
[36] Cheikh Anta Diop, Civilization *or Barbarism: An Authentic Anthropology (*Brooklyn New York: Lawrence Hill Books, 1991), xviii.

So African Ancestors started out like all others in Mesopotamia when the floodwaters receded and the Ark rested and they drifted to East Africa until the Eastern African Empires fell. Then later they made it to the Sahara to continue building the Empires of Ghana, Mali and Songhai.

Cushite Empire Spanned all the way from West To East:
From Africa to India

CHAPTER THREE

AFRICA'S SAHARA ROOTS

Do not call the forest that shelters you a jungle. (African proverb)

The trend of migration was mostly southbound, from Mesopotamia to Egypt and down into Ethiopia after the fall of the Northern Empires. When the Egyptian Empire fell, the people drifted in waves southward to Ethiopia and onward to Western Sudan or Northwest Africa, which is Sub-Sahara Africa. That is why the ancient Ghana Empire rose up as soon as the Egyptian Empire fell.

Migration from Mesopotamia to the Interior of Africa:
Exodus to Sahara

The people who were driven out of Egypt and other parts of Mesopotamia, Canaan and Carthage, went to the interior of Africa and continued to do what they knew to do best—build empires. Beside other empires, they built these three major Empires: Ghana, Mali and Songhai, spanning from 300 B.C. to 1600 A.D. Windsor traces the migrations:

> The Cushites [also known as the Ethiopians] inhabited east Africa along the coast and parts of the interior. More Ethiopians and Black Semites crossed the Red Sea from the southern tip of Arabia and traveled into the interior of Africa. The entire continent of Africa was populated from the north and the east. Mary Hastings Bradley, during her journey through Tanganyika, relates a story of the experienced Watusi of Rwanda. She says they have an exact theology of the account of the creation of the world, and a tradition that they came down from the north. Also Hermann Norden writes about the people of Uganda having a legend of crossing the Nile centuries ago. Uganda is south of the Nile and east of the Congo.
> The third son of Ham is Phut, sometimes written Put. The descendants of Phut have been found in the entire area below the Sahara Desert. They use the names Futa, Foul, Fulas, Poul, Poulbe, and Fulbe. These tribes have disseminated themselves across Africa from Somaliland to Senegal. Professor Godbey says they have prefixed their name to almost every district of any extent that they have ever occupied. They have Futu-Torro near Senegal;

19

Futu-Jallon and Futa-Bondu to the north of Sierra Leone. There is also Futu-Kasson, Futa-Zora, Futa-Ferlo and Futa-Dugu.[37]

Included in the group of the descendants of Phut, brother of Cush and Mizraim would be "The Peuls, Pouls, Foulahs, or Foutes who are scattered today, from Senegambia to Darfur; dark-complexioned, red, bronzed, copper-colored, *(recalling the warm tones of c ertain Egyptian types),* the oval face, aquiline nose, the smooth hair, they stand out above the surrounding Negroes."[38] Simon of Cyrene who carried the cross for Jesus might have been a descendant of Phut. His two sons were Ruphus (Mark 15:21), an obvious link to father Phut, and Alexander named after an Egyptian city taken over by Alexander the Great.

Interestingly enough, in Ghana along the Coast of Central Region among the Fantees are a people called "Afutu-fo", meaning the "Futu people." There are also the Hutus and the Tutsis of Rwanda. In Guinea-Conakry, Burkina Faso, Mali, Nigeria, Niger, Cameroon and Chad are a people called the Fulani.

So in modern Africa, we find living proofs of the remnants of the children of the third Son of Ham called "Fut" (often written Phut). All these are historical indications of our ancient migration from the East, generally Mesopotamia and specifically Babylon, Canaan and Egypt, and from Ethiopia to the present locations in Africa. *A Ghanaian historian describes th e migratory patterns from North-East Africa thus:*

> The Migrationist School holds that Ghana was uninhabited until the first settlers arrived, according to them, from Mesopotamia, the Biblical cradle of life. This is contained in the Garden of Eden episode, supported by the city and Tower (of Babel) episode. Dr. J.B. Danquah, who belonged to this school, traced the Akans to the valley of Tigris and Euphrates from where they left in the company of other tribes like the Gonja, Bantu, Ewe, and Ga, to various parts of Africa. This was before 750 B.C.[39]

Akan Migration within Africa: Exodus from Sahara

"The Dankyira, whose kingdom emerged on the ruins of Adanse claim to have migrated from the source of the Nile, through Muslim country and settled at Nkyiraa (in Wankyi District) before finally establishing in the Pra

---

[37] Rudolph R. Windsor, From Babylon to Timbuktu: A History of Ancient Black Races Including the Black Hebrews (Chicago Illinois: Windsor's Golden Series, 1988), 55.

[38] Joseph John. S.J. Williams, *Hebrewisms of West Africa, from Nile to Niger with the Jews.* (New York: Biblo and Tannen, 1967), 244.

[39] K. Nkansa-Kyeremateng, *The Akans of Ghana their History & Culture* (Accra: Sebewie Publishers, 1996), 30.

and Offin basin"[40] in Ghana. The "source of the Nile" would be Ethiopia or Egypt and "Muslim country" would be the Songhai Empire when the Muslims in North Africa chased the Akans in jihad from the Sahara. "The pattern of migration was reminiscent of the Exodus embarked on by the Israelites (Ex. 12: 34, 37-38).

In these movements the people carried clan stools; symbols of unity. Whereas, the Israelites were organized in 12 tribes and moved simultaneously, the Akans were in 8 [tribes,] with sub clans, and moved at different times. Each group had its totem represented in an animal."[41]

Kyeremateng goes on to list the tribes as follows: Aduana-Aberade, Agona, Aseneε, Asona, Ayokoɔ, Bretuo/Tena, Ekoɔna and Asakyri."[42] It must be noted here that different authors have used clan and tribe interchangeably. *One is a general* description of a group and the other is a specific group within a group. Clan and tribe have also become synonymous because of intermarriage among Akan people: so clan and tribe would be used interchangeably in the book.

Akan Royal Staff and Tribal Symbols

The four-headed Totem means "Wisdom does not reside in one man's head"

---

[40] K. Nkansa-Kyeremateng, *The Akans of Ghana their History & Culture* (Accra: Sebewie Publishers, 1996), 29, 30.
[41] Ibid., 34, 35.
[42] Ibid., 36-39.

Akan Royal Staf and the Lion Symbol

The Lion Staff and Symbol in the Akan Culture indicates that the Ruling Tribe of that Village comes from the Lion Tribe of the Akan People.

Real similarities exist between Akan and Hebrew cultures. Akan culture is full of Biblical symbols. An Akan Totem is what the Bible calls banner, insignia or standard. All ancient Israelite tribes had their symbols that represented them. It is very interesting to note that both the Aberade or Aduana Akan tribe/clan and the Tribe of Judah have the same Tribal Lion symbol.

One can also easily identify a lion totem on the top of the staff in African gatherings, or the portrait of a lion on top of the traditional stool and on their palaces, and know that Aberade the lion tribe rules in that city. Some members of Aberade tribe at Agona Nkum in the Central Region of Ghana like the Ashantees, believe that the Akan tribe of Aberade and the tribe of Judah belong together and that Jesus was a member of the Aberade tribe.

The Original Heritage Bible commentary confirms their suspicion in this way, "Ashanti tribe who are said to have descended from the tribe of Judah settled on the west cost of Africa. Many of the ancient Israel's cultural traits and customs are found among the Ashanti"[43]

Short Narrative of the Saharan Empires

To provide a perspective on the foregoing discussion, you will need to understand the context in which the forthcoming discussion can be properly placed. We will explore the Western Sudanic Empires, namely, Ghana, Mali, and Songhai.

Ghana Empire

The following are the stories of Akan migration from ancient Mesopotamia through ancient African Saharan Empires: Ghana, Mali and Songhai, to the present location in Ghana. "The ancient Empire of Ghana was located in the western Sudan, at least 500 miles from modern Ghana. It included parts of modern Mali, Mauritania, and Senegal. The Empire arose around the 3rd Century B.C. and flourished for more than a thousand years. Ghana was an important center of trade, and its wealth was so great that Arabs called it, "the land of gold" and its ruler, "lord of the gold."[44]

African ancestors established their origins in Mesopotamia at one time or another and when their empires began to fall, they migrated southwestward through Egypt then to Sub-Sahara (western Sudan, Timbuktu, etc.) and then to the rest of Africa. The last migrants were said to have fled south after the fall of Timbuktu by the Muslim conquests.

Incidentally, it was in the Third Century B.C., that the Egyptian Empire fell and Diop reminds us that Saharan African Empires began. After the migration from Mesopotamia and Egypt, our ancestors continued to build Empires. The first Empire they built in the Western Sudan, was the Ghana Empire, which endured for over a thousand years. Diop shows a pattern: "Thus combined, these histories would lead to a *properly patterned* past in which it would be seen that (ancient) Ghana rose in the interior (West Africa)

---

[43]Felder, Cain Hope, *Original African Heritage Study Bible,* (Iowa Falls, Iowa: World Bible Publishing, 1998), 665.
[44]*Royalty in Ghana, A Very Brief History of Ghana.* (*Cinderella* 2002) *http://www.royalty.nu/Africa*

of the continent at the time that Egypt began to decline, just as the western European empires were born with the decline of Rome."[45]

Bruce Willis further elaborates on the trend of African migration in the following:

> Oral traditions, or oral accounts, of Ghanaian history refer to the origins of the Ghanaian people as having migrated from the kingdoms of the Western Sudan about the thirteenth century A.D. After the fall of the Roman Empire, the empire of Ghana, which was located in the Sahel, north of the Niger River on the edge of the Sahara Desert in the area of present-day Mali and Mauritania, was to rise as the most important state and dominant civilization in that part of the world. It was especially important in the ninth century A.D. when it controlled the Wangara area (between the upper Niger and the Senegal Rivers) that provided much of the gold for trade across the Sahara.
>
> The empire of Ghana coordinated trade for metals, merchandise, and the all-important salt produced in the north, and sold imports from the north to the miners and farmers of the agricultural and gold-mining lands of the upper Niger and Senegal Rivers. By selling the latter's products to northern traders and levying taxes on that trade, the empire of Ghana prospered, grew rich, and became more powerful than all its neighbors. The empire of Ghana lasted about eight hundred years, from about A.D. 300 until the year 1076. Gold was the most important export of this region. In 1076, the Almoravides arose among the Western Sahara Berbers and unified Morocco. They eventually initiated a jihad (holy war) that led to the invasion and eventual fall of the empire of Ghana, which eventually split into a number of smaller states. [46]

The failure of past empires did not deter the African spirit from further empire building. Even though some left and migrated south, others remained to continue building yet another empire on the ruins of Ghana. This became the Mali Empire.

The Mali Empire

Bruce Willis writes that:

> The next Empire to evolve in this area was Mali. The rise of the Empire of Mali was largely due to the efforts of the Mandinka

---

[45]Cheikh Anta Diop, *Civilization or Barbarism: An Authentic Anthropology* (Brooklyn New York: Lawrence Hill Books, 1991), xviii.
[46]Bruce W. Willis, The *Adinkra dictionary: A Visual Primer on The Language of Adinkra* (Washington, DC: The Pyramid Complex, 1998), 10.

24

of Kangaba, a small state on the banks of the Upper Niger. Led by Sundiata, the Keita people expanded and assumed the role that the Empire of Ghana had lost. Sundiata created a much larger Empire with political and military power that enabled producers and traders to prosper over a wider area of the Sudan. The Empire of Mali lasted for about two centuries and was at its peak about the middle of the fourteenth century.[47]

In his book about the migration of people from the empires that collapsed in the sub-Saharan West Africa region, K. Nkansa-Kyeremateng states:

> Evidence is not unavailable that since the seventh [century] CE there have been waves of migration in the West African sub-region. The period coincides with the time Christianity was engaged in Crusades with Islam for control of the Holy Lands of the Middle East. The spillover effect was the refugees who moved in all directions propagating the new faith.
>
> West Africa was already known in the north for her wealth in gold, which attracted traders. Timbuktu was a popular commercial centre. By the eleventh century, however, interest in West Africa had developed religious wings. Islamization of the region had begun and this was heightened when Mansa Musa, King of Mali made an epoch pilgrimage to Mecca during which he advertised the wealth of the region on an unprecedented scale. The peace of the zone hereafter came to be disturbed and refugees were forced southwards who eventually peopled the forest zone. It is therefore not uncommon to hear in some traditions that their ancestors (the Akans) bothered by Almoravid domination, fled, wandered, and finally settled at the confluence of Pra and Offin rivers. Mention is made in many sources of flourishing kingdoms, in the Niger bend in about the tenth century CE but which were no more by 1000 CE because they were destroyed by an Islamized people, the Berbers.[48]

Akan as part of African history started from Mesopotamia as J. B. Danquah, an African historian describes, and moved southwest upon the fall of the Hamitic Empires in the north and east. Other tribal migrations joined them as the Egyptian Empire fell. The people moved south of Egypt gradually onward to the Sahara region. It was there that the Ghana, Mali and later Songhai empires were founded. The next African Empire was the Songhai.

---

[47]Bruce W. Willis, *The Adinkra dictionary: A Visual Primer on The Language of Adinkra* (Washington, DC: The Pyramid Complex, 1998), 12.
[48]K. Nkansa-Kyeremateng, *The Akans of Ghana their History & Culture* (Accra: Sebewie Publishers, 1996), 33.

The Songhai Empire

Referring to Willis, we find incontrovertible evidence to affirm and collaborate what other scholars have suggested with respect to the Empires that thrived in the West Africa sub-region:

> The next great Sudanic Empire to evolve was the Empire of Songhai. It is believed to have begun in the ninth century when the Berbers gained control over Songhai farmers along the Niger River. The empire of Mali was dependent on Songhai boatmen for vital connections along the Niger River. Sonni Ali, who came from a Songhai royal family, established the Songhai Empire in the late fifteen century. It was centered on the trading city of Gao. Over the next one hundred years at least ten different rulers succeeded each other as the state became increasingly divided and fragmented. It is thought that the main cause of the decline of Songhai was the internal struggle for power that weakened its government. Its downfall occurred when the Moroccans, who controlled the areas north of Songhai, eventually, routed the Songhai army. In 1591, a column of three thousand Moroccan soldiers led by Juda Pasha, a Spaniard in service to the Sultan of Morocco, crossed the desert, attacked Gao, and defeated the Songhai or its authority in that area.[49]

History indicates continuity from the Egyptian to the Saharan Empires. The work called *Hebrewisms of We st Africa* shows the connection between the Egyptians and the rest of the Africans within the Songhai Empire. "The Songhai seemed to have adopted an imitation of ancient Egyptian architecture in clay and wood instead of stone. They in turn subdued the Mandingoes . . . in the city of Jenne, at the confluence of the Niger and the Bani. From Jenne radiated over all the Western Sudan a diluted Egyptian influence in architectural forms, in boat building, and other arts."[50] From all appearances, the Saharan Empires (Ghana, Mali, and Songhai) were a continuation of the Eastern Sudanic Empires—that is, Mesopotamian, Ethiopian, Egyptian, etc. John Henrik Clarke asserts that:

> In that period in Western African history, the University of Sankore at Timbuktu was flourishing, and its great chancellor, the last of the monumental scholars of West Africa, Ahmed Baba reigned over that university. A great African scholar, he wrote 47 books, each on a separate subject. He received all of his education

---

[49] Bruce W. Willis, *The Adinkra dictionary: A Visual Primer on The Language of Adinkra* (Washington, DC: The Pyramid Complex, 1998), 12.

[50] Joseph John. S.J. Williams, *Hebrewisms of West Africa, from Nile to Niger with the Jews,* (New York: Biblo and Tannen, 1967), 306.

within Africa; in fact, he did not leave the Western Sudan until he was exiled to Morocco during the invasion in 1594.[51]

It is reported that about 700 thousand African documents have been found in Timbuktu in North Africa to date![52] Unfortunately, the African kingdoms did not last forever. Their end came like other empires before them. However, historical accounts have shown that Black people emerged ruling the world from the womb of history. They maintained world dominance all the way from Babel, Egypt and Summer to the Babylonian Empire of which God confirmed Ham's leadership in the ancient world, in the statement made to the King of Babylon, "Thou Art the Head of God" (Daniel 2:38).

After the fall of the Eastern Hamitic kingdoms, world political dominance went to the hands of Shem and Japheth represented by Medo-Persia and fell permanently into the hands of Japheth represented by Greece, Rome and through the Ten Divisions of Rome into Europe, to America till the coming of the "Kingdom of the Stone." "And in the days of these kings shall the God of heaven set up a kingdom, which shall never be destroyed: and the kingdom shall not be left to other people, but it shall break in pieces and consume all these kingdom, and it shall stand for ever" (Daniel 2:44).

Prophetically speaking, it was just a matter of time before African political dominance would come to an end. In the third century B.C. the eastern empires fell and in the seventeenth century the western empires came to an end. "The year 1660 is considered by historians as the time when the medieval kingdoms of the Sudan came to an end."[53] This period of the fall of the last of the African Empires was the lowest point of the African civilization. Since then Africans have not regained world political dominance.

Geographically, the old Ghana is 500 miles north of the present Ghana, and occupied the area between Rivers Senegal and Niger. Some inhabitants of present Ghana had ancestors linked with the medieval Ghana. This can be traced down to the Mande and Voltaic people of Northern Ghana--Mamprussi, Dagomba and the Gonja. Anecdotal evidence connected the Akans to this great Empire. The evidence lies in names like Danso shared by the Akans

---

[51] Clark, John Henrik, Christopher *Columbus and the African Holocaust* (Brooklyn New York: A & B Publishers Group, 1993), 82.

[52] Justin Pearce, (BBC News website, Johannesburg) (700, 000 manuscripts found in Timbuktu and its surroundings to date, a living testimony of a highly advance civilization on the Continent of Africa. Mali's written treasures.url, Alida Jay Boye/Undesco/afrol News and News $ Notes, January 1, 2007.

[53] Bruce W. Willis, The *Adinkra dictionary: A Visual Primer on The Language of Adinkra* (Washington, DC: The Pyramid Complex, 1998), 12.

of present Ghana and Mandikas of Senega-Gambia who have strong links with the Empire. There is also the matrilineal connection.[54]

The population of North Africa was Black. Chancellor Williams affirms this view by stating, "For until the Islamic "flood" which began in the middle of the seventh century A.D., the vast majority of the Egyptians were what modern scholars like to characterize as "Negroid."[55] Thus, it is a noble act for Whoopi Goldberg to trace her Akan roots to Ghana via Mande!

Akans in Modern Ghana

Modern Ghanaians have always believed they came from Mesopotamia via the Ancient Empires of Ghana, Mali and Songhai with culture and tradition. The migration from the north of Africa began at the fall of Mali and continued after the fall of the Songhai Empire. It is understandable why J. B. Danquah and Kwame Nkrumah named the Gold Coast after the ancient Empire of Ghana as a tribute to the roots of her people. "'Every Fante knows that at one time his ancestors lived in Takyiman.' This assertion by Christensen, though [an exaggerated] statement, shows the direction of the

---

[54] www.ghanaweb.com/GhanaHomePage/history,Posted,1994-2005, 4/24/2005
[55] Chancellor Williams, *Destruction of Black Civilization (*Chicago: Third World Press, 1956), 74.

movement of the Fante groups. Fante constitute about the first batch of Akans who crossed the forest belt to found kingdoms along the coast."[56]

A division of Akan tribes called the "Agona" claim to have arrived around the middle of the 16th century as refugess from Mande. They settled in Bono Manso and became a sub-clan of the Anona. In 1580, however, they migrated and founded their own kingdom based on Ntuntumbe Apeanyiase. They waxed in power until their king, Mumuromfi (Werempi Ampem) defeated Akyerekyere and established the kingdom of Dankyira with its capital at Abankeseeso where modern Oboase stands. At the height of its power the kingdom was very oppressive, a situation which caused its defeat at the hands of her vassal states led by Kwaman under Osei Tutu.[57]

Again, historians affirm Akan tribal migration to the present location of West Africa from the thirteenth century all the way to the sixteeth.

Another Fante group led by Nana Okesedu arrived in Bono Manso as refugees from Timbuktu at about the time Adiaka Fante left for the coast. This group also left for the coast towards the end of the 16th centrury during the time chaos reigned in Bono, following wars with Mande. They settled at Mankesim and in the group were the Djomo (Anona) and the Adininadze (Asona). Quarrels between the groups were common and the Anona, migrated under their king Kwanza and founded Ekumfi while the Asona group also left and founded Anomabo (the palace of the bird shaped rock).[58]

"The modern Republic of Ghana is located on the coast of the Gulf of Guinea. Today's Ghanaians seem to be descendants of immigrants from different parts of Africa, including the ancient empire of Ghana. . . . After European traders arrived in the 15th century, the area came to be known as the Gold Coast because its residents traded gold for European goods."[59] That was the beginning of sorrows and the end was not yet in sight!

---

[56] Nkansa-Kyeremateng K. *Akan Heritage*. Accra: Sebewie Publishers, 1999), 46.

[57] Ibid., 36.

[58] Ibid., 47.

[59] *Royalty in Ghana, A Very Brief History of Ghana* (Cinderella, 2002) http://www.royalty.nu/Africa/Ghana.html,

CHAPTER FOUR

THE TRANSATLANTIC SLAVE TRADE

When the cock is drunk, he forgets about the hawk. (African proverb)

Exodus to the Americas and Beyond

As we review the history of the Akan migration to the present-day Ghana, we realize that the Akan people escaped from the Muslims in the north, crossed the forest area, and attempted to settle in the interior forested area of Africa.

Meanwhile, this was also about the time Europeans actually discovered and invaded Africa. They exploited the land, and took the people into slavery. The Africans had no time to settle before the Europeans invaded the Continent. This was the beginning of the Trans-Atlantic Slave Trade in the fifteenth century.

The Silent Trade

"The Ghanaian writer, A. Adu Boahen, in the article, 'The Coming of the European (c. 1440-1700),' gives us the following information about this significant event in history:

> "Africa, south of the Sahara has been known to Europeans since Greco-Roman times, but it was not until the fourth decade of the fifteenth century that they began to arrive in numbers on its shores. The first to come were the Portuguese. They were followed in the 1450's by the Spaniards, who soon after abandoned Africa to explore America; toward the end of the century some English and French adventures and traders arrived.[60]

There was a kind of trade between the Europeans and the Africans that has not been revealed in the West. It was called the "Silent Trade." The Silent Trade was the means by which business was transacted in the beginning when neither the Europeans nor the Africans spoke each other's language.

---

[60] John Henrik Clarke, Christopher *Columbus and the African Holocaust* (Brooklyn New York: A & B Publishers Group, 1993), 47.

30

Europeans would bring their goods to the harbor, line them up at the shore and then go back into their ships. The Africans would then come and take a look at the items, weigh them and offer gold in exchange for the European goods. They would therefore leave both the goods and the gold and wait for the Europeans to come back to check the offer. If it was acceptable, business was transacted and the European would take the gold and leave the goods and the Africans would later come to claim the goods. For the Africans, trust was the basis of the trade.

The Liquor Content of the Trade

Unbeknownst to the Africans, however, were the sinister intentions of their counterparts in the trade. Not all the goods brought from Europe were innocent. Much of it was alcohol. The Europeans brought alcohol to the African shore to trade for gold and as the Africans opened the bottles and began to ingest the drinks, they became drunk. Some did not make it home but fell right along the shore for the Europeans to snatch them and send them to Europe as servants or later to the West Indies. (The problem of drug use and proliferation in the African community and the resultant addiction- crime and the incarceration, are the same tactics used in times past to enslave Africans). These were among the first groups to be tested for endurance on the plantations. The Silent Trade was the genesis of the Transatlantic Slave Trade. Adu Boahen continued:

> "After the Portuguese seafarers finished displaying the four men they kidnapped from the Gold Coast, they gave the men as presents to their merchants and financiers. These Africans from the Gold Coast were the first to be introduced into European servitude, and soon African servants became prized possessions and symbols of affluence in wealthy Portuguese homes. To satisfy the demand for African servants in Portugal, the Portuguese sailors that went to the Gold Coast made a habit of capturing and kidnapping more and more Africans in each expedition.[61]

The Gunpowder Content of the Trade

The second batch of captured people was secured as a result of tribal wars the Europeans instigated. When the natives learned the European language, they formed alliances against the other tribes. Europeans would supply gunpowder to one tribe, making that tribe more powerful than the other and thus tilting the balance of power in the area. In such situations, any

---

[61] Nana Banchie Darkwah, *The Africans Who Wrote The Bible.* (White Plains, MD: Aduana Publishing, 2002), 160.

little conflict became a trigger for war and something that could have been resolved easily, escalated into a major tribal war. Whole villages were ransacked, houses torched, men killed and families displaced.

The most amazing thing was the gradual evolution of trade in human cargo—the Europeans were interested in buying the captive victims of the tribal or ethnic wars. There was good money for the captives of the wars. The tribes made powerful by European gunpowder rose against weaker tribes, pillaged their villages, and took their people for sale to the European traders.

An Antislavery Medallion of the Early 19th Century

Gang Warfare - A Logical Conclusion

Things worsened when gangsters joined in the trade. They had no mercy for any life; old or young, and no respect for property. They would go from place to place looking for vulnerable villages to rob, rape, ransack, and kill those who resist, capture the rest, and sell them to the Europeans. In one sense therefore, drugs, guns, "gangsterism", incarceration and the loss of voting rights in the black community have their genesis in the slave trade that caused Africa's demise. Its strategy worked and it is still working today.

Traditional African Slavery

Without condoning it, African traditional slavery needs to be presented for all to compare with European slavery. Clarke compares them:

> The word slave in West Africa had an entirely different meaning than it had when used by the Europeans. The slave in Africa did not lose her/his humanity. Some African chiefs or kings

32

became corrupt and went into the slave trade because they wanted to. The Europeans sold firearms to one African group to either protect themselves or capture another group. The European gunpowder, rum, and cheap bric-a-brac coming from the embryo of what will eventually become the European Industrial Revolution, was traded for slaves. In every slave fort in West Africa, there is a door of no return. The captured slaves went out of this door to the beach and subsequently to the boats that would take them away from their home forever.[62]

The Slave Trade was similar to the drug cartel today, only that it was backed and sanctioned by powerful governments. Therefore, it was a vicious and merciless business. It reduced every participant to the level of the brute. By dehumanizing another human being before the Unfallen Intelligent Universe, we dehumanize ourselves as humans. And therefore redemption of the black man is a blessing for all!

From Colonization to Independence

Clarke continued:
Various kingdoms and empires dominated Ghana during this time, including the Akwamu Empire and the Asante (or Ashanti) Empire. The African rulers did not permit Europeans to settle inland, but did allow them to build castles and forts on leased land along the coast to protect their trading interests.
Starting in the late 19th century, Europeans conquered and colonized most of Africa. Modern-day Ghana is comprised of Britain's Gold Coast colony and the British part of Togoland, a German protectorate that eventually fell under the control of Britain and France.
Ghana became independent in 1957. Its prime minister (and later first president), Kwame Nkrumah, named the new country after the great ancient empire of Ghana. 'We take pride in the name of Ghana,' he said, 'not out of romanticism, but as an inspiration for the future.'[63]

In a nutshell, Africans especially Ghanaians and particularly the Akan people trace their history back to the Songhai, Mali, and Ghana Empires all the way to the Mesopotamian Empires. Their history is connected to the Cushite or Ethiopian Empires back to the Egyptian Empire.

And so herein lies the narrative of Black Civilization and Africa's connection to the Divine in relationship to the Biblical history of the Flood.

---

[62] John Henrik Clarke, *Christopher Columbus and the African Holocaust* (Brooklyn New York: A & B Publishers Group, 1993), 78.
[63] *Royalty in Ghana, A Very Brief History of Ghana* (Cinderella 2002) http://www.royalty.nu/Africa/Ghana.html.

There we trace Ham as the father of Black people through Cush, Mizraim, Phut and Canaan. There can be no African history without Ham, the father of Africans. The God of Noah is therefore the God of the Africans. This part of African history has been severely suppressed in the history of the ages. Now you the reader have been introduced to that stifled history.

There are two things that cannot be denied in our historical narrative and in our noble past and ought to serve as sources of inspiration for our future achievement and fulfillment. They are our collective genius to survive and our sense of spirituality.

We should therefore, strip ourselves of every sense of inferiority and brace ourselves to meet the challenges of our times. However, we must depend on God just as our ancestors did and were able to produce civilizations, which still challenge the modern mind, and technology today.

Knowing what we now know, the time is ripe for us to strip ourselves of the borrowed or imposed garments of inferiority. It is now time to brace ourselves to face the challenges of our times in the spirit of our ancestors, who depended on God for guidance. Like our ancestors, our dependence on God will produce the wisdom needed to face the challenges of our modern world.

CHAPTER FIVE

AFRICANS FROM ANTIQUITY TO THE ADVENT

He who learns, soon teaches. (African proverb)

From volume one of Sankofa Heritage Series: <u>*Africa's Roots in God*</u>, we have learned that Biblical, as well as historical evidences show that Africa knew God in an intimate way before the Europeans set foot on the Continent. One may wonder just how Biblical truths such as the knowledge of God as the Creator, the memorial of Creation, the knowledge of His sacrificial system and blood atonement, knowledge of divine Tetragrammaton; the Covenant Name, principles of redemption and many other such Biblical truths found their roots and understanding in Africa?

One simply has to trace Africa's origins in the Biblical context. And one will find Africa's history linked to the Biblical history of the patriarchs, prophets and the kings. In essence, Africa's Biblical history goes back to the Garden of Eden. However, African people could have only been identified after the flood when humanity spread out.

Robinson and Sinnegen showed that in the *Ancient History*, "The human family spread itself from Ancient Mesopotamia in the region of Euphrates and Tigris,"[64] (Genesis 2:8-13). "And the LORD GOD planted a garden eastward in Eden; and there he put the man whom he had formed. And the river went out of Eden to water the garden; and from thence it was parted, and became four heads. And the name of the second river is Gihon: the same is it that encompasses the whole land of Ethiopia.

It is Biblically accurate for historians to start the history of Africa from Noah's youngest son, Ham. Ham's sons, Cush, Mizraim and Phut migrated into the vast Continent of Africa after the Flood. Ham's last-born son, Canaan became the ancestor of Melchizedek, a Jebusite king of Salem and the priest of the Most High God, through whom God blessed Abraham, the father of the Hebrews.

The NIV Zondervan Bible commenting on Genesis chapter 10 says: "The Hamites were located in the Southwestern region of Africa. Cush, the

---

[64] Robinson Jr., C.A., and Williams, S.G. *The Ancient History* (New York, 1981), 50.

descendant of Ham, migrated to the upper Nile region south of Egypt. Mizraim, which means two Egypts, referred to the upper and lower Egypt. Phut might be Libya or a land ancient Egyptians called Punt (Modern Somalia)."[65] The descendants of Ham spread throughout the Continent of Africa with the knowledge of their fathers and concepts of the worship of the patriarchs with animal sacrifice and other rituals, which are still prevalent in the African culture today.

The Land of Cush

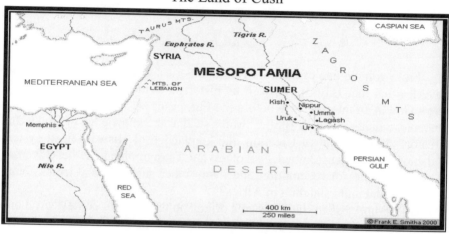

"The Cushites appeared to have spread along tracts extending from the higher Nile to the Euphrates and the Tigris rivers. History affirms many connections between Babylon, Arabia, and Ethiopia. There is more than adequate evidence that the ancient nations of Babylon, Akkadia, Sumer, and the Chaldea were inhabited by Cushite tribes (Ethiopians), on all sides of the Tigris and Euphrates rivers."[66]

To keep things in perspective, Chancellor Williams reminds us that "at various periods in ancient times, the "Land of the Blacks" meant all Ethiopia, all Ethiopia meant all Africa, and all Blacks were Africans or Ethiopians or Thebans"[67] So Modern Africans are direct descendants of Hamitic children of Mesopotamia, Egypt and Ethiopia, to name a few.

Nana Darkwah observes that, "Apart from the Kwehu people of Adiabene having lived in the Euphrates and Tigris valley in ancient times, there is evidence that Akan people lived in Canaan in ancient times. The people named their place of dwelling, 'Adom' meaning providence. This was

---

[65] *NIV Zondavan Bible* Commenting on Genesis (Chapter 10), 22 margin

[66] William Smith, Bible Dictionary, 155.

[67] Chancellor Williams, *Destruction of Black Civilization* (Chicago: Third World Press, 1956), 105.

the ancient Akan name that became Biblical Edom. The land of Adom was known as Adomea simply meaning a place of Adom."[68]

Ancient Mesopotamia and the Modern African Connection
Linguistics:

What are the Akan linguistic connections to ancient Egypt, Ethiopia, Mesopotamia, and Canaan? "We do know, however, that the Akan people were the earliest and the most dominant group in Ancient Egypt."[69] Nana Darkwah went on:

> The kingdom of Akka was not Akkadia and the people were not Akkadians. Linguistic and cultural evidence shows that a lower king or sub-chief in Akka's kingdom was called an *Ensi* (see H. W. F. Saggs, *Civilization Before Greece and Rome*, 1989, p. 37) The kingdom of Akka was originally called the *Ensiman*, meaning the nation of the Ensi, where the suffix "man" is also Akan, meaning nation or state. The ancient people of King Akka are the modern *Ensiman* people. These people today inhabit the southwestern corner of Ghana in West Africa. The so-called Sumerians did not vanish from the face of the earth as Western historians have assumed or their historical accounts have implied. The Sumerians moved towards Ancient Egypt and joined the Ancient Egyptian tribes in the Exodus, towards inner Africa. The Sumerians were black people then, and they are still black…. Today, the ancient name Ensiman is written as Nziman. …The greatest Nziman personality the world may remember was Dr. Kwame Nkrumah, the first President of Ghana."[70]

Akan Mesopotamian Names

There are common names passed down from ancient to modern Hamitic people that connects them both. For example "Sumani," is a Ghanaian name, which simply means a person from Suma. Since both are descendants of Ham, it is possible that some Ghanaians could be Sumerians. Darkwah says, "This is confirmed by the fact that the indigenous name of the great god of Sumeria was called Shama and not Shamash as Western historians have transposed it."

---

[68] Nana Banchie Darkwah, *The Africans Who Wrote The Bible* (White Plains, MD: Aduana Publishing, 2002), 237.
[69] Ibid., 246.
[70] Ibid., 201.

Shama is still a name of a town belonging to Fante people of the Akan stock."[71]

Indigenous Akan Names for Ancient Egyptian Objects

The surname Tutu, Futu, Khuffu, Fufu and Akenten are all Akan names. The most basic problem of modern people missing the African connection to ancient African ancestors has come about because the Europeans who translated some of these words could not pronounce African words properly. Therefore, they wrote these ancient African words the way they could make sense of them, and that was to Europeanize them. That is why the true African rendering of certain historical words is hidden from view. This is why Chancellor Williams admonishes, "I have urged that, high up on the list of research fields yet to be explored, there should be one devoted to the rediscovery of African names and their meaning. For, obviously much of the African past was rather effectively blotted out by blotting out African names along with other indexes to black achievements."[72] From *The Africans Who Wrote the Bible*, Darkwah continues:

> In earlier discussions, I revealed the indigenous Akan names of ancient Egyptian Pharaohs, people, cities, and the indigenous Akan names of the most important ancient Egyptian gods. I revealed that the indigenous Akan name of the Pharaoh Psammetichus I is Asamaoa Ateko I, Akhenaten is Akenten, Djekara-Isesi is Gyakari Asaase, Khuffu is Akuffu, Djedefra is Dade Afre, and Chephren is Okyere (Ochere) Afre. The indigenous Akan of the most popular Ancient Egyptians are known in Egyptology as Djesekaraseneb Gyasi Krasenboo. Osiris is Osoro, and Isis is Asaase."[73]
>
> "For example, the Greeks transposed the indigenous African tribal name of the Ancient Egyptian priest who wrote the history of Ancient Egypt for the Ptolemys from its indigenous Akan name of Omane Anto to Manetho. This means the indigenous African name of the Ancient Egyptian personality we call Manetho, was not Manetho. It was Omane Anto. This is an Akan name, but it is specifically the name of the Akuapem and Kwahu tribes of the Akan group. This name in Akan simply means Omane the posthumous child.
>
> The Greeks also transposed the indigenous and very important Akan names of Ancient Egyptian sky god from Osoro Kantamanto

---

[71] Nana Banchie Darkwah, *The Africans Who Wrote The Bible* (White Plains, MD: Aduana Publishing, 2002), 214a.

[72] Chancellor Williams, *Destruction of Black Civilization*. (Chicago: Third World Press, 1956), 89.

[73] Darkwah, 202.

to Osiris Khentimentiu. . . . It was through Greek linguistic corruption and transposition of Ancient Egyptian names that the indigenous Akan name of popular boy king Tutu Ankoma became Tutuhamun, Akuffu became Khuffu, the ancient Akan city of Mamfe became Memphis, Dade Afre became Djedefra, and Okyere Afre became Chepheran. The entire history of Ancient Egypt was transposed into the Greek language in the same corrupt manner.[74]

European scholarship makes it appear that these ancient Egyptians, Sumerians etc, are extinct. However, to the modern descendants of the ancient Egyptians, Ethiopians and Mesopotamians, these names are not extinct. They are still used in Ghana and other African Countries and can be traced to Akan dynasties, tribal names, and places.

One of the most enduring cultural practices that have come down from ancient Egypt to the present day Africans to authenticate the Hamitic ancestry of Akan is the matrilineal system. Chancellor Williams confirms that, the "Egyptian dynasties' were Africa-founded and were nothing more or less than the African traditional lineage system; matrilineal in character except when it was made patriarchal, after Asian conquests of the great Egyptian transformation."[75]

Hebrewisms of West Africa credits Diodorus with the following observation: " . . . the laws of the Egyptians were in substance, the same as those of the Ethiopians. According to the established order of succession amongst some Ethiopic nations, upon the death of the king, his sister's son mounted the throne,' and Joseph Williams adds, "This is, as noted before, the rule among the Ashanti."[76] And I might add, the Fantees and all the Akan people of Ghana and the Ivory Coast practice the same system to date.

The dominance of the black woman in the African American family may have less to do with slavery and more to do with cultural memory. The Matrilineal system is still among us in spite of many years of living in a patrilineal or patriarchal society of the West.

African Pronunciation of Egyptian and Mesopotamian Names

- *Ancient Egyptian god Apoahis [African name Akpofe] and Tutankhamen [King Tutu Ankoma][77]*

---

[74] Nana Banchie Darkwah, *The Africans Who Wrote The Bible* (White Plains, MD: Aduana Publishing, 2002), 105.

[75] Chancellor Williams, *Destruction of Black Civilization.* (Chicago: Third World Press, 1956), 88.

[76] Joseph John. S.J. Williams, *Hebrewisms of West Africa, from Nile to Niger with the Jews* (New York: Biblo and Tannen, 1967), 39.

[77] Nana Banchie Darkwah, *The Africans Who Wrote The Bible* (White Plains, MD: Aduana Publishing, 2002), 214.

- *Sumerian King Uruk worshiped a virgin goddess whose indigenous Akan name was [Anani]. This refers to a fourth child in the Akan language. Western historians orthographically transposed the name of this virgin goddess to Innini.*[78]
- *The god of irrigation of the Sumerians was called Naagyensu meaning "great one" here it is transposed as Ningirsu.*[79]
- *The quite sorrowful mother, goddess of Sumeria was called [Nimkasa] meaning "one who knows how to speak." Western historians identify this goddess as Nimkarsag.*[80]
- *...Sumerians were the [Nzima and Ahanta] people who can now be found in the Western Region of Ghana in West Africa.*[81]
- *..."Ancient 'international power in the north of Syria called [Kheta'] was the Ewe people whose story is the biblical story of Kpotufe or Potifar'*[82]
- *"King Nebuchadnezzar of Babylon built himself a shrine called the shrine of [Ekua] at Esagil" (see Lloyd Graham, 1995, p. 255). Ekua is a day name given to a female born on Wednesday among the Akans in Ghana to date.*[83]
- *[Arabah] in Joshuah 18:18. Araba is a name for Akan girl born on Tuesday. (Italics Author)*
- *"In the book, Egypt Revisited, edited by Ivan Van Sertima, in a chapter by Asa Hilliard, Tut's relationship to Akhenaton is mentioned, among other things (page 231): 'Ankh-en-Aten is well known as the husband of Nefertiti. He is described as a visionary. He was the son of Queen Tiye and Amenhotep III. He was the brother of King Tut-Ankh-Amum...Ankh-en-Aten led a religious revolution toward a new form of monotheism.'*[84]

Evidence showing Akan connection to Mesopotamia is beyond a reasonable doubt.

Akan Migration from Mesopotamia

From antiquity, the Akan people along with other African tribes of Hamitic stock migrated from one place to another. Like all people, the Hamites started from Mesopotamia but unlike others, moved southwest by way of Egypt/Ethiopia to Western Sudan and finally journeyed to their present location in West Africa.

In a book titled, *The Gold Coast Akan*, an Akan scholar called Dr. J. B Danquah asseverated that the Akan people migrated from the valley of the Tigris and Euphrates Rivers with other tribes such

---

[78] Ibid., Nana Banchie Darkwah, *The Africans Who Wrote The Bible* (White Plains, MD: Aduana Publishing, 2002), 202.

[79] Ibid., 202.

[80] Ibid., 202.

[81] Ibid., 202.

[82] Ibid., 202.

[83] Ibid., 221.

[84] Dr. Freeman, http://**www.**freemaninstitute.com.

as the Gonja, Bantu, Ewe, and Ga to their present locations in West Africa. The genetic discovery of the Lemba tribe, a Bantu-speaking people of Southeastern Africa, whose tradition states that a leader named Buba led them out of Judea to southern Africa also confirms that the black people of modern Africa used to live in the Middle East in ancient times…

According to Dr. Danquah, the migration of the Akan people from the valley of the Tigris and Euphrates Rivers took place before 750 BCE. The Kwahu tribe, one of the Akan tribes, lived in the valley of these rivers in ancient times. The Kwahu were the people that western historians believed were the vassal kingdom of the Parthian Empire.[85]

We have confirmation of the connection between the Akan people of modern Africa and ancient Mesopotamia, Egyptians and Ethiopians.

Cushite Empire Spanned From East to West

---

[85] Nana Banchie Darkwah, *The Africans Who Wrote The Bible* (White Plains, MD: Aduana Publishing, 2002), 234.

CHAPTER SIX

THE AFRICAN JEWS

A man does not wander far from where his corn is roasting. (African proverb)

A very crucial point to make is that the ten lost tribes of Israel may not have been lost after all. Moreover, given the experience of the people, how could they just get lost, without a trace? Where did they 'get lost'?

The Israelites' migration was similar to that of the Akan people. Through Shem, the Israelites started in Mesopotamia and then in Babylon, and moved to Canaan through Abraham. Later, with their father Jacob, the Israelites moved from Canaan back to Egypt. Israel mingled with the Africans at various levels and moved with the Africans in the mixed multitude to Canaan.

The Northern kingdom of Israel was finally displaced by the Assyrian invasion of 722 B. C. and later also assimilated into Babylonian life. After the fall of the Babylonian and Egyptian empires, the Hebrew inhabitants of these kingdoms joined in the migration south of Egypt where they likely further mingled with the Africans. Indeed there were waves and waves of migration from Mesopotamia to Africa.

The so called lost tribe of Israel could be traced among the mixed population: Cushites mingled with Israelites, Canaanites mingled with Israelites, Babylonians mingled with Israelites, Egyptians mingled with Israelites, and Assyrians mingled with Israelites who eventually migrated from Mesopotamia to Africa.   George Lichtblau confirms:

> Claims of a historic presence of Jewish communities in certain regions of Africa, notably West and Southern Africa, seem esoteric when first mentioned. This presence goes back not just centuries, but even to Biblical times. Of course in two areas such a communal presence on the African continent remains a firmly acknowledged part of Jewish history and experience (North Africa and Egypt/Ethiopia). A Jewish presence in Egypt and the former Kingdom of Cush are described in the Book of Exodus.[86]

The waves of migrations with their resultant mingling of genes, culture and theology might explain the phenomenon of the African Jews; the Falashas

---

[86] George E. Lichtblau, *Jewish Roots in Africa* http://www.ubalt.edu/kulanu/africa.

in Ethiopia, and Jewish Africans; the Bantus or the Lembas of South Africa. The origin of the people along with documentation of their migration, explains why the Falashas in Ethiopia can be both Israelites and Africans at the same time. We shall consider the records below:

The Falasha Jews

Windsor writes:
> The word Falasha in Amharic, the official language of Ethiopia, means immigrants. The Falashas did not call themselves by this name; they used the name "Bet Israel" (the house of Israel), but the Abyssinians called them Falashas. Because the other tribes in Ethiopia called the house of Israel Falashas or immigrants, this would suggest that perhaps the Falasha Jews came to Abyssinia at a later date; therefore they were ostracized because they did not accept Christianity.[87]

Numerous documentation show that the descendants of Ham and Shem were mixed culturally with each other in Mesopotamia, Ethiopia, Cyrenaica, Nubia, Carthage, Canaan and Egypt. The ten tribes were not lost to history. They were 'lost' through the cultural and familial intermixing with Africans. With available documentation, it is not difficult to understand why anthropologist and religious historians look for the so-called, lost tribes of Israel in Africa. The following are some documented accounts:

> Near the eastern part of Malagasy on the Isle of St. Marie, there exists a group of black Jews who call themselves Zafin Ibrahim, "descendants of Abraham." . . . . Like the Jews of Ethiopia, Uganda, and Wasambra, there are multiplicity of Jewish cultural survival, complexes, patterns, and traits found functioning among the Jews of Madagascar such as the following: the day counted from sunset to sunset, many feasts, the eating of beef, the New Year festival, the making of a small fire on the first evening of the feast; rituals of the purification of the people, the sprinkling of blood ritual upon the doorposts at New Year's. The latter ritual could be reminiscent of the Passover ceremony, which is observed in the month of Abib; this month is the first month of the Jewish civil New Year. In this month the kings of Israel were inaugurated.[88]
> In addition to the Jewish tribal groups in Senegal who claim to be descendants of the tribe of Dan, the Ethiopian Jews also trace

---

[87] Rudolph R. Windsor, From Babylon to Timbuktu: A History of Ancient Black Races Including the Black Hebrews (Chicago Illinois: Windsor's Golden Series, 1988), 80.
[88] Ibid., 82.

their ancestry to the tribe of Dan. Some of these transmigrants established communities in such still renowned places as Gao, Timbuktu (where UNESCO still maintains notable archives containing records of its old Jewish community), Bamako, Agadez, Kano and Ibadan. A notable number of Berber and African nomad tribal groups joined up with the Jewish communal groups trying to resist aggressive Arab Islamic efforts or as bulwark against Christian proselytizing, sometimes going so far as to convert to Judaism. Notable among these were some Tuareg, Peul and Ibadiya groups.[89]

The waves of migration and the presence of a "mixed multitude," explain the possibilities of why the Bantu or Buba clan of the Lemba people and other Africans to be both Israelites and Africans. Finally, after many years, there is scientific and genetic vindication of the assertion that an African people were derived from the Biblical Aaron, the brother of Moses. Their claim that Aaron was their ancestor was brushed aside as a myth for many years until recently when scientists confirmed it as factual. This finding supports the reason why Canaanites in Africa could demand that Alexander the Great restore the land of Canaan back to them. Before the fall of the Egyptian Empire, there was an East-West trend of migration. Professor Godbey points out, "When the Israelites under Joshua Ben Nun invaded the land of Canaan, many of the Hamitic-Canaanite tribes migrated to North Africa."[90]

All these are in concert with the Biblical position that the descendants of the four children of Ham, that is, Ethiopians, Egyptians, Phut; Libyans and Canaanites, saw themselves as brothers and sisters. They moved freely among each other. They all came from Ham, son of Noah. Here is the story:

> One Tosefta, *(Shabat 18)* quoting an older source, says that when Joshua approached Canaan . . . the Girgashites, among others, preferred to withdraw into Africa. The Tosefta goes on to say that the Amorites, the Kadmoni, the Kenites and the Kenezites—some of whom figure among the founders of Carthage—also went to Africa. These traditions date from a period when communication between Africa and Phoenicia was continuous." "The Talmud" *(Babylonian Talmud, Sanhedrin 9 1a.)* says that the Canaanites in Africa asked Alexander the Great to restore to them their country, which had been taken from their ancestors by Joshua Ben Nun." "These traditions . . . have been ratified by the Fathers of the Church; thus St. Jerome calls to witness the Talmud to support his statement that the Girgashites established colonies in Africa; *(Onomastica Sacra)* and Saint Augustine designates the natives of

---

[89] George E. ichtblau, *Jewish Roots in Africa* http://www.ubalt.edu/kulanu/africa.
[90] Allen Godbey, *The Lost Tribes a Myth* (Durham, N. C.: Duke University Press, 1930), 206.

44

Africa as 'Canaanites.' 'When our peasants are asked what they are, answering after the Punic fashion Chenani, having corrupted the word as is usual with their kind, what else do they answer but Canaanites.'"[91]

Interestingly "ni" at the end of "Chena" is an Akan suffix, making Chenani mean literally "one from Canaan" in Akan language. If the Phoenicians truly spoke in this manner, and the Carthaginians understood them, then they all might have likely spoken some Akan language to some extent. Here is a curious fact: The way the Canaanites talked after the Punic fashion was purely Akan. Augustine's illustration is precisely how Akan people still speak today. They only have to add "ni" at the end of the noun of a place to identify the person from that place. So for example we would say, Sumani, Ghanani, Fanteni, Americani, or Jamaicani. One thing is certain. Mesopotamian peoples especially the Shemites and the Hamites in the ancient times indeed intermingled. That is why most indigenous Africans still practice Biblical cultural traditions. This also explains why some Modern Jews still carry traditional African names.

That is why scholars who follow the Mesopotamian migration trend, have tended to search for the lost tribes of Israel in Africa and have reported finding them there. The reason really is that somehow, most ancient Egyptians, Ethiopians, Babylonians, Canaanites and Israelites through migration and intermarriage have been fused together in Africa and can be traced among the numerous tribes on that continent.

Yoruba Jews of Nigeria

The fact cannot be denied that common Biblical thread runs through all the so-called Jews in Africa. That thread can also be seen among the Yorubas of Nigeria:

> "There are black Jews in southern Nigeria known as the "Emo Yo Quaim," or "Strange People," by the native Africans. These black Jews called themselves by the Hebrew name "B'nai Ephraim" or 'Sons of Ephraim." The B'nai Ephraim claimed that their ancestors emigrated from Morocco; a fact, which Godbey says, is "supported by the language, a mixture of Maghrebi Arabic and local Negro speech. Thus *abu* ("father") has become *yaba,* umm ("Mother"); Hebrew em is ima." Nevertheless, most of their language is similar to the black Yorubas around them. The Yorubas have influenced these Jews largely in their external social life; the

---

[91] Rudolph R. Windsor, *From Babylon to Timbuktu: A History of Ancient Black Races Including the Black Hebrews* (Chicago Illinois: Windsor's Golden Series, 1988), 106-7.

crocodile is considered the sacred animal for all; the customary sacrifices of the Yoruba appear to be the same for the Jews.

The assertion of these Yoruba Jews is that their ancestors were driven from locality to locality by Moslem persecution; they did not find rest even when they arrived at Timbuktu. . . . Yoruba Jews lived in the Ondo district when Godbey wrote in 1930; this district was nine hundred miles southeast of Timbuktu. When Godbey wrote, they numbered about two thousand people in twenty small hamlets.

The Hebrew political structure and culture of the Yoruba Jews included seven hereditary heads of the community; their leadership was that of priesthood. They were known to have had copies of portions of the Torah (Old Testament) preserved in a "most holy place," however, their social life is not Torah-controlled like many of the Hebrew cultural traits among the Ashantee Jews. These black Jews observed certain Jewish customs, among which were the great holy days. In almost every way, these black Jews were like the Yorubas and were hardly distinguishable from them. There were some outstanding Hebrew observances. One of the most notable among these black Jews was a young man names Bata Kindai Amgoza, ibn Lo Bagola, who was taken from Whydah, Dahomey, to Scotland. After he had received four years of the white man's education, he returned to his home in Africa.[92]

The point made here again is that the Africans were mixed with the Jews and particularly that the Yoruba Jews were indistinguishable from the Yorubas in general.

The Black Jews of Dahomey

The Biblical thread runs through the indigenous people of Dahomey in Africa as well:

Dr. J. Kreppel reported in 1926 that there existed a large Hebrew community of black Jews in the interior of Dahomey, West Africa. These Hebrews had their own central temple where animals were sacrificed. In the temple, many laws were engraved on tablets that were attached to the temple walls. The community consists of a High Priest and a large number of priestly families, whose members walk from house to house rendering educational and religious instructions to each family. Moreover, these Jews have their own Chumash (the five books of Moses) written on old parchment in Hebrew letters. They have no other books. What little Judaism they possess was transmitted to them from their ancestors. Dr. Kreppel

---

[92] Allen Godbey, *The Lost Tribes a Myth* (Durham, N. C.: Duke University Press, 1930), 244, 5.

says that they observe the Sabbath and other Jewish customs, despite the pressure from their pagan environment.[93]

The point needs to be emphasized that there is no distinction between Africans and these ancient Jews in Africa, they have become one group.

The Jews Among Ashantees

Rudolph R. Windsor asserts that:
> Among the Ashantees of the Gold Coast (Ghana) are found Jews who observe many Hebrew customs: They don't fight on Saturday but they rest. They celebrate the New Year of the Jews which occurs in September or early October; they used the word "Amen" at the end of their hymn of thanksgiving; like the Hebrews of old, they marry in their tribe only; they perform cross-cousin marriages. The Ashantee Jews also observe the laws of uncleanness after childbirth, purification ceremony of the fortieth day, the menstrual seclusion law, and ceremonial ablutions. The Ashantee Jews have a breastplate like the High Priest in ancient Israel and it is divided into twelve parts, representing the twelve tribes of Israel. Also, they have the misnefet or headdress, with its gold disc in front, which in ancient Israel bore an inscription – 'Holy Unto the Lord.'[94]

The description in the above quote fits all Akan people, not only the Ashantees. This means that all Akan people are Jewish or Jews are Akans or both Jews and Akans were mixed in antiquity. This is supported by the history of inter-marriage or inter-mixing between Ham and Shem or Africans and Hebrews in the past. Indigenous Africans do not consider themselves Jews per se but in all likelihood intermingled with Israelites in antiquity. Here is a collection of African Nations, which were believed to have been mixed with ancient Israelites. Windsor sums this up in the following:

> Some scholars have located black Jews within the entire Niger River bend; the countries in this territory that have contained black African Jews include the following: Upper Volta, Ivory Coast, Ghana, Togo, Dahomey, and Nigeria. Joseph Dupuis, concerning the Jews in 1824, says: "The lands occupied by these people cover a wide extent, between Massina and Kaby. Massina is located in

---

[93] Rudolph R. Windsor, From Babylon to Timbuktu: A History of Ancient Black Races Including the Black Hebrews (Chicago Illinois: Windsor's Golden Series, 1988), 131.
[94] Joseph John. S.J. Williams, *Hebrewisms of West Africa, from Nile to Niger with the Jews* (New York: Biblo and Tannen, 1967), 65. also Windsor, 130

southern Mali, inside the Niger River bend; and Kaby is found in the southern part of the Ivory Coast.[95]

There can be no legitimate reason for racism or ethnocentrism, for we are all of one blood going back to antiquity. George E. Lichtblau told a relevant story:

> A related story about surviving memories of Jewish roots in West Africa was told to me around 1976 by former Israeli Prime Minister Shimon Peres. He had just returned from a meeting of the Socialists International, during which he had met with then president Leopold Senghor of Senegal. In the course of their discussion about the possibility of normalizing Senegalese-Israeli relations, Senghor had told him that he too had Jewish ancestors. At that time we both smiled somewhat incredulously. Yet, indeed, there are a number of historical records of small Jewish kingdoms and tribal groups known as Beni Israel that were part of the Wolof and Mandinge communities. These existed in Senegal from the early Middle Ages up to the 18th century, when they were forced to convert to Islam....
>
> Jewish presence is said to have been introduced into Senegal, Mauritania and numerous other West African countries south of the Sahara in part through the migration of Jewish Berber groups and later through some exiles who had been expelled from Spain, had first settled in North Africa, and had then crossed the Atlas mountains. Other even earlier arrivals are said to have come from Cyrenaica (now part of Libya, Egypt, the Sudan and Ethiopia), having crossed the Sahara to West Africa and eventually also moved further south.[96]

Ten Tribes Lost into Africa

Ephraim, one of the sons of Joseph by Asenath, an Egyptian African woman, could have eventually returned to Africa where he came from in the first place. After being inducted into the tribe of Israel by the patriarch Jacob, Ephraim became so prominent in Israel that his name became synonymous with the whole Northern Kingdom of Israel. Collectively, the Assyrian kingdom took the Ephraimites, and possibly, they ended up returning to Africa from where they started. It is therefore, not surprising that Yoruba Jews are called 'B'nai Ephraim or sons of Ephraim.

The year was about 721 B.C., when the House of Israel or Ephraim was finally driven out of their own land—out of their homes and cities—and

---

[95] Rudolph R. Windsor, From Babylon to Timbuktu: A History of Ancient Black Races Including the Black Hebrews (Chicago Illinois: Windsor's Golden Series, 1988), 130.

[96] George E. Lichtblau, *Jewish Roots in Africa* ttp://www.ubalt.edu/kulanu/Africa.

carried captive to Assyria, on the southern shores of the Caspian Sea! "Therefore the Lord was very angry with Israel, and removed them out of His sight: there was none left but the tribe of Judah only" (II Kings 17:18).

As indicated above, the lost tribes of Israel might not be lost after all; they were transplanted from the Northern Kingdom of Israel into Mesopotamia among Assyrians and Babylonians, and among Cushites, some later migrating to the continent of Africa.

"Interestingly, the Akan people are made up of eleven tribes. These modern Akan tribes are of present Akuapem, Akwamu, Akyem, Asante, Assini, Bono, Fante, Kwahu, Sefwi, Wassa and Denkyira"[97] They are actually ten tribes (of eight clans or eight tribes of ten clans depending on definition) also because the Fantes and the Asantes were one tribe/clan which divided during the migration from Timbuktu to the modern Ghana. Fantees and Ashantees split when the "Asantes" decided to settle in the interior of Africa but the Fantes decided to continue their journey to the Coast. It was there the Fantes began to refer to their kin they had separated from as "Asante." The Fantes said to them, "wo aso antse or literary "aso ante," meaning "your ears don't hear" or you are "stubborn."

The number of the ten Akan tribes/clan that migrated from Mesopotamia corresponds to the ten lost tribes of Israel. It is possible that some of the ten tribes scattered and were infused into all African tribes including the Akan tribes/clans. At the least, this evidence allows that the lost tribes of Israel were not lost but mixed at the biological level with the children of Africa.

Israelites have mingled with Africans from ancient times. It would not be surprising if DNA were discovered to unequivocally show that greater numbers of Africans carry Jewish DNA or vice versa. Further, it would be interesting to determine a genetic link between Jamaicans, (who are also Ashantees) and King David, Trinidadians with Moses, and Guyanese with Joshua.

Scientific proof has already vindicated the Lemba's claim that they descended from Aaron and that they share the same Y Chromosome DNA with the Cohen priestly tribe of Israel. The Rastafarians' insistence on being members of the lion of the tribe of Judah, biologically speaking, may not be far fetched. Most Jamaicans, of which Rastafarians are a part, come from Ghana, especially from the Akan people.

The Lion Tribe is Represented even now in the Akan Culture

---

[97] Nana Banchie Darkwah, *The Africans Who Wrote The Bible* (White Plains, MD: Aduana Publishing, 2002), 252.

49

Lion Tribe of Ghana

Among the Akan people of Ghana are many tribes/clan including the Aberade Tribe, which is the Lion Tribe of Ghana. This tribe may have an affinity with the tribe of Judah or other Israelite tribes through the Hebrews,

Lion, the Symbol of the Aberade Tribe of the Akan People of Ghana	**Author Shaking Hands with Nana Nyarko Etua III of Agona Nkum with the Lion Totem in the Background**

who likely encountered the Akans in Egypt. It is not a coincidence that Rastafarians hold this opinion. Among the Rastafarian group are legitimate members of Aberade, the Akan Lion clan of Ghana or Africa from the Fante or Ashanti tribes.

> "Before Dr. Godbey published his book, *The Lost Tribes a Myth*, Rabbi Matthew organized a Hebrew congregation in 1918 and proclaimed that the black people of the United States and the West Indies are the original black Hebrews. (The synagogue of Rabbi Matthew is presently located at No.1 W. 123rd Street, in the Harlem section of New York City.) Thousands of Bblack African Hebrews are scattered throughout the United States. Black Jews reside not only in the urban areas, but also in the rural communities of this nation. With the revelation of ample historical evidence, the authenticity of these black Hebrews can no longer be questioned. However, the purity of their Judaism among some of these Jews is not certain."[98]

---

[98] Rudolph R. Windsor, From Babylon to Timbuktu: A History of Ancient Black Races Including the Black Hebrews (Chicago Illinois: Windsor's Golden Series, 1988), 133.

It is becoming clearer and clearer that the Akan people of Africa of whom numerous slaves were taken to the Americas had a common heritage with the children of Israel.

"Some evidence can also be derived from surviving tribal traditions of some African ethnic groups, including links to Biblical ancestors, names of localities, and ceremonies with affinities to Jewish ritual practices. Moreover, the writings of several modern West African historians and two personal anecdotes indicate that the memories of an influential Jewish historical past in West Africa continue to survive."[99]

Based upon Dr. Allen H. Godbey's postulation that the Jews were driven to the area that is now West Africa from the Central Sudan by Moslem propaganda, his knowledge of the Black Jews in the United States, allowed him to develop this conclusion:

> "These facts have peculiar significance when the presence of Judaism among American Negroes is to be considered. Hundreds of thousands of slaves were brought to America from West Africa during the days of the traffic, beginning nearly four hundred years ago. How much more of Judaism survived among West African Negroes in that earlier time? As persecuted communities, they were rather more in danger than other Negroes of being raided by war parties and sold as slaves. It may be considered certain that many partially Judaized Negroes were among the slaves brought to America. How many of them might still hold some Jewish customs here is another question."[100]

They may not recall their ancient concepts of God but their genetic memory still hold these precious truths. The knowledge of God is fixed into the African mind through the oral tradition from ancient times, though the use of the tradition has declined over the years.

However, the fact cannot be denied that most modern Africans are a mixture of indigenous Africans and the lost tribes of Israel. Time and DNA have already vindicated the facts in the Lemba tribe of South Africa.

---

[99] George E. Lichtblau, *Jewish Roots in Africa* ttp://www.ubalt.edu/kulanu/Africa.

[100] Allen Godbey, *The Lost Tribes a Myth* (Durham, N. C.: Duke University Press, 1930), 206. Also Windsor, 133.

CHAPTER SEVEN

AFRICANS ON THE MOVE

Don't laugh at your neighbor when you see his beard on fire, get water by yours.
(African proverb)

The First Major Migration

From the above discussion, we have established that the first major migration of Africans in general and of Akans in particular was from the Eastern Sudan to Western Sudan, from the Euphrates, the Nile and the Jordan River valleys to the Niger River Valley in the sub-Sahara Africa. This migration also moved from Ur, Memphis and Salem to Timbuktu and from Mesopotamia to the interior of Africa in the days of old.

The first major African migration therefore consisted of all minor migrations that took place westward into Africa in ancient times from the fall of the Tower of Babel through the fall of the Sumerian Civilization, from the Babylonian, Assyrian, Egyptian, and Carthaginian Empires until the establishment of Sahara Empires of Ghana, Mali and Songhai in the North Western part of Africa. The ancestors of Africa ruled the world in Mesopotamia before migrating to the Sahara.

J. A. Rogers had this to say:

> "Thus, at the time when Ethiopia was leading the civilized world in culture and conquest, East was East, but West was not, and the first European [Grecian] Olympiad was yet to be held. Rome was nowhere to be seen on the map and sixteen centuries were to pass before Charlemagne would rule in Europe and Egbert would become the first King of England. Even then, history was to drag on for another seven hundred weary years, before Roman Catholic Europe would see fit to end the Great Schism, soon to be followed by the news of the discovery of America and by the fateful rebirth of the youngest of World Civilization.[101]

---

[101] J.A. Rogers, *World's Great Men of Color,* Vol. 1. (New York: A Simon & Schuster, 1996), 27, 28.

That was ancient African history contrasted with Western history in a nutshell. "The history of Africa was already old when Europe was born."[102] The ancestors of Africans lived in East Africa, Mesopotamia and its surroundings before migrating to the interior of the African Continent.

The Second Major Migration

Joseph Williams speaks of the second major migration of the African people, and of the Akan people in particular when he said, "We may also conclude, that the Ashanti are not autochthonous to their present habitat, but are comparatively recent arrivals from their district of the Upper Volta, whither they had in all probability been driven from the vicinity of the Niger by the advance of Islamism."[103] The Muslims declared a jihad on the Akans to force them out of North Africa to the West Africa in their present location.

Unfortunately, for the African Empire, "In one of a number of holy wars, or jihads, Ghana was invaded by the Almoravides under the leadership of Abu Bekr of the Sosso Empire in 1076, A.D. This conquest brought an end to Ghana's age of prosperity and cultural development.

And finally, "In 1591, a column of three thousand Moroccan soldiers led by Judar Pasha, a Spaniard in service to the Sultan of Morocco, crossed the desert, attacked Gao, and defeated the Songhai people in the Battle of Tondibi. No power arose to take the place of the empire of Songhai or its authority in that area."[104] It was around this time that the Akan people and other African tribes finally left North Africa to Islam and settled in the present locations.

After the fall of the Sahara Empires particularly the Old Ghana Empire, the Akan people began to move from the north down to their present location in West Africa. Many other African tribes including the Hausas, Yorubas, Igbos, Ewes, Ga's, Dagombas and many more also went through similar migration.

The Third Major Migration and the Present Reality

The third major migration of Africans was from West Africa into the Diaspora. This migration was involuntary and caused the relocation of millions from the continent into the Diaspora.

---

[102] John Henrik Clarke, *African People in World History* (Baltimore, Maryland: Black Classic Press, 1993), 17.
[103] Joseph John. S.J. Williams, *Hebrewisms of West Africa, from Nile to Niger with the Jews* (New York: Biblo and Tannen, 1967), 42.
[104] Bruce W. Willis, *The Adinkra dictionary: A Visual Primer on The Language of Adinkra* (Washington, DC: The Pyramid Complex, 1998), 12.

"At that time most Europeans were ignorant about the shape of the world and some of them thought it was flat. The Portuguese set out to disprove this and about the middle of the Fifteenth Century, they began trading with the people along the west coast of Africa, to which they gave the name "guinea" after the Sudanic Empire of Ghana. At first they traded mainly in gold but before long they began to take slaves."[105]

Here is where Africans (mostly Akan) began to spread throughout the whole world. They were moved from Africa to the West Indies, England, the Americas and the rest of the world. However, in spite of this, individuals and groups of the Diaspora can still be traced back to their various tribes in Africa because of their peculiarities. Linguistic and cultural characteristics would tell us that Jamaicans who are mostly Akan and the Maroons who are Ashantees were taken via Koromatse in Ghana. Antiguans are Akan, specifically Gomoa (a clan of the Fantees) still using names like Kojo, Kweku, Oware and Dukuno and cooking like Ghanaians. The Barbadians are also Akan specifically Fantees. Grenadians are the same. Trinidadians are mostly Nigerians from the Yoruba and Igbo tribes. Some Bermudans are Senegalese and others Akan.

Some of the islanders and others in the Diaspora still use some African words. All those whose vocabulary still contains the following words are linked to the Akan tribes or clans like: Ashantees, Fantees and Gomoas. Examples of these words include: Accompong town (after the name of God – Onyankopon), Oware or Ware, Dokono - Dukuno, Fufu, Kuku, Fungi, Ananse - Anensi, Kofi, Kojo, Koromatse (Chromates), Kwame, Kweku, Obeah, etc.

The traditional African can easily identify the African region of one's origin based on natal, family or tribal names, birthmark, unique features or personality. No matter how far removed from one's ancestral home, the African still carries as much Africanness with him or her as possible.

Origins of well-known African-Americans could be traced by simply observing their features or mannerisms. Mike Tyson could be a Ga, Oprah Winfrey may come from the Kpelle tribe of Liberia but she carries some Akan spirit in her genes. Kwesi Mfume is either Ga or Ewe. He may be predominantly Ga. Bill Cosby is as Fante as super O.D. - a Fante comedian who actually comes from the author's village of Agona Abodom. Colin Powell leans toward Ashantee heritage. They are known for their war genius and strategic skills demonstrated in colonial times. Condoleezza Rice has maintained even her Fante pride and tenacity. Whoopi Goldberg is definitely Akan from Nzima in the western region of Ghana. Her connection to Mande in the north is possible because it's from there our Akan ancestors migrated in the 1500s to the present location in Ghana.

---

[105] John Henrik Clarke, *Christopher Columbus and the African Holocaust* (Brooklyn New York: A & B Publishers Group, 1993), 53.

Movement of Yah People

We have come this far all the way from Eden in Mesopotamia to the New World. We have seen much on our way in our migration and this poem seems to capture it all. All Africans, on the Motherland and in Diaspora can share in this poem. It is our story captured by Langston Hughes:

> "I've known rivers:
> I've known rivers ancient as the world and
> older than the
> flow of human blood in human veins.
> My soul has grown deep like the rivers.
> I bathed in the Euphrates when dawns were
> young.
> I built my hut near the Congo and it lulled me
> to sleep.
> I looked upon the Nile and raised the pyramids
> above it.
> I heard the singing of the Mississippi when
> Abe Lincoln
> went down to New Orleans, and I've seen its
> muddy
> bosom turn all golden in the sunset.
> I've known rivers:
> Ancient, dusky rivers.
> My soul has grown deep like the rivers."[106]

---

[106] Langston Hughes, *The Collected Poems* (Alfred A. Knopf, Inc.).

CHAPTER EIGHT

HOW DID EDENIC CONCEPTS BECOME AFRICAN?

Every time an old man dies it is as if a library has burnt down. (African Proverb)

The concept of creation was universal among the dwellers of Eden. In those days, truth was not written down but passed on from parents to children in a mode of transmission called the oral tradition, which is still practiced by indigenous Africans and some Africans of the Diaspora. Much of the Bible was first received and kept in the oral tradition for over three thousand years before Moses wrote it down. The first book to be written was the Book of Job, followed by the five Books of Moses on the continent of Africa, in east of Egypt, on the Sinai Peninsula.

In the oral tradition, coming from the Garden of Eden the concepts of God as the Creator and blood sacrifice have been encoded in the "Protoevangelium" in Genesis 3:15. This was exemplified in the first animal sacrificed. Its skin was given to Adam and Eve for covering. It was also depicted in the sacrifice of Abel in the beginning. After the Flood, Noah performed sacrifices as worship unto God. The children of Noah were not strangers to the Biblical concepts contained in the oral tradition. This tradition had descended from the Garden of Eden down through the ages. Therefore, the concept of a Creator God and His sacrificial system was universal Edenic theology, which was known and practiced by the patriarchs. This theology was transmitted to their children, some of whom migrated to Africa.

In short, Biblical knowledge was passed from father to son in the beginning. It is the contention of this author that Adam, (Genesis 5) passed the Biblical Edenic knowledge down to Seth, who passed it down to Enos, who passed it down to Enoch, who in turn passed it down to Methuselah. Methuselah passed it down to Lamech who also passed it down to Noah.

Noah passed this same knowledge down to his three children (Genesis 10:6). Shem, the Semitic was acknowledged to be the father of the Jews. Japheth was the father of Caucasians and "Ham" which means hot; was the father of the sun-kissed, dark hued chocolate colored people. Ham then passed on the knowledge of God he had learned from his fathers from the Garden of Eden through his father Noah, to his four children. Cush, Mizraim, Phut, and

Canaan received the knowledge of God through oral tradition. Therefore, with the knowledge of God in their hearts, Cush settled in Ethiopia and Nubia, which was around the horn of Africa. Mizraim, which means two Egypts, settled in the upper and lower Egypt. Phut settled in Libya, North Africa and Canaan in Palestine.

Universal Biblical Edenic concepts of the God of creation made it to the continent of Africa, through oral tradition from the patriarchs to their children and all the way to modern indigenous Africans. The oral tradition in ancient times was replete with Biblical concepts.

Although distorted here and there by certain recipients of the ancient world, the core Biblical knowledge was preserved. For instance, "Enuma Elish," the Babylonian Creation Story might have been wrong on how things came about but maintained the fact of divine creation. The *Gilgamesh* Epic, the Babylonian flood story, might be wrong on the "wherefores" but is accurate regarding the concept of a historical flood in the ancient world. Hammurabi could not have known about the Sinaitic Code but he was certainly aware of a moral code. Hammurabi was an instrument of morality for the ancient Babylonians. The Code or the Law of Hammurabi was a testimony that ancients were not devoid of the knowledge of the God of creation.

There were universal Biblical concepts shared in common among the Ancients. It becomes even obvious by observing that Jonah did not teach the people of Nineveh about God, prayer or fasting. He only preached his gloom and doom message and left the people to perish. However, someone knew how to appeal to the mercy of God. The King of Nineveh surprised everyone by demonstrating superior knowledge of the will of God. He certainly demonstrated a greater knowledge and faith in God than did Jonah, who refused to obey the call that came to him the first time. The king already knew about fasting and prayer. He called his people to fast as an indication of their repentance to God. The actions of the king were an indication that he was not as pagan as some might think. His actions reflect that his people knew God.

Theologians promulgate the belief that Africans were pagans and idolaters. The Biblical text itself communicates a different story. All ancient people, including Africans, shared some concept of the true God and maintained various Biblical principles.

Ancient Biblical Stories

All ancients had either creation or flood stories. The Phoenicians, the Africans, the Chinese, the Egyptians, the Native Americans and many other indigenous peoples share these stories. No matter how the devil sought to distort the historical knowledge of mankind from Eden through the Antediluvian world, somehow remnants of the truth managed to filter through many traditions. These remain in many indigenous societies today. Like the Athenians, the apostle Paul did not emphasized what was different between him and the Greeks. Paul found a common ground in the "Unknown God" whom they worshiped and therefore preached the Gospel for all to hear.

Instead of exploiting the ways in which we are different, let us seek to find the common ground by connecting their dots (hence what I call "The Dot Evangelism," from which we can minister to indigenous people of the world about the Gospel. Depending on their memory to keep the oral tradition meant that the indigenous world was going to lose some information over time but certainly they did not lose everything altogether. That is why the concept of redemption is still alive in many indigenous cultures of Africa in many places of the world.

Who Are Pagans?

Pagans are people who are totally devoid of the knowledge of God! Are there such a people in this world? Certainly! There are those whose knowledge of God is insufficient. However, few people are totally devoid of the knowledge of God altogether. God ensured that the Gentiles who did not have the written word of God, had nature and the oral tradition by which to teach and remind them of Him.

Apart from the oral tradition, which was handed down from Adam through Noah through the ages, indigenous people also had nature's book from which to read; "*The heavens declare the glory of God; and t he firmament sh eweth his handiwork. Day unto day uttereth speech, and night unto night sheweth knowledge. [There is] no speech nor language, [where] their voice is not heard*" *(Psalms 19:1- 3)*. If we are humble, the so-called pagan can teach us something about God.

However, here is the distinction. "*Then said Jesus unto them again, Verily, verily, I say unto y ou, I am the door of t he sheep. All that ever came before me are thieves and robbers: but the sheep did not hear them. I am the door: by me if any man enter in, he s hall be saved, and shall g o in and o ut, and fi nd p asture*" (John 10:7-9) (emphasis Author). "All that ever came before me" is an over-generalization referring to all other religions including Moses and Judaism (John 9:28-29) as insufficient channels of light. Therefore their only role was to lead to the greater light, Jesus the Way. They served as streams leading to the main stream, which is Jesus the Way. They were paths leading to the only way – Jesus! All other ideas, philosophies and theologies are incomplete statements leading to the Word of God. They are man's attempt to reach God, but Jesus is God's way of reaching humanity.

The divinity of Jesus is what sets Him apart from all religious gurus. Everyone has some light but only Jesus is the complete or true light by virtue of His divinity and atonement. These are the basis of our salvation.

It is not surprising that the three pillars of ancient theology: The knowledge of God as the Creator, Saturday as God's Memorial Day, and the practices of blood sacrifice came down through the oral tradition from Adam through Noah to Ham. Hamites went to Egypt, Ethiopia, and Nubia, which is North East Africa from which we all migrated.

Africa preserved the knowledge of the original true seventh-day Sabbath, Saturday (Genesis 2:1-3), as God's day in her oral traditional culture. Africa is replete with various Biblical concepts. The concept of the kin's man Redeemer (Leviticus 25:25), the idea that only someone in your family or a kin can buy back what you have sold out was Edenic (Genesis 3: 15), and therefore universal but was kept in the African culture. African moral concepts, which are also Biblical, were not all from the same era. Some of these moral concepts predate Sinai and others are Sinaitic.

The majority of these concepts that preserved the knowledge of God were Edenic and Noachian because they were principles passed on down through the Antediluvian world to Noah and to his children. They all originated from the Garden of Eden. They either were from Eden through the Patriarchs or were learned from mingling with the Israelites who also practiced the oral tradition before the printed page became a necessity.

With this oral tradition, the ancient merges with modern Africa. This is how Edenic knowledge came to be the knowledge of the indigenous Africans. This is also how Africans have kept an unbroken link to the ancient world from generation to generation until now. Africa knew the God of creation and practiced principles of redemption long before the Europeans arrived on the continent. What was new about the message the missionaries brought to Africa was not the concept of God, but the principles of the Gospel. Not knowing Jesus is not to be equated with not knowing God, or else the Jews would be considered pagans; but no one dares call Jews pagans!

African Roots go way back to Noah's youngest son Ham, to Cush, his son who migrated to Ethiopia in Africa, to Egypt in Africa, to Phut who populated Libya or Somalia in Africa and to the last born son Canaan, who settled in Palestine in the Middle East. As pilgrims, we have come a long way across the flood, settling in Mesopotamia along the banks of the Two Rivers, to the Memphis of the Nile River Valleys, to the Timbuktu's of the Niger River bend, to Madagascar and all the way to the Islands of the sea. We have come to the Manchester of the Old World and to the Mississippi of the New World. We have come a long way. We have come from Eden to go to Eden. Africa knew God but did God know Africa?

PART 2

THEOLOGICAL AFRICA

Theological Reflection On The Motherland

CHAPTER NINE

THE SECRET BEHIND OUR BROKENNESS

If Yahmeh won't kill you mankind fights a losing battle.(African proverbs)

Why has our Kind Suffered so Much for so Long?

Do You Know Why?

Standing true to our God and our Native Land also means taking responsibility to establish the truth about our humanity in God. It is no secret that Black people are treated with contempt the world over. But do you know why?

We know how Black people are abused and misused, robbed and raped around the world and even in this country. But do you know why?

What is the root cause of the mess we suffer everyday: the dysfunctional family, the black on black crimes, the culture of poverty in all our communities, the high child mortality rate, the high teenage pregnancy rate, the high school dropout rate and the unabated high incarceration rate. Again I ask, do you really know why?

How could historic people of such power, prominence and royal majesty be reduced to servitude, poverty and inferiority complex? How could a people who initiated civilization, invented writing, laid the foundation for engineering, science and technology, started architectural construction, irrigational agriculture, built the pyramids, created long lasting empires: Ethiopian Empire, Egyptian Empire, Babylon Empire, Ghana Empire, Mali Empire and Songhai Empire; masters of Civilization, rulers of Kingdoms and Nations be reduced to servitude in modern society? What happened? Do you want to know why?

Why are Black people, a people of power be so segregated from modern economic powers and made to feel so helpless? Is there a reason?

A people, Isaiah describes in the Bible as "tall and smooth skined", "people feared near and far, a nation mighty and conquering, whose land the rivers divide" (18:2) become comfortable with defeat, and even believe in the lie that was concocted to defeat them. Do you know why?

A people, Herodotus, commenting on their academic excellence said, "Greeks were always proud to have them for their teachers". A people about whom, the Greeks complained as being "the most notable priests in the ancient world" Should they accept their modern condition of fragmentation and powerlessness? How has the Hawk become like a chicken? Does anyone know why?

Why has our kind suffered so much for so long and still suffer? Do you know why Black people suffer so much today and if not, how then can we stop it?

Do the civil rights architects really know why? Could the civil rights movement, as beneficial as it may be, only be dealing with the symptoms of racism, the outward sign of discrimination, hatred, and racial remarks and not the root cause or the core of the problem? Do you know why people behave the way they do towards Black people across the world? If you and I are serious about finding the cure for this disease, we must then look for the root cause.

What Is The Secret Behind Our Brokenness And Suffering?

For years, I have been struggling with this question. And finally, the answer is clear. There is a reason we are catching it and not pitching it. The disturbing discovery is that Black people are destroyed in the name of the Lord! Our problem stems from misinterpretation and misapplication of one text of Scripture.

We suffer today not because of the content of our character but because of the content of false theology; bad theology about a purported reason for the color of our skin. This is the reason for our perennial suffering. The reason we are so broken today in the Americas is because of Bad interpretation of the Biblical Text. Racists' theologians misinterpreted and applied Genesis 9:20-25 to black folks. Here is where they stumbled: The Bible says, "And Noah awoke from his wine, and knew what his younger son had done unto him. And he said, Cursed [be] Canaan; a servant of servants shall he be unto his brethren" Genesis 9:20-25.

Racists' theologians seized upon the "Curse of Canaan" text and twisted it into the "Curse of Ham" and added to it the "Curse of Cain" and applied it to Black people around the world. And that was the beginning of our suffering in the world.

"Some Biblical scholars see the "curse of Canaan" story as an early Hebrew rationalization for Israel's conquest and enslavement of the Canaanites, who were presumed to descend from Canaan."[107] The Bible

---

[107] Donald E. Gowan, *Genesis 1-11: Eden to Babel*, (Wm. B. Eerdmans), 110-15.

nowhere says Ham uncovered his father's nakedness (Lev. 20: 11) nor that Ham was cursed.

"Unfortunately, 'The "curse of Ham" had been used by some members of Abrahamic religions to justify racism and the enslavement of people of Black African ancestry, who were believed to be descendants of Ham."[108]

The truth is that neither God nor Noah cursed Ham. But racist theologians, trying to justify their diabolical mistreatment of Black people, managed to twist the scriptures to create the notion that Ham was cursed, and that this curse has been extended to all Black people around the world.

The Beginning of Our Suffering

Jewish Rabbis in the 6th Century AD began this assault on the Black. They are credited with creating the "Curse of Ham" interpretation. We are told, the Torah assigns no racial characteristics to Ham. "Despite this, a number of early Jewish writers have interpreted the Biblical narrative of Ham in a racial way."[109]

These Rabbis, working around the 6th Century AD, invented the idea that Ham was marked by dark skin as a result of his conduct in the Ark. The Babylonian Talmud created an extra Biblical idea about Ham.

The Sanhedrin 108b states,

> "Our Rabbis taught: Three copulated in the ark, and they were all punished — the dog, the raven, and Ham. The dog was doomed to be tied, the raven expectorates [his seed into his mate's mouth], and Ham was smitten in his skin."[110]
> Since this rabbinic creation, history records that the "curse of Ham" has been used by many religious organizations and nations to justify dehumanization of African people.

Could the motivation for this fallacy be the avenging of their forefathers suffering at the hands of Black people in their Egyptian Captivity?

Islamic Contribution to our Suffering

Islamic historians also misinterpreted scripture and considered Ham and his progeny as inferior by linking them to this stereotype: the "curse of Ham. "Writer Muhammad Ibn 'Abdullah al-Kisa'i's book *Tales of th e Prophets'*

---

[108] http://en.wikipedia.org/wiki/Curse_of_Ham#cite_ref-0.
[109] http://en.wikipedia.org/wiki/Curse_of_Ham#_note-1#_note-1.
[110] {Talmud Bavli, Sanhedrin 108b}.

(Qisas Al-anbiyâ), written in the 6th century AH, expounds on the curse with Noah reputedly calling blackness on Ham for his offences."[111]

Another Muslim historian named, l-Mas'udi describes blacks as being the accursed progeny of Ham. Al-Mas'udi portrays everything about Black people as a curse. He manufactures a bizarre detail about black folks.

> "Stricken in his semen because of his sexual relation with his wife in the Ark" and marked by "kinky hair, thin eyebrows, broad noses, thick lips, sharp teeth, malodorous skin, dark pupils, clefty hands and feet, elongated penises and excessive merriment".[112] Ibn Khaldun, concluded, "Therefore, the Negro nations are, as a rule, submissive to slavery because [Negroes] have little human and have attributes that are quite similar to those of dumb animals."[113]

These Muslims continued from where the rabbis left off and embellished "the curse" as being the black skin color, and eventually extending it to all attributes of Black people; reaching all the way to Ham's semen, to the unborn. As a rule, Black people are submissive "because they have little humanity." With a theology like that in the name of the Lord, the door was open wide to justify any dehumanizing act against them and that's just what happened historically. But we are admonished: "Add thou not unto his words, lest he reprove thee, and thou be found a liar" (Proverbs. 30: 6).

Christian Application of the Curse of Ham

Early European Interpretations

The Rabbis and the Imams already sowed the seed and the Europeans were all too eager to reap its financial benefits all in the name of the Lord. "In the middle ages, European scholars of the Bible picked up on the Jewish Talmud idea of viewing the "sons of Ham" or Hamites as cursed, possibly "blackened" by their sins. Though early arguments to this effect were sporadic, they became increasingly common during the slave trade of the 18th and 19th Centuries."[114]

"The justification of slavery itself through the sins of Ham was well suited to the ideological interests of the elite; with the emergence of the slave trade, its racialized version justified the exploitation of a ready supply of African labour."

---

[111] http://en.wikipedia.org/wiki/Curse_of_Ham#_note-1#_note-1.

[112] Akbar Muhammad, (*Slaves and Slavery in Muslim Africa, vol. I*), 68.

[113] Ibid., 68.

[114] Wikipedia.org, note-3#_note-3.

"Historically, many Christians have interpreted the Biblical passages so that the "mark" is thought to be part of the "curse". In the 18th century, America and Europe commonly assumed that Cain's "mark" was black skin, and that Cain's descendants were black and still under Cain's curse. This doctrine was used to support a ban on ordaining blacks to most Protestant clergies until the 1960s in the U.S. and Europe. And based on this some churches practiced racial segregation as late as the 1990s, including Pentecostalism."[115]

Mormon Church under Joseph Smith

"The Latter Day Saints movement was founded during the height of white Protestant acceptance of the curse of Cain doctrine in America, as well as the even more popular "curse of Ham" doctrine, which was even held by many abolitionists of the time."

Joseph Smith, Jr. in his "Manuscript History" indicated his belief in the curse of Ham theology in as early as 1831 and theologized about the cursed of Cain as black in his translation of the Bible, in Moses 7:22, he writes: "And Enoch also beheld the residue of the people which were the sons of Adam; and they were a mixture of all the seed of Adam save it was the seed of Cain, for the seed of Cain were black, and had not place among them."[116]

However, according to other parts of Smith's theology, the descendants of Cain were destroyed in the flood. And since this is true, therefore it debunks the first idea that Black people descended from Cain. "Despite Smith's insistence that Cain's descendants did not "mix" with Adam's descendants, Smith's successors later concluded that Cain's descendants did indeed survive the flood via the wife of Ham, son of Noah."[117] In fact, no seed of Cain survived the flood. Cain's descendants were destroyed in the flood. And that was the main reason for the flood in the first place.

Mormon Church Policy Under Brigham Young

"After Joseph Smith, Jr., came Brigham Young, the church's second president. He became the vocal advocate of the doctrine that people of African ancestry were under the curse of Ham, and that this curse was a rationalization for slavery and societal bans on interracial marriage."[118] Young also believed that the curse of Cain or Ham remained in people with even a single black ancestor. As a result, Black people were banned from the Mormon priesthood.

---

[115] http://en.wikipedia.org/wiki/Curse_of_Ham.
[116] Blacks and The Church of Jesus Christ of Latter-day Saints.
[117] http://en.wikipedia.org/wiki/Blacks_and_the_Latter_Day_Saint_movement.
[118] Ibid,.

In 1852, as the church's president, Young, stated: "Any man having one drop of the seed of Cain (black) ... in him cannot hold the priesthood and if no other Prophet ever spoke it before I will say it now in the name of Jesus Christ..."[119] Racism is never effective even in high places except in the name of the Lord.

In February 5, of that same year Young queried: "What is that mark? You will see it on the countenance of every African you ever did see upon the face of the earth, or ever will see.... I tell you, this people that are commonly called Negroes are the children of old Cain."

In October 9, 1859 He went beyond color to include other black features in the curse. He adamantly maintained: *"The Lord put a mark upon Cain, which is the flat nose and black skin . Trace mankind down to after the flood, and then another curse is pronounced upon the same race—that they should be the 'servant of servants;' and they w ill be, until that curse is removed; and the Abolitionists cannot help it, nor in the least alter that decree."*[120]

When was the curse supposed to be removed? If the cross did not remove Noah's curse, what was he thinking could remove it?

Building on Young's fallacy, another Mormon President, John Taylor, in 1881 theologized that black folks are representatives of the Devil. "And after the flood we are told that the curse that had been pronounced upon Cain was continued through Ham's wife, as he had married one of that seed. And why did it pass through the flood, he asked? "Because" he answers, it was necessary that the devil should have a representation upon the earth as well as God."[121] By these sentiments in the name of the Lord, theologians of the establishment were able to demonize black folks in the mind of others for generations to come.

Mormon Church, since then may have sensed their error and reinstated the priesthood to Black people but have not renounced or repudiated the fallacy of the doctrine of the curse of Ham that caused our pain and suffering in the first place. Are black folks cursed or was the supposed curse, a figment of racist's imagination? This is an important question that the Mormon Church needs to answer and we demand the answer now!

Jehovah's Witnesses Preoccupation With Miraculous Curing Of The Black Skin Color In The Restitution

---

[119]Address to the Territorial Legislature, 16 January, 1852, recorded in Wilford Woodruff Journal, 1852.

[120] *Journal of Discourses, Vol. 7, 290-91.*

[121] Ibid., 22:302, *22:304,* 28 Aug. 1881; 23:336, 29 Oct. 1882.

The "curse of Ham" and the healing of the black skin doctrine is discussed in the Watchtower's answer to the question "Can The Ethiopian Change His skin color?

The Watchtower Society's official response is: "No. But... what the Ethiopian cannot do for himself God could readily do for him. God can change the Ethiopian's skin in his own time." Watchtower provides some examples:

> "Julius Jackson, of New Frankfort, Montana, a negro boy of nine years, began to grow white in September, 1901, and is now fully nine-tenths white. He assures us that this is no whitish skin disease; but that the new white skin is as healthy as that of any white boy, and that the changed boy has never been sick and never has taken medicines"[122]

To the Jehovah's Witnesses, black skin is a disease that only God's intervention can cure. This supposed cure, the Watchtower argues, is an indication that God can and will change "Ethiopians" (blacks) into whites in the New World. "Actually, Mr. Julius Jackson was likely suffering from Vitiligo, a skin disease involving a loss of melanocytes which affects about one percent of all Americans."[123]

However, The Watchtower insists that blacks need to become white to remove the curse of Ham, which they have inherited, and this would be done in "the Restitution." "The change in skin color...was needed to remove the "curse" of dark skin which was a major part of the whole curse by God."124

They infect you with symptoms of a fallacy, which leads to psychosomatic malady, and then try to offer theological encouragement to help you endure it.

> "In an effort to provide encouragement for the World's blacks, the Watchtower Society gave hope that they can become white in an article entitled: "Restitution Can Change The Ethiopian's Skin". The story is about a person whose skin color changed--today we know this person was suffering from Vitiligo. The Watchtower reported that this is the third case they have seen, and this suggested to them "the process of restitution [is] soon due." The story "From Black to White He Slowly Turned" they took as a miracle from God, and it vividly illustrates their racist's beliefs and their teaching that in the new world, all blacks would turn white. The item reads:
>
> ... Rev. William H. Draper... gave a living affirmative answer to the famous Biblical question, "Can the Ethiopian change his skin or the leopard his spots?" Though once as black as charcoal, the Rev. Mr. Draper is now white. His people say that his color was

---

[122] Zion's Watch Tower, February 15, 1904: 52-53.
[123] Ibid., July 15, 1902:216.
[124] http://www.seanet.com/~raines/discrimination.html.

changed in answer to prayer. Many years ago a fair-skinned man employed Draper, and he was often heard to remark that if he could only be white like his employer, he would be happy. While in the white man's service Draper 'experienced' religion."

From that day forward he prayed constantly and fervently that he might become white.... He first experienced a prickling sensation on his face, and upon close investigation found a number of small white spots scarcely larger than the point of a pin. He became alarmed, thinking he had some peculiar disease but he did not suffer and aside from the prickling sensation felt nothing unusual. Gradually the white spots became larger and extended themselves, until now, after the change has been in progress for over 30 years, Draper has not a single dark spot on his body"[125]

Now you know the logical justification for Michael Jackson's identity Maladjustment

Whatever doctrine would make a Reverend seek a miracle to change his God-given rich melanin is a serious matter. If the Reverend in Jehovah's Witnesses denomination would believe that, how can we blame Michael Jackson, a child of the same faith who had the means to achieve it (restitutional miracle) by plastic surgery?

This theology that God had cursed Black people was the basis of all the evils perpetrated against blacks and our own inferiority complex. And this was what Europeans used as a Biblical justification for racism, slavery, a ban in interracial marriage and denial of the priesthood to blacks. "Things became so bad, most 19th and early 20th century Southern Baptist congregations in the southern United States taught that there were two separate heavens; one for blacks, and one for whites."[126]

"The doctrine was used to support a ban on ordaining blacks to most Protestant clergies until the 1960s in the U.S. and Europe. It is significant to note that the Coptic, Ethiopian, Orthodox, Thomasite, and the Catholic Church did not recognize these interpretations and did not participate in the religious movement to support them. Certain Catholic Diocese in the Southern United States did adopt a policy of not ordaining blacks to oversee, administer sacraments to, or accept confessions from white parishioners."[127]

Reasons For Segregated Fellowships

---

[125] Zion's Watch Tower, October 1, 1900:296-297.

[126] Dana Martin, *The American Baptist Convention and the Civil Rights Movement: Rhetoric and Response,* 1999, p. 44.

[127] http://en.wikipedia.org/wiki/Diocese.

Residual effects of the decision to separate from other Baptists in defense of white supremacy and the institution of slavery have been long lived. A survey by SBC's Home Mission Board in 1968 showed that only eleven percent of Southern Baptist churches would admit Americans of African descent.128"

'African Americans gathered to develop their own churches earlier on, including some before the American Revolution, to practice their distinct form of American Christianity away from attempts by whites at control. Within the Baptist denomination, in the late 19th and early 20th centuries, African Americans established separate associations.'

During the conservative resurgence, the Southern Baptist Convention of 1995 voted to adopt a resolution renouncing its racist roots and apologizing for its past defense of slavery."129 The resolution repenting racism marked the denomination's first formal acknowledgment that racism played a role in its early history."130

Implications of the Curse of Ham

Systematic segregation continues among the churches, and sadly to say even among conferences in the same denominations. The curse of Ham doctrine must be removed from all organizations and especially religious ones and the truth published and made official.

Racial Neutrality of the Bible

"Whatever the claims and counterclaims of various racial doctrines, the Biblical passage [in the] Book of Genesis 9:20-27, which people use [to teach] the "curse of Ham," makes no reference to skin color or race...Whatever the ethnic origins or skin colors of the Cushites, no curse is pronounced on either Ham, or Cush."[131] Noah cursed his grandson Canaan, one of Hams' four children. "Servant of servants," just meant they would serve the children of Israel who themselves had become slaves under the hegemony of the Egyptians.

If God endorsed the curse, the way theologians applied it, why would He use an "accursed seed" to be the instrument of His Blessing? Melchizedek

---

[128] Dana Martin, *The American Baptist Convention and the Civil Rights Movement: Rhetoric and Response,* 1999, p. 44.

[129] Priest, Robert J, L. Nieves, Alvaro ed., *This Side of Heaven: Race, Ethnicity, and Christian Faith.* (Oxford University Press, 2007), 275 and 339.

[130] Salmon, Jacqueline L. "Southern Baptists Diversifying to Survive: Minority Outreach Seen as Key to Crisis" Washington Post Feb. 16, 2008.

[131] http://en.wikipedia.org/wiki/Curse_of_Ham#_note-7#_note-7.

who blessed Abraham was a Jebusite, son of Canaan, son of Ham. The Bible contradicts the alleged inferiority of the Hamitic descendants. In the Bible, descendants of Ham developed and maintained a variety of sophisticated civilizations, ranging from the kingdoms of Egypt to the empire building of Nimrod, a descendant of Cush, (Genesis 10: 6-11); to the fortifications of the Canaanites in the book of Joshua).

The Die-Hard Still Hold on to the Curse of Ham Doctrine

The curse of Ham and the mark of Cain interpretation have been largely abandoned even by the most conservative theologians since the mid-20th century, "although the theory still has some following among white supremacists and an older generation of whites, as well as a very small minority of Christian churches."

> "African colonization was the result of God's curse on people with black skin or of African descent through Cain or through the curse of Ham, and some churches practiced racial segregation as late as the 1990s, including Pentecostalism. Today, however, official acceptance and practice of the doctrine among Protestant organizations is limited almost exclusively to churches connected to white supremacy, such as the Aryan World Church and the New Christian Crusade Church."[132]

Modern Christian Reactions Against Racial Interpretations

Other Christian Arguments Include the Following:

- That Moses' wife Zipporah, Job, Queen of Sheba, Ebed-Melech, Tirharkah, and the Ethiopian Treasurer of Queen Candace, Hagar, Egyptians, and other Black people in the Bible were not mentioned as being partakers of the curse. Had the curse affected Black people, at least one instance of it would have been mentioned in the Bible in reference to these people.
- That the racist interpretations of scripture did not exist before European colonization. These interpretations were likely introduced by ethnocentric ideologies that were codified into the Western mindset. This ideology adversely influenced the Protestant reformation and enlightenment period.
- That objectively making the idea of a Cain's mark into a change of skin color would require Biblical passages to equate the two...133 No such passage exists.

[132] http://en.wikipedia.org/wiki/Pentecostalism#History.
[133] http://www.xmission.com/~country/reason/black_1.htm.

If servant-hood is a curse Israelites would have been under a curse in Egypt. And Jesus' model of servant-leadership would have been discredited. Jesus said in Mark 10:44, 45; "And whoever would be first among you must be slave of all. For even the Son of Man came not to be served but to serve, and to give his life as a ransom for many."[134] We may be suffering now, but we should not forget that we ruled the ancient world as the Babylonian, Ethiopian and the Egyptian Empires and we enslaved others including the children of Israel.

Even if Noah cursed Black people (which is untrue) Jesus would have abolished the curse on the cross. Such nonsense should never apply in the modern world. Jesus' redemption washed away all human curses!

"He was made sin for us who knew no sin that we might become the righteousness of God in him. Jesus was also made a curse for us that we might be a blessing, for it is written, cursed is every one that hangeth on a tree" (2 Corinthians 5: 21; Galatians. 3: 13.)

Let us therefore delete Noah's curse from memory and install the blessings of Jesus in its place. If Noah's curse continued after the cross, Jesus death would have been in vain. Count your blessings and name them one by one

How do you deal with the fallacy of the curse of Ham?

You stop its effects from reaching the unborn of generations to come by:
- Establishing the truth about the curse
- Confronting the lie which underlies the curse
- Celebrating your blessings in Jesus
- Demanding an apology in all media
- Undoing the curse (in all media) because they spread the lie all world!

You Establish The Truth In The Scriptures.
- The Bible mentions no curse of Ham. God never cursed Black people. The writings of Moses pronounce no curse on Ham.
- I ask the questions again, if God endorsed a curse on Ham:
  - Why did He allow Moses to marry Zipporah a Cushite and descendant of Ham?
  - Why did He use a descendant of Canaan (Melchisedek) as His instrument of Blessing to Abraham?
  - Why did he allow Hamitic black blood (Rahab) to flow into the genealogical line of Jesus the savior of the world?

---

[134] *The Holy Bible : English Standard Version.* Wheaton : Standard Bible Society, 2001, S. Mk 10:44-45

71

The 'Curse of Ham' theology therefore was a lie concocted from hell in the name of the Lord to subjugate Black people to servitude in the world. Don't believe everything you hear – check it against the Bible.

The only way the devil succeeded in turning our blessings into a curse and used it against us is because we believed his lies. And sad to say, some Black people still believe they are cursed and are trying to change their skin color and adjust their noses! Everything said in the name of the Lord is not from the Lord! So establish the truth, check everything anyone says 'in the name of the Lord' against the Bible. "To the law and to the testimony if they speak not according to this word it is because there is no light in them" (Isaiah 8:20).

Why do we need to Confront the Theology of the Curse of Ham?

- Because it is a sin against the commandment and an insult to God
- Because Europeans of old lied in the name of the Lord to gain advantage over Black people – it's not just a sin, it's a crime against humanity in the name of the Lord
- Because, dealing with civil right on the social level cannot undo the deep seated psychological undercurrent which drives the engine of racism
- Because just a ban on the Word Nigger won't reverse racism
- Because racism cannot be stopped unless the source of its power is destroyed.
- Because, no one thinking less of me is qualified to talk well of me.
- Because there are people who still believe Black people are cursed, who teach black children in schools, across the country
- Because, it is hypocritical for anybody who believes I am cursed by God to be my doctor, my teacher, pastor, my theologian or even cab driver.
- Because Martin Luther King's Dream will be empty unless society reverses the "Curse of Ham" doctrine.
- Because, only by confronting the lie, can we reverse the curse that exists in the mind of the racist, and is manifested in his attitudes and treatment of blacks.
- Finally, because if God cursed Black people to be slaves, He would not have fought against America to liberate them.
- We are duty bound to confront the lie that lies at the root of the curse.

Inspirations say slavery and all its baggage originated from the pit of hell:

"Satan was the first great leader in rebellion. God is punishing the North that they have so long suffered the accursed sin of slavery to exist; for in the sight of heaven it is a sin of the darkest dye. God is not with the South, and He will punish them dreadfully in the end. Satan is the instigator of all rebellion. ...Your views of slavery cannot harmonize with the sacred, important truths for this time.

72

You must yield your views or the truth. Both cannot be cherished in the same heart, for they are at war with each other.[135]

Slavery (the byproduct of the lie about Black people) originated with Satan and he used men to do his diabolical deed. God was against it and He punished the perpetrators for it. Consequently, as we confront the lie, we should begin to view our worth in the eyes of God who bought us at the price of the blood of His Son Jesus. And then let's celebrate our blessings in God. We are children of the King! Royal Blood runs through our veins. We are "Somebody!"

Part of the lie also stated that the curse made us black. But how ironic that something as important as melanin can even be considered as a curse? If it's a curse, why would people pay thousands of dollars to go to the Caribbean and other parts of the world to get a little tan to enrich it?

Although:

> "In the past, melanin was considered by "western scientists" to be a waste product of body metabolism and served no useful function within the body. Recently however, scientists have discovered that melanin is a refined, complex, multifunctional chemical that has a wide variety of important functions within the human body and in the environment. All aspects of our lives are centrally involved and controlled by melanin."[136]

God never gave us melanin because he hated us. That ebony skin, as dark as the velvet of the night has always been a blessing and never a curse! Melanin has a major significant function in the body. It protects the body by absorbing ultraviolet (UV) radiation from the sunlight during exposure. UV radiation can damage the skin without melanin and produce skin cancer.

We are told melanin is a living molecule, a life chemical, and it is charged like a battery and operates like a battery. And that Melanin is found in many vital organs of the body and in nature: in animals, in the soil, in the bark of trees, rivers, streams, and seas. That's why our food should be as natural as possible and the fastest way to die is by eating the fast foods of our modern world!

In explaining the significance of melanin in African physiology, Professor T. Owens Moore, in *The Science of Melanin*, likened melanated people to plants: "A melanated human body is synonymous with chlorophyll in plants. Like chlorophyll, which converts solar energy for plants, Melanin is

---

[135] Ellen G. White, *Testimonies for the Church vol.1* (Mountain View, CA: Pacific Press Publishing Association, 1948), 359.

[136] Ronald G. and Emile J. Lewis, *Black Survival in Crisis: The Plight of Afrikans in the Globalization of Western (European) Culture,* (Mpambo Multiversity Conference on Jinja, Uganda), June 8 - 11, 2004/ http://www.blackherbals.com/black_survival_in_crisis.htm.

a converter of physical energy. Just as the pigment chlorophyll is necessary for all vegetation, so Melanin is important for proper human physiology."[137]

One thing about battery is that it needs charging to function better. And thank God we don't need to pay to charge our melanin battery. We can get charged just by exposure to the light of the sun. Melanin is not a curse it's a blessing! We've got a durable skin! Don't bleach it to damage it, recharge to enjoy it!

Also they said we have excessive merriment (too much fun) and it's not good according to Muslim historian, Ibn Khaldun. Well, it may not be good but it's way better than blowing ourselves to bits.

Undo the lie and celebrate your blessings for Jesus' redemption has washed away all curses and that was 2000 years ago! "God so loved the world (Africa included). And those who believe on Him, He gave the power to become children of God.

Greater than Noah is here to reverse all curses; no one in Christ is under any curse! Black folks are blessed not cursed. Undo the lie thereby undoing the curse!

Then you demand apology (on the media). They lied in the name of the Lord. They must apologize in the name of the Lord (in all media). They spread it around the world - they must reverse it around the world. Obama's America must confront racism like she confronts Terrorism.

THE SECRET BEHIND OUR BROKENNESS IS THE FALLACY OF THE "CURSE OF HAM" PROPAGATED BY RELIGIOUS PEOPLE IN THE NAME OF THE LORD.

Now the time has come to undo the "curse" in the name of the Lord!

Understand that the fallacy came from the Devil. But why is the devil bent on destroying us so bad? Because we are worth the world to God! We are children of the king, we are bound for glory. Jesus says, "Blessed are you when men hate you, and when they exclude you and revile you, and cast out your name as evil, on account of the Son of man! Rejoice in that day, and leap for joy, for behold, your reward is great in heaven; for so their fathers did to the prophets" (RSV Luke 6:22, 23).

The Devil lost heaven and he vows to make it impossible for everyone to get there – but he is a liar! We are not going to curse God and die! We know our Redeemer liveth! And weeping may endure for the night but joy comes in the morning. Never give up! For we are bound for glory!

Finally, they said our endowments and other black features are all evidences of a curse. It is evident by now that jealousy is actually the major reason for these stereotypes that were heaped upon us and that they have no

---

[137] Moore, Dr. T. Owens, *The Science of Melanin: Dispelling the Myths,* (Beckham House Publisher, 1995).

74

basis in theology, in anthropology and in scientific thinking and now is time to reject them out right. So give thanks for your endowment and celebrate your blessings.

But by all means confront the lie, establish the truth, undo the curse and rejoice in Christ because you are blessed! For the "curse of Ham" is a lie!

CHAPTER TEN

THE FALLACY OF THE CURSE OF HAM

Quarrels end, but words once spoken never die.(African proverb)

Dismantling the Curse of Ham!

We discussed earlier that our time has come to bless! However, there are two very sobering questions that confront us: *first,* can a cursed people be the instrument of blessings to others? And *second,* would others accept the blessings of a people they believed are cursed? Something is very wrong if people still believe that Black people were cursed by God. And so the record must be set straight.

It is therefore theologically imperative to deliver the black soul from the psychological effects of the so-called "curse of Ham." Was Ham indeed cursed in the Bible and by extension did this curse reach to all Black people down the ages past the cross of Christ?

Any diligent reader of the Bible knows that Ham was not cursed any where in its pages. Yet, many repeat the refrain "Ham was cursed and therefore Black people were cursed." People actually taught these lies as facts in churches and schools across the Atlantic. However, nowhere in the Bible does it say that Ham was cursed or that Black people were cursed. Many generations who have come and gone believed and treated Black people as accursed things. It was this belief without foundation that led to the enslavement of African people by Europeans. There are many living that still treat Black people with disdain because of their belief in the "curse of Ham."

Therefore, it is important to know the truth so the truth can set us all free. "In the African context, and in the Bible, salvation as a theological concept cannot be complete without liberation as a social/political concept."[138] In order to undo the effects of a curse that was not cast, the truth must unequivocally be told in the pulpit where it was perpetrated in the first place. The truth is that there was no curse placed upon Ham or on all of Ham's descendants!

---

[138] Robert Earl Hood,. *Must God Remain Greek?: Afro Cultures and God-talk.* (Minneapolis: Fortress Press, 1990), 83.

To those who believe that there was a curse, remember that the mission of Christ here on earth was to take away humanity's curse. Therefore, had there been even a curse, Christ's death and Resurrection absolved mankind of every historical curse. *"He was made a curse for us" (all of us), "Christ hath redeemed us from the curs e of the law, being made a curse for us: for it is written, Cursed [is] every one that hangeth on a tree"* (Gal 3:13). Every human being in Christ is free from whatever historical curse there might be. Therefore, honest Bible students ought not to have used Noah's curse as a justification for man's inhumanity to man. No one living today has any Biblical or theological right to harbor any racist views based on a mythical curse. Racism is a disease caused by lies of which only the truth can cure.

Bad theology and hatred were the twin evils of slavery and racism. Humanity must not repeat the process that initiated these evils. Here is how Adu Buahen described it:

> "To set the process in motion, the African was totally dehumanized in the minds of the Europeans. So far as most of them were concerned, the Africans were outside of the grace of God; Africans became living commodities in a world trade system that laid the basis for modern capitalism. The middle passage, the condition of the transfer of the Africans across the Atlantic to the various ports of embarkation where they were to be sold as slaves, is the most tragic story of forced migration in human history."[139]

In the Bible, we are all equal by creation and by redemption. By becoming a curse Himself, Christ has redeemed all humanity from whatever curses that might have existed. Christ's redemption has allowed all to participate as full citizens in the family of God.

Unfortunately, not all have heard such good news and continue to dehumanize their black neighbors by denying them full participation in such redemption. True redemption is holistic; it implies wholeness of body, mind and soul. It is unjustifiable to stand in the way of some groups in attempts to deprive them of God's blessings, spiritually, economically or academically. Therefore, any barrier raised by any group that attempts to prevent the full participation of others in the redemptive process of Christ's sacrifice, is a sin and an insult to the God of creation. For God has made of one blood all nations of men for to dwell on all the face of the earth...(Acts 17: 26).

To make redemption a holistic experience, all barriers set up by racism must be removed so that all of God's children can be set free indeed not only spiritually but also mentally and economically. The "powers that be" cannot be content to give Black people a message that saves only their souls but

---

[139] John Henrik Clarke, *Christopher Columbus and the African Holocaust* (Brooklyn New York: A & B Publishers Group, 1993), 78.

condemns their bodies to raw poverty, psychologically and economically. We need redemption from any condition that holds us in the physical as well as the mental bonds of slavery. That is what the truth does; it sets people free! We need deliverance from any condition that enslaves us so that we can be effective instruments in the hands of God to finish the work of redemption for all humanity.

Were Black People Cursed?

God did not curse Ham
God did not curse Black people
God did not curse all Black people
God did not curse Canaan
Noah cursed Canaan!

There was a curse pronounced by Noah the prophet. However, Ham was not the object of it. *"And Ham, the father of Canaan, saw the nakedness of his father, and t old his two brethren without"* (Genesis 9:22). However, it is unbiblical to curse the son instead of the father, for the sins of the father. Ham did the deed but Noah pronounced a curse upon Canaan. "And Noah awoke from his wine, and knew what his younger son had done unto him. And he said, Cursed [be] Canaan; a servant of servants shall he be unto his brethren" (vs. 25).

Did God endorse the denouncement of Canaan? Here is God's position: *"The soul that sinneth, it shall die. The son shall not bear the iniquity of the father, neither shall the father bear the iniquity of the son: the righteousness of the righteous shall be upon him, and the wickedness of the wicked shall be upon him"* (Ezekiel 18:20). The justice of God demands the punishment of the sinner. The one who did the deed, and not another, must be held responsible for the deed.

There was something wrong for a man of God to curse his grandson for the sin of his son. The Bible gives us a clue; Noah had allowed himself to be mocked by wine. "Wine [is] a mocker, strong drink [is] raging: and whosoever is deceived thereby is not wise" (Proverbs 20:1). Noah was a prophet, no question, but Noah was operating under the influence of a hangover when he pronounced the curse; "And Noah awoke from his wine, and knew what his younger son had done unto him" (Genesis 9:24).

The curse at best was a father's reactive response to a bad situation by his son. At best, the curse was a wish; it was Noah's impulsive wish *(may a curse be upon Canaan),* not God's will that a son be cursed for the sin of the father. God could not be forced to endorse it. If it was an impulsive wish of Noah then it could only be as conditional as "all other threatening and blessings alike" and not an automatic blanket judgment decreed by God against Canaan. It meant that as long as Canaan did what was right, no curse would fall on him. However, if Canaan deviated and fell from righteousness into sin similar to the one committed by his father, he would suffer the consequences of the curse. In other words, the most rudimentary sins would trigger the curse of Noah.

In recounting: Noah cursed his grandson, Canaan, when he rose up from his drinking stupor. The curse was not in the indicative mood as a statement of fact but in the subjunctive mood, conditional, indicating a wish. Therefore, it could not have been an automatic universal decree upon all Canaanites of all times. The curse could only be activated when Canaan fell, became depraved, the condition on which the curse was pronounced.

Historically, as Canaanites were doing the will of God, they were blessed and there was no curse working against them. A Descendant of Canaan was chosen by God to be the high priest of the Most High God. Melchizedek was a Jebusite king, and a priest of the Most High God. Melchizedek was known as the king of righteousness and the king of peace or Shalom. Shalom or Salem was the capital city of the Jebusites in the land of the Canaanites. The Jebusites were descendants of Canaan. It was a Jebusite city called Salem, which became Jebus' Salem, which eventually became Jerusalem.

In those days when the children of Israel were going to Jerusalem, they would say they were going to Jebus. *"And David and all Israel went to Jerusalem, which [is] Jebus; where the Jebusites [were], the inhabitants of the land" (1Ch 11:4). But the man would not tarry that night, but he rose up and departed, and came over against Jebus, which [is] Jerusalem; and [there were] with him two asses saddled, his concubin e also [was] with him"* (Judges 19:10). Jebus or Jebus' Salem, Melchizedek's dwelling place, was what later became Jerusalem.

Jebus' Salem was already chosen by God for His name and His glory and was flowing with milk and honey before the Jews arrived. The Canaanites lived there not under a curse but under Divine blessings. The most important names in the Bible besides the Godhead are Jerusalem and the Land of Canaan. The city of Jerusalem was originally the capital of the Jebusites who descended from Canaan, a descendant of Ham. All were Hamitic!

If Noah's curse upon Canaan was an automatic curse that spanned from Noah's time to the end of time, then God could not have used Melchizedek, a Canaanite as a high priest of the Most High God to be a channel of blessing to humanity. God certainly could not have used him to be the channel of blessing to Abraham. Yet, the Bible clearly teaches that Melchizedek blessed Abraham and Abraham paid tithe to him, a Jebusite or Canaanite at that!

Clearly, the "so called curse" was not automatic but conditional and was not a blanket curse across the board. It was specific, triggered by a degrading sin. It was not until Melchizedek, the righteous king passed from the scene of action to be followed later by a king who did not follow the Lord that God transferred the land and the priesthood from the Canaanites to the Hebrews so they could continue the ministry the Lord had entrusted to the Canaanites under Melchizedek.

When Adonizedek, king of Jerusalem and other Canaanite kings departed from the spirit of Melchizedek; king of righteousness, that God overthrew the Canaanites and gave them over to Joshua to be servants. "And Joshua made them that day hewers of wood and drawers of water for the congregation, and for the altar of the Lord, even unto this day, in the place which he should choose" (Joshua 9:27).

> "Wherefore Adonizedek king of Jerusalem sent unto Hoham king of Hebron..., Come up unto me, and help me, that we may smite Gibeon: for it hath made peace with Joshua and with the children of Israel. Therefore the five kings of the Amorites, the king of Jerusalem, the king of Hebron, the king of Jarmuth, the king of Lachish, the king of Eglon, gathered themselves together, and went up, they and all their hosts, and encamped before Gibeon, and made war against it...So Joshua ascended from Gilgal, he, and all the people of war with him, and all the mighty men of valour. And the Lord said unto Joshua, *Fear them not: for I have delivered them into thine ha nd;* there shall not a man of them stand before thee" (Joshua 10:3 -8).

Well, servant-hood in itself was not a curse. If it had been, the Israelites would have been the first to be cursed in Egypt. By departing from the will of God, Canaan had sunken into sin and fulfilled the condition of the curse and therefore forfeited the land to a new nation that would bring forth the fruits. This fulfilled the prophecy God made to Abraham of transferring the land of Canaan unto his descendants. The land was not transferred then because the Canaanites were not under a curse yet they sunk into iniquity.

> "And he said unto Abram, Know of a surety that thy seed shall be a stranger in a land [that is] not theirs, and shall serve them; and they shall afflict them four hundred years; And also that nation, whom they shall serve, will I judge: and afterward shall they come out with great substance. And thou shalt go to thy fathers in peace; thou shalt be buried in a good old age. But in the fourth generation they shall come hither again: <u>for the iniquity of the Amorites [is] not yet full</u>" (Genesis 15:13).

God in particular chose the Land of Canaan in general and Salem for the purpose of doing the ministry of Yahweh. It was given to a nation willing to bring forth righteous fruits to God's glory. And such blessing was not limited to Israel alone.

CHAPTER ELEVEN

DID GOD KNOW AFRICA?

To love the king is fine but a king's love for you is many times better. (African proverb)

Yahweh-African Connection

Did God know Africa?
Good question!

Yes! Africa knew God and Africa is rooted in the Bible!
But did God know Africa?
Was there any interaction between the true God and Africans?
Can we find God in our heritage?
Good question!

Where did God choose to reveal the Ten Commandments to humanity?
On Mount Sinai on the Sinai Peninsula!
And where is that?
Egypt!
And where is Egypt?
Africa!
Did God know Africa?
Good question!

Where did God send the children of Israel for food, when there was famine in the world?
Egypt!
And where is Egypt?
Africa!

Did God know Africa?
Good question!

When Jeremiah was thrown into a dungeon, whom did God use to bring him out? (Jeremiah. 38:7-13)

Ebemelech! And who was that?
An Ethiopian!
And where is Ethiopia?
Africa!

Did God know Africa?
Good question!

When King Herod, the Roman governor was hunting down baby Jesus to kill Him, where in the world did God choose to hide His only begotten Son the Savior of the world?
Egypt!
And where is Egypt?
Africa!

So God could proudly say, "Out of Egypt (Africa) have I called my Son!"

Did God Know Africa?
Good question!

When His own refused and rejected Him, and shouted "Crucify him" and when the Romans made Him a heavy cross he could not carry and no one would help Jesus so that He fell under the weight of the cross, who came to his aid by carrying the cross?
When God needed someone to help His Son carry the cross, who did He choose from the foundation of the world to carry Jesus' cross?

Simon of Cyrene, a black man from Libya!

And where is **Libya**?
Africa!
Did God know Africa?
African people have carried crosses ever since. But our God will never forget!

Did God know Africa?
The bush that burned with fire and not consumed was an African bush.
It was from the African bush, that God revealed Himself as Yahweh to Moses.

Did God know Africa?
Good question!
It was in Africa that He told Moses to tell Pharaoh to "Let my People go" and proclaimed Himself to be the "I AM THAT I AM."

Did God know Africa?
No wonder the Akan people of Africa call Saturday Memeneda" meaning "I AM THAT I AM'S DAY. It came from the God of the African burning bush!

Did God know Africa?
The two tablets of stone on which the Ten Commandments were written were African tablets from Mount Sinai: on the Continent of Africa!

Did God know Africa?
We are God's people, we are "Somebody"! Royal blood runs through our veins. God is our Father, Jesus is our Brother, The Holy Spirit is our Comforter, and so we shall overcome someday!

Did God know Africa?
I say good question!

Each time God wanted to preserve anything of value He used Africa!
He used Africa to preserve:
The original sound of His name Yahweh, the Akan people call Him Yahmeh!
The original true Sabbath from creation!
Israel from famine and death!
Jesus from the wrath of Herod, the Roman governor and other teachings of ancient theosophy.

Did God know Africa?

When God wanted to preserve His covenant children, He used Africa
Joseph was preserved in Egypt in Africa
Israel was preserved in Egypt in Africa
Moses was preserved in the palace of Egypt in Africa
Jesus was preserved in Egypt in Africa

No wonder, He preserved the knowledge of
Himself as the Creator,
Saturday as His day and the sacrificial system in the oral tradition of Africa!
We are rooted in God!

Did God know Africa?

Hear me, children of Africa, you can run but you can't hide from God. Religion is a part of you. It is in your roots. You can't shake it off. You have to know your religious roots. Young Black men on the street pour libation every day. The first thing they do when they open the top of their drink is to pour some on the ground and that is libation, a drink offering; offering of the first fruits to God before man partakes of the rest (Numbers 28:7).

This concept was not taught to them, it was passed down to them unconsciously. They have proven the African proverb that says religion is not taught but caught. Therefore, we ought to know our heritage and get connected to God so we can bear some fruits.

Did God know Africa?
God has used Africa in the past! Expect God to use the descendants of Africa: Black people in the last days.

Did God know Africa?
"Yes He Did!"

84

CHAPTER TWELVE

THE COLOR, THE CURSE, THE COMMISSION

It's not what you are called, but what you answer to. (African Proverb)

Are Black people black in color because of a curse? Many people including the Mormons and the Jehovah's Witnesses actually taught that people with black skin color are that way because originally humanity started white. In their theology, everyone was white until Black people were cursed. It is clear that when a story begins in error, that same story will end in error. If humanity started white, there would be a problem in accounting for the presence of Black people. It is genetically impossible for two whites to produce a black offspring. Two recessive genes cannot produce a dominant. Under this theory, the only way to account for the presence of blacks in history is to create theological genocide by the fabrication of the 'curse of Black people.'

Only the truth that humanity started out at least brown will account for all people on the face of the earth. Because two brown can produce black, brown, red, yellow and white. There must be more melanin, in order, to produce children with more or less melanin. If there is less to start with, it is impossible to produce more. Therefore, two whites cannot produce black.

Generally speaking, melanin determines skin color. The more melanin in the body, the darker the person is. Lighter skinned individuals have less melanin. The original people had to have more melanin and not less melanin in order to produce children of all shades. Therefore, human beings could not have started white; otherwise, they could not have produced black. The presence of blacks refutes any argument that identifies the first humans as being white.

Prejudice against Negroes is a cardinal tenet of the Mormon religion. Black people are considered accursed and so are all their offspring with white people. The Mormon prophet Joseph Smith had the 'Lamanites', a white people, changed to black by God for their sins. The book of Mormons, II Nephi, Chap. 5, verses 21-23, reads, "And he caused the cursing to come upon them, yet, even a

85

sore cursing because of their iniquity. For behold they had hardened their hearts against him that they had become like flint; wherefore as they were white and exceedingly fair and delightsome that they might not be enticing unto my people, the Lord God did cause a skin of blackness to come upon them…and cursed shall be the seed of him that mixeth with their seed; for they shall be cursed with the same cursing.[140]

According to Joseph Smith, Black people were white at a certain point in history and because of a hardness of their hearts God Almighty cursed Black people with blackness that should extend throughout all generations. Otherwise, they were white and "exceedingly fair and delightsome" and in order not to entice his children, the white people, God cursed not only Black people but also those white people who mixed with blacks. Can you imagine the absurdity of that and yet some still believe that lie!

About two-thirds of the population of this world is brown or have black ancestors. Therefore, regardless of their character, all Black people carry a curse in their heritage. Blacks must be guilty or they would not be black - they would be white. What a tragedy!

It is a tragedy because this notion of the curse of Black people is still the modus operandi of many people. People make decisions about Black people based on this false theology and widely held belief. They still would not marry Black people for fear of also being "cursed with the same cursing." The tragedy is that there is not one shred of truth in this teaching of the Mormon prophet. He said God has spoken when God has not said a word about cursing Black people!

Many people, blacks and whites, have had their lives destroyed because of the belief in this unsubstantiated curse. There are countless numbers of whites, trapped in racism because of this faulty thinking. The consequences of this type of thinking have been grave. Many have lost their lives, unjust laws and 'de facto' practices have caused the death and defamation of many thousands. Is there any wonder that Utah law punished mixed marriages so severely?

The following is an example of the result of bad policies from false theology at work:

> Negroes are permitted to attend Mormon services but they are not welcome as devout Mormons do consider them as accursed 'race." They are ineligible for Mormon priesthood and incapable of redemption. Not so the Japanese, however, thanks to their lighter color. 'Several Japanese,' says Carey McWilliams (Nation, N.Y. Jan. 26, 1946, p. 98) 'are members in good standing of the Mormon

---

[140] J.A. Rogers, *World's Great Men of Color,* Vol. 1. (New York: A Simon & Schuster, 1996), 4.

*Church and eligible for the priesthood and are not segregated.'
Negroes, he says, are treated quite differently in Utah and in the
Mormon Church.*[141]

Melanin, Determines Color Not a Curse

Melanin determines human skin pigmentation or skin color. The presence or absence of melanin determines lightness or blackness of skin color. Whiteness is an indication that there is little melanin. Melanin comes from Melan—French or Melas – Greek and it means black. Blackness is an outward sign of a greater amount of melanin. Color, therefore, does not determine one's innate spiritual nature or condition. The greater the levels of melanin present in the human body, the greater the ability of the skin to withstand harmful levels of the sun's ultraviolet rays.

Melanin is a protective shield designed by God for the human skin. Moreover, an increased level of melanin may be a potential preventative measure against skin caner. There is no way in God's universe that the presence of melanin would be the determining factor in one's salvation, such a belief is a doctrine of devils. Melanin was a blessing, not a curse. The original ancestors, Adam and Eve had to be equipped with more melanin to be able to produce offspring with different colors of people. Therefore, Adam, Eve, and their progeny could not have been white as the Mormons teach.

In conclusion, Black people did not come into existence because of a curse. The original people were dark-skinned, brown or ruddy. The original color of Adam was a ruddy, reddish brown that reflected the colors of blood and melanin. The investigations of science, altogether independent of historical evidence, lead to the conclusion that God "hath made of one blood all nations of men for to dwell on all the face of the earth" (Acts 17:26).

It is also an observable fact that when blood dries it gets dark, and rich blood is darker not white. So original rich blood plus melanin of the original man would make him dark not white. Whiteness is a mutation of the melanin gene; it is a depletion of the brownish pigmentation. It is the loss of something that was there and if it is depletion, then it cannot be original.

The Song of Solomon helps us peer into the ancient world to see their color identity. Solomon's wife breaks into poetry as she identifies herself to the reader," *I [am] black, but comely, O ye daughters of Jerusalem, as the tents of Kedar, as the curtains of So lomon"* (Song of Solomon" 1: 5). In (verses 10 and 11), she describes Solomon himself in these words; "My lover is radiant and ruddy, outstanding among ten thousand. His head is purest gold;

---

[141]J. A. Rogers, *World's Great Men of Color,* Vol. 1. (New York: A Simon & Schuster, 1996), 4.

87

his hair is wavy and black as a raven."[142]   This is how King James Version renders verse 11, *"His head [is as] the most fine gold, his locks [are] bushy, [and] black as a raven." The Bible u sed the same word ruddy to describe David. "And he sent, an d brought him i n. Now he [was] ruddy, [and] withal of a beautiful countenance, and g oodly to look to. A nd the Lord said, Arise, anoint him: for this [is] he"* (1Samuel 16:12).

The most basic meaning of ruddy is reddish-brown or brownish-red. The colors are fused together. The red emanates from the color of human blood and the brown is from the color of melanin. Adam was made from the earth, "Adama," and in the Hebrew, Adama was ruddy, which was reddish-brown and not white. An authoritative Bible student closed the case when she wrote:

> "As Adam came forth from the hand of his Creator, he was of noble height, and of beautiful symmetry. He was more than twice as tall as men now living upon earth, and was well proportioned. His features were perfect and beautiful. His complexion was neither white, nor sallow, but ruddy, glowing with the rich tint of health. Eve was not quite as tall as Adam. Her head reached a little above his shoulders. She, too, was noble--perfect in symmetry, and very beautiful.[143]

Blackness is not a curse. It's a blessing! It is therefore pathetic for any among us to buy into the racist's oppressive notions about their blackness by stewing their hairs, fixing their noses and bleaching their skins as if to say that God made a mistake by creating them with a dark complexion. Don't tell me that what God gave me is bad! Don't tell me I've got bad hair! I have good hair--kinky, wooly and wavy all at the same time. I have obedient hair that will stay where I put it until I move it. I have got a good nose specially designed to withstand the tropical African heat. I have good skin equipped with enough cancer fighting properties to block the merciless rays of the sun to prevent cancer and to promote health. I am still fearfully and wonderfully made. I was made in the image of God. I am blessed and not cursed. Let no one call accursed what the Almighty God has blessed! Doing so risks the condemnation of God.

Black people are blessed! Therefore racism has no Biblical foundation on which to stand and slavery was unjustified. These twin sins could only have come about through the instigation of the devil and God should not be held responsible any longer. God will hold people accountable for their participation in these twin sins of racism and bigotry. Therefore, we ought to reject what God has not endorsed, no matter where it comes from. God never

---

[142]*Compton's Interactive Bible NIV.*, (SoftKey Multimedia Inc.11996)
[143]Ellen White, *Spiritual Gift* 3 vol. 1864 (Battle Creek, MI: Seventh-day Adventist Publishing Association, 1945), 33. Also *The Spirit of Prophecy.* 3 vol. 1878,

cursed Black people and the truth must set all free. And whomever the Son sets free is free indeed. What great news! This truly, is good news.

Instead of the so called "curse of Ham" attributed to Black people which has no foundation in the Bible, or any creditable source, Black people are rather blessed and entrusted with a mission of reaching out to everyone in the world for God (Psalms 68:31-32). Ethiopia is now stretching her hands unto God on behalf of the world. We are blessed with a mission manifested in the ministry of Melchizedek to bless the nations, to help the weak, to set the captives free and to preach the Good News to the poor. Ours is a blessing and not a curse. Africa! Know yourself, accept yourself, arise, take up your mission, and be a blessing to all humanity. That is your calling; this is our calling, for our time has come to bless the world!

Oral Tradition Meets Written Document

Whenever the oral tradition meets the written document there has been a renewed interest in divine things, a passion for God, a new zeal and fervor for the gospel. A new wine is created and new wine skins are made. Whenever the African oral tradition meets Biblically written documents, a new people of spiritual zeal is born. The (African) Ethiopian Eunuch who was well versed in the African oral tradition came across the gospel narrative and a new life emerged. The African Queen of Sheba, great student of the African oral tradition encountered the Wisdom of Solomon and a new life emerged.

African slaves, bathed in the wisdom of the African oral tradition confronted the Biblical document in the West and a new American experience in religion, culture, poetry and music surfaced, resulting in a renewed interest in spirituality, a passion for God and a new zeal and fervor for the gospel. God has done it before and He will do it again. Rise up and answer to your name for your time has come to bless!

CHAPTER THIRTEEN

EVANGELISM TO AFRICA IN A NEW KEY

Tomorrow belongs to the people who prepare for it today.

It is time to acknowledge that the prevailing negative stereotypes about Africa have done far more harm than good regarding evangelism. Beyond this acknowledgement, efforts need to be made to correct these erroneous beliefs. These negative ideas stem from the portrayal of renaissance stereotypical notion of Africa as a pagan society devoid of the knowledge of the true God. The belief that Africa was a dark continent was a fabrication of the West to justify the enslavement of blacks for the purpose of economic exploitation. Unfortunately, all have by and large accepted this falsehood: The educated and the ignorant, the blacks and the whites, the clergy and the layperson. For too many centuries these inaccurate representations of Africa have gone unchallenged and unmitigated.

In a 2003 news story, Pastor Earl Carter, Founder of Christ Ministries Church of God in Christ in Orlando, Florida, states that God allowed the enslavement of African people to occur as a punishment for the 'crimes' that were committed through the worship of idols.[144]

Pastor Carter's theology is a typical example of how this falsehood has become so ingrained in us and illustrates how we ignorantly have become its proponents. It is therefore not surprising that this lie has gained currency in our community and is being perpetuated by our own ministers. In his book, Pastor Earl Carter, claims to have an answer to that old perplexing question and claims that there is no need for an apology. He proposes that slavery was orchestrated by God to cure Africans of the sin of idolatry. This is heresy indeed.

However, greed was the main reason for slavery and Europeans have found other reasons to justify it. Dr. John Henrik Clarke laments,

> "The greatest destroyer of African culture, the greatest exploiter of the African, was the plantation system of the New

---

[144] *Maranatha Christian News Service* 2003 http://www.charismanews.com (Post date: January 5, 2003).

World. The African was transformed into something called a Negro. He was demeaned. This is the thing that is uniquely tragic about the African slave system. Of all the slave systems in the world, no other dehumanized the slave more than that started by the Europeans in the fifteenth century. Using the church as a rationale, they began to set up myths that nearly always read the African out of human history, beginning with the classification of the African as a lesser being. The Catholic Church's justification for slavery was that the African was being brought under the guidance of Christendom and that he would eventually receive its blessings. This rationale was that slavery was a blessing to the African. It was not."[145]

Well, no matter how we think of slavery, the end does not justify the means. Both the means and the end must be moral. A bad tree cannot produce good fruits. The major problem with Pastor Carter's conclusion is that, first, it is the same old Catholic justification and second, his analysis of African paganism is based on what he was told by the Slave Master and he cannot show whether that assertion is true or not. I can confidently say that many who purport to speak for Africans have never set foot on the continent to know the whole truth.

Those who have been there to study the African way of life have come away with different conclusion from what Pastor Carter claims. "When we fully understand that God was behind our enslavement . . . then no apology is necessary." Carter adds: "If the white man was just the instrument, we must face the reality that we committed a crime. The crime was idol worship."[146] This has always been the old strategy of blaming the victim and hoping the problem will go away. But no! We must deal with it until we find the solution, which can only be found in the truth.

Positive Historical Accounts

Historians, sociologists and theologians who have done in-depth, honest research in Africa have come to the conclusions that are diametrically different from those of Pastor Earl Carter. Kenneth Carlston, who did such studies in *Social Theory and African Tribal Organization* discovered a totally different Religious phenomenon in Africa from what Carter has propagated in his book. Carlston referring to Africans says, "Contacts with the Supreme Being were maintained directly in the household."[147] The fact is not that

---

[145] John Henrik Clarke, *Christopher Columbus and the African Holocaust* (Brooklyn New York: A & B Publishers Group, 1993), 83.

[146] *Maranatha Christian News Service* 2003 http://www.charismanews.com (Post date: January 5, 2003).

[147] Kenneth S. Carlston, *Social Theory and African Tribal Organization* (Chicago: University of Illinois Press, 1968), 125.

Africa did not know God, rather even though they knew Him, they did not make an image to represent Him. Contact with God was personal in the household, fulfilling the African adage that says no one teaches the child to know God. It is taken for granted that once children live in the home they will grow up to know God because in Africa, religion used to be caught and not taught.

James Fly, corroborating the story says: "The Akan peoples of Ghana worshiped the Creator on Saturday long before the first Portuguese ship anchored off the coast of Ghana in 1471. Gradually the Christianity introduced by European missionaries supplanted Akan rites and traditions to some extent:"[148] James Fly gives us some important details of the African religious experience practiced from ancient times about which many are not knowledgeable. The reason the missionaries missed that was because they did not understand the Old Testament sanctuary system with its blood atonement and Sabbath observance. Otherwise they would have found a connecting link between the Bible and the African culture.

He continues, "Historians suggest that Ashantis are one of the last African tribes to retain many of their ancient traditions in the face of Colonialism and post independence development. Though European Missionaries replaced some aspect of African culture, providence preserved a people in the heart of the continent who kept the Sabbath until now. Saturday "Memeneda" was associated with God Oyamee Kwame the God of Saturday."[149] And then under the title "The Jews among Ashantees" Rudolph R. Windsor writes,

> "Among the Ashantees of the Gold Coast (Ghana) are found Jews who observe many Hebrew customs: They don't fight on Saturday but they rest. They celebrate the New Year of the Jews, which occurs in September, or early October; they used the word "Amen" at the end of their hymn of thanksgiving; like the Hebrews of old, they marry in their tribe only; they perform cross-cousin marriages. The Ashantee Jews also observe the laws of uncleanness after childbirth, purification ceremony of the fortieth day, the menstrual seclusion law, and ceremonial ablutions. The Ashantee Jews have a breastplate like the High Priest in ancient Israel and it is divided into twelve parts, representing the twelve tribes of Israel. Also, they have the misnefet or headdress, with its gold disc in front which in ancient Israel bore an inscription – "Holy Unto the Lord."[150]

---

[148] James Fly, "Ghana Ashantis" *Afritell,* (1988), 8.

[149] Ibid., 8.

[150] Rudolph R. Windsor, From Babylon to Timbuktu: A History of Ancient Black Races Including the Black Hebrews (Chicago Illinois: Windsor's Golden Series, 1988), 130.

Professor Owusu Mensa, in his *Akan God of Saturday* adds his voice when he says, "But for the European missionaries who brought Christianity to Akanland, the Akan would never have known about a Sunday God. The only thing they knew and had lived with throughout the ages was that God is called "Oyamee Kwaame and that His day of worship is Saturday. Christ indeed was in Akanland before the Christianity in its Sunday garb made its debut."[151]

The truth is that for centuries Africans have known the one true God and have kept the knowledge of God intact in their culture. Just like the Children of Israel, Africa was susceptible to idol worship, but that did not negate her knowledge and worship of the Supreme God, Creator of the Universe. Here is a prophetic insight into the African past before the arrival of the European missionaries unto the continent of Africa. In her book, *The Great Controversy,* Ellen White says:

> "The Churches of Africa held the Sabbath as it was held by the Papal Church before her complete apostasy, the churches of Africa hidden for nearly 1000 years did not share in this apostasy. When brought under the sway of Rome they were forced to put aside the truth and exalt the false Sabbath, but no sooner had they regained their independence than they returned to obedience to the Sabbath of the forth commandment."[152]

You cannot worship on the Sabbath for 1000 years and not have other concepts of God along with it. It is most unfortunate that, to a greater degree African missiology has not been based on the truthfulness of the African religious experience but rather on the faulty conception of Africa as a pagan society. As a result, there has been a spirit of suspicion and mistrust on the part of the indigenous African. This will not change unless there is a change in the attitude of condescension on the part of the missionary.

African missions would exceed far beyond its present successes if the indigenous understanding of God were critically incorporated into the principles of reaching Africans for Christ. The time has come for those who work for the salvation of Africa to cease and desist from stigmatizing indigenous form of worship, while accepting only the European style. If there were a shift in attitudes, it would not be surprising to one day see the whole Continent accepting the gospel of Jesus Christ.

Akan Theology Of God Summarized

---

[151] K. Owusu Mensa, *Onyamee Kwamee: The Akan God of Saturday* (Accra Ghana: The Advent Press,1990), 45-53.

[152] Ellen White, The Great Controversy Between Christ and Satan 1911 (Mountain View, CA: Pacific Press Publishing Association, 1911), 577.

In volume one of our Sankofa Heritage Series; *Africa's Roots in God* we demonstrated that Africa was not a pagan society without the knowledge of God and gave evidence to support that.

What therefore, did Africa know about God that can help the missionary in his efforts to evangelize Africa for Christ? Africa held various religious concepts and ideas that were synonymous with Biblical theological concepts and ideas about God. Numerous symbols in the African culture reveal a very profound knowledge relative to the God of the Bible. In summary, here are a few Biblical Akan concepts:

The God of Creation

Africans knew about the God of creation. The Akan name for God the Creator is 'Odomankoma Boadi', which literally means the Gracious Creator, the One who created things. 'Boadi' means Creator. This is the Supreme God of the Akans who is believed to dwell in Heaven. So the traditional priest in performing libation would look up into the Heavens and declare, "You who say no, and no one else can say yes, and say yes, and no one else can say no, from you I ask permission." The Akan people knew 'Oboadi' as the Supreme God whose decree, no one can contradict. They considered Him to be the God above all other gods.

Among the Akans is also the concept of 'Onyame Dua.' This means God's tree. The most interesting thing about this tree is that it has three Branches, a perfect theological symbol of the Triune God.

Then there was "Gye Nyame," the symbol in the Akan culture that sums up the concept of the omnipotence and the creatorship of God. This theology attributes all creation to God by stating. ***"This great Pano rama of creation dates back to time immemorial. No one lived who saw its beginning and no one lives who knows its end, GYE NYAME: EXCEPT GOD."*** Our ancestors did not do systematic theology but their concepts and symbols demonstrated their belief in the true God of creation. And their understanding and knowledge of God have been passed down to posterity through their oral tradition.

The Biblical Sabbath

As noted earlier, through oral tradition, our Fathers also kept the idea of Saturday as Creator's Day. The personal name for God is 'Onyame Kwame,' for short or 'Twereduampon Kwame.' 'Twereduampon' simply means a friend whom you can lean on or depend upon and you will never fall because He will never let you down. His last name, 'Kwame', is a day name given to any male born on Saturday. So the concept of the Supreme God whose day is

Saturday is in our oral tradition. He is in essence the God of Saturday, not Sunday, or Friday, as Creation Week attest.

Apart from the last name that connects God to the Sabbath, the literal meaning of Saturday itself contains a profound theological insight. Saturday in the Akan language is 'Memeneda.' Memeneda is a compound word; the first part 'Memene' is a repetition of the first person singular of the verb 'To Be,' so "Memene" simply means "I am that I am."

The second part of the compound 'da,' means day. When you put them together Saturday literally means "I AM THAT I AM'S DAY." And this profound concept is alive in the culture of the African people. Behind the Akan language is "Someone" claiming ownership of Saturday as His Day, and He is none other than Yahweh, known as Yahmeh in the Akan culture.

The Sacrificial System

There is this strong concept in the Africa culture that says evil cannot be eradicated without the shedding of blood. Any significant sin calls for blood atonement. The chief cannot re-enter the palace after attending a funeral or after coming in contact with a corpse unless a lamb is sacrificed to cleanse him of defilement. Epidemics result from sin, and blood is the means of its eradication.

For the Akans, blood is the means of purification and atonement. The sacrifice must be spotless; the blood is poured on the sacred stone before the palace at festivals. Annually it is sprinkled in the sacred room on the sacred stool, which is the seat of government of the indigenous people.

Also there are two kinds of sacrificial animals. One is killed the other is left to wander in the bush or wilderness just like the Biblical "scape goat." The most significant thing about the African sacrificial system is that the sacrificial lamb is not allowed to make any noise during the sacrifice. The bleating sound of the lamb during the offering of the sacrifice is considered some kind of protest, and the sacrifice is rendered unacceptable. Therefore the lamb's mouth is always gripped tightly, so that it may not utter a sound.

With this aforementioned insight, anyone can see how the Ethiopian Eunuch, an African, would readily accept the Savior upon reading about the Sacrificial Lamb in Isaiah 53. The concept of the lamb not making a sound made sense to him and his interest was directed to finding who that could be and when Philip expounded the gospel of Jesus to him, he was ready to accept the Lamb of God, which takes away the sins of the world. This was to be the model of African evangelism. Like Philip, the missionary ought to find a common ground with what the Africans already know and practice. The missionary then needs to connect the dots from what they know to what they do not know, in leading them to Jesus. In other words, it is leading them from the known to the unknown.

95

God has not left Africa in darkness without a witness. He has given to Africa ample indications of who He is and how He operates so that a child of Africa familiar with the African oral tradition can be led through its sacrificial system to Christ, the ultimate sacrifice.

Mission to Africa

A good starting point for missionaries to Africa, if success were to crown their efforts in winning Africans to Christ, is for them to accept the fact that the African culture and the Old Testament Biblical worldview are similar in many respects. They need to see the similarities in traditions, symbols and shadows. The evangelist's duty is to acknowledge their theological significance of all these and point Africans beyond the symbols to Christ. There are so many things that ancient Israel did in the Bible that Africans do and have kept alive in their culture until today.

Africans can now be said to be the keepers of many Biblical traditions in the modern times. We cannot overlook these facts as we minister to them. Africans are the keepers of oral traditional culture, which was the original way of passing down knowledge to posterity. Africans are keepers of the creation concept, the original doctrine of the origin of the universe; keepers of the memorial of Creation, Saturday, the original day of the God of creation; keepers of the sacrificial system, original mode of atonement; keepers of the culture of dress, the djampa and the wrap—the two garment system, the original and authentic mode of dress; keepers of the culture of redemption, the original Biblical way of redeeming slaves; keepers of the "village life," marriage of joining two families rather than two individuals together, which is the involvement of extended families in the marriage covenant; keepers of table fellowship, original or Bible way of eating from the same bowl together; keepers of the tribal system, the original way of organizing the community or the "village"; keepers of the patriarchal system, the original way of handing down inheritance to descendants; keepers of the judicial system, the assembly of tribal elders, the original way of adjudicating village issues; keepers of the royal system, original way of governing the village; keepers of ceremonial system, original way of dealing with the dead, defilement and sin; and keepers of the divine names, the original sounding of Yahweh from the root Yah, which Africa knew as 'Yahmeh' (spelt Nyame) and the Amen or Amon, and "Memeneda" of the Akan which means "I am that I AM's day."

These and other Biblical concepts are practiced daily by Africans throughout the continent and yet missionaries the world over have not come to terms with their significance in their efforts of bringing Christ to Africa. I contend that success in the African work largely depends on incorporating the African religious experience and worldview into missions to Africa. The effective missionary must find the African dots and connect them to Jesus!

Paul's Practical Example

From a theological standpoint, therefore, missions to Africa should follow the Apostle Paul's example in his ministry to the Gentiles in Athens. In Acts 17, Paul was able to use the indigenous knowledge of the Athenians to lead them to the understanding of the Gospel of Christ and called them to accept Jesus. He simply connected their dots. Consider the following:

> And Paul stood in the midst of the Areopagus, and said, Ye men of Athens, in all things, I perceive that ye are very religious. For as I passed along, and observed the objects of your worship, I found also an altar with this inscription, To An Unknown God. What therefore ye worship in ignorance, this I set forth unto you. The God that made the world and all things therein, he, being Lord of heaven and earth, dwelleth not in temples made with hands; neither is he served by men's hands, as though he needed anything, seeing he himself giveth to all life, and breath, and all things; and he made of one every nation of men to dwell on all the face of the earth, having determined (their) appointed seasons, and the bounds of their habitation; that they should seek God, if haply they might feel after him and find him, though he is not far from each one of us: for in him we live, and move, and have our being; as certain even of your own poets have said, For we are also his offspring. Being then the offspring of God, we ought not to think that the Godhead is like unto gold, or silver, or stone, graven by art and device of man. The times of ignorance therefore God overlooked; but now he commandeth men that they should all everywhere repent: inasmuch as he hath appointed a day in which he will judge the world in righteousness by the man whom he hath ordained; whereof he hath given assurance unto all men, in that he hath raised him from the dead. Now when they heard of the resurrection of the dead, some mocked; but others said, we will hear thee concerning this yet again. Thus Paul went out from among them. But certain men clave unto him, and believed: among whom also was Dionysius the Areopagite, and a woman named Damaris, and others with them. (Acts 17:22-34)

Lessons for the Missionary to Africa

Paul did not condemn the Athenians as pagans even though they had built shrines for their numerous other gods. Neither did he reject their indigenous religious foundations but used what they knew about God as a springboard or a basis from which to teach them the Gospel, to introduce what they did not know. *"And Paul stood in the midst of the Areopagu s, and said, Ye men of Athens, in all things, I percei ve that ye are very religious. For as I passed along, and observed the objects of your worship, I found also an altar with this ins cription, To An Unknow n God. What   therefore y e worship in ignorance, this I set forth unto yo u"* (Acts 17:22 ASV). He simply connected their dots.

The principle here is that in the work of saving souls for the kingdom, the evangelist has to learn to meet the people where they are, and to establish a common ground; and then move them to where they ought to be. And, as I have said before, the best policy is to start from the known to the unknown. Ministry to African people should not be any different.   Jesus Himself followed this same principle of bringing people from the known to the unknown, especially in His use of parables.

The Apostle Paul under the influence of the Holy Spirit has set an important example for us. Like Paul, the evangelist must realize that there is something in everybody's culture to connect them to Christ, and it is our duty to find it. Failure to do so will disqualify us from reaching many diverse groups for Christ. For instance, how can we reach a group like the Rastafarians if we are not willing to find their dots or speak their Reggae language and to meet them where in order to bring them to Jesus!

Well, my point here is that Africans knew God and held on to the Old Testament Biblical concepts of God. What most did not know was how Jesus fulfilled these shadows of things to come. When we start from their understanding of the knowledge of God, connect their dots to the Gospel, and then lead them to Jesus as the center and the fulfillment of all religious activities, the African is ready to accept.

Paradigm Shift and Personal Experience

As stated before, Paul and Philip's example should form the bedrock of the theology of African mission or evangelistic thrust to the whole of Africa. This is a paradigm shift from conventional methodology to a more accurate Biblical evangelistic model that works for Africa.

The African field is white and the harvest is ready. All it needs are evangelists who are attuned to the effective means by which African work must be done. These individuals must understand the Old Testament Scriptures and the African worldview and must be willing and able to connect the dots in their efforts to lead the African to Christ.

In the course of writing this book I went to Ghana and interviewed churches and royalties in their palaces. I visited African kings at Swedru, Nyakrom and Nkum in the Central Region and interviewed them regarding the knowledge of God in the African culture since they are the ones who have preserved the accumulated wisdom of the ancients. Each of them confirmed beyond a shadow of doubt the knowledge of the creatorship of God in their culture, Saturday as the Creator's day, blood Atonement. They even pointed

98

to a tradition they said was handed down from the days of Joshua as the basis for Akan Royal houses keeping 'Sacred Stones' on which they pour sacrificial blood in front of their Palaces. "And Joshua said unto them, Pass over before the ark of the Lord your God into the midst of Jordan, *and take ye up ever y man of you a stone upon his shoulder, according unto the number of the tribes of the children of Israel"* (Joshua 4:5).

The implication of what the kings told me is that deep down in their hearts they believe they share some kind of theological bond with ancient Israel. The fact of the matter is that the royal houses like the Ethiopian Eunuch are waiting for a "Philip" to put the missing piece of the theological puzzle, or connect the dots to complete the African puzzle. Like the Ethiopian Eunuch, Africa will cry out, "Here is plenty of water, what hinders us from being baptized?" Royal and the indigenous Africa alike are ready to confess Christ. Our duty is to connect their dots to Him!

General Conclusion

African paganism is as a myth as the 'broom crossing marriage ceremony,' that was purported by the West to be of African origin. It was a myth created by the slave masters to make fun of the slaves. It was fiction uncritically accepted as fact. After peeling off skins of the great myths of African paganism, we come away with a simple fact collaborated by numerous sources that Africa knew God, the Great Creator of the heavens and the earth, and not only did they worship Him, but God also interacted with them. Now Jesus can be presented to Africa in the rich currency of African religiosity to prepare the children of Africa for the great Camp Meeting in Heaven.

CHAPTER FOURTEEN

UNSHACKLED!

Until lions have their own Historians tales of the hunt will always glorify the hunter. (African proverbs)

The thief cometh not, but for to steal, and to kill, and to destroy: I am come that they might have life, and that they might have [it] more abundantly (John 10:10).

Breaking Out Of the Last Chains of Slavery!

And ye shall know the truth, and the truth shall make you free (John 8:32).
All truth is God's Truth! All Lies Come From The Devil!
And the truth is not against people, it's against error!

Do you ever wonder why "everything black is bad" in America? Why is the Devil black and Jesus white? Who attached goodness to whiteness and badness to blackness? The word "black," even in the dictionaries, is a metaphor for evil and is the epitome of badness. Ask Webster, and he will tell you; Black is devilish, ugly, grotesque, sad, solemn and dismal. Webster defines Black in these terms:

> "Relating to any of various population groups having dark pigmentation of the skin <black Americans> (2): of or relating to the African-American people or their culture, thoroughly sinister or evil: wicked, indicative of condemnation or discredit; connected with the devil, very sad, gloomy, or calamitous, marked by the occurrence of disaster, characterized by hostility or angry discontent: sullen <black resentment filled his heart." [153]

And since white is the opposite of black, it must be pure, innocent, holy and just.

Otherwise, why Black Market, Black Sunday, Blackout, and Black Death! What makes black magic worse than white magic, a black lie more evil than a white lie, a black cat more mischievous than a white cat? What makes the black skin bad and ugly? And why do some of us feel the need to bleach our skins and adjust our noses? What makes the Black person a nobody, the color black ugly, black music inferior, black expressions sacrilegious and black instruments demonic and, therefore, unacceptable in church worship?

Why did the world go to war against Germany in Europe to stop the genocide, to Bosnia in Europe to arrest the genocide, but refused to go to Rwanda to stop the genocide of one million Africans, or to Sudan to stop the genocide which has spread to Chad even now? Is the African life not worth saving? What then makes the African life so cheap around the world? I will tell you why! *The thief came to steal, to kill, and to destroy: by lies, deceptions and fraud—Lies!*

Satan lied and humanity fell. Satan lied to Adam, who bought into the lies and Satan stole Adam's dominion, killed Adam's dream and destroyed Adam's destiny. Humanity fell and Adam lost it all, because Adam accepted the Devil's lies. Similarly, Hitler lied about the Jews, and Germans bought the lies and 6 million Jews died in the holocaust.

Slave masters lied about Africa to steal her wealth, her dignity, her historic achievements, and killed her dreams, her destiny, and her heritage. No lie is innocent; because all lies are dangerous, calculated to destroy, deadly and demonic. No one can buy into Satan's lies and still hold on to the dignity of his or her roots, heritage, and humanity!

And yet like Adam, we have bought into some of his lies about humanity in general and Black people in particular. The result? The world has been the worse for it!

---

[153] Webster's Ninth New Collegiate Dictionary (Springfield Massachusetts, 1989), "Black."

Isn't it true that, in this world, people treat others based on their views of them? Unless the Word of God detoxifies society and Black people are unshackled by the truth of God, it matters little how much "emancipation" we proclaim. It matters little how often we sing, "We shall overcome" and how many Civil Rights legislations we pass. Black people will continue to be treated as inferior, or subhuman, and evil as long as these lies shall remain unchallenged and unrefuted! Racism is a disease of which lies are the cause, destruction the effect, and for which Truth is the only cure!

Three Basic Chains of Lies

There are three basic historic chains of lies that blind and bind humanity, poison society, and rob Black people of their historicity, dignity, and their destiny. The first lie is responsible for the inferiority complex and the perennial dysfunctionalism in the African or Black Community.

The First Chain of Lies:

The first lie is the idea that humanity came out of three distinct races of people. Built in this theory is the notion of superior and inferior races in general, and, in particular, the superiority of the white man and the inferiority of the black man. If ever there was an idea that has socially damaged humanity and black folks in particular, it was this lie uncritically accepted as fact. Racism, racial prejudice, segregation, bigotry, hate crimes, and anti-Semitism came from this idea of three distinct origins of humanity.

It is popularly believed that humanity started out in prehistoric times as "Hominids," animal-like humans, then developed into "Homo Habilis," a little more human and then eventually, Man raised himself up on two feet and became "Homo Erectus," who evolved to have common sense and to use tools and so became "Homo Sapiens," an intelligent human being, whose offspring we are.

There are two scenarios for this concept—on the one hand, it is said that human beings evolved from Africa, branched out in Asia and then arrived in Europe for his final destination. On the other hand, it is also suggested that different species of man evolved in different parts of the world, but some became extinct leaving three distinct species: the Negroid (the African people), the Mongoloid (the peoples of Asia), and the Caucasoid (the European people). This theory has been made into a theology about Noah's children in the Bible.

The fact is, nowhere does the Bible teach the concept of three distinct races of people. This is an evolutionary concept disguised as Biblical truth created to divide humanity along racial lines, thus putting white folks on a pedestal as superior to the inferior black folks.

This was how society lied about the Lord to exploit the Bible to dehumanize Africans, justify racism and rationalize slavery. This was how African life came to mean nothing in America. This was why the death of more than 80 million Africans being transported across the Atlantic was no big deal, and meant little to so many. All the evils perpetrated in the name of race have taken place under this lie. Don't buy into it.

The Second Chain of Lies:

The second chain is the lie that "man was created white"—the idea is that humanity came white from the hand of God, and that the original ancient people were all white. This presents us with the belief that Adam and Eve, Abel and Seth, Enos and Enoch, Lamech and Methuselah, Noah and all these holy men of the Bible were white. This lie seems innocent enough until you discover its impact and implication on the life of Black people. This is the lie that fosters false conditioning born of false association in our youth and raises serious questions about the origin of Black people.

In early childhood our children manifest the effects of this lie by associating everything white with being good and beautiful and everything black with the bad and the ugly, and by this they are conditioned to accept inferior status. An experiment was conducted with black girls playing with dolls to see how they value themselves. They gave them black and white dolls and asked them to choose which was beautiful. The black girls chose the white dolls! Surprised? The reality of this insidious lie that makes whiteness good and beautiful, and blackness bad and ugly is at the root of the suffering of Black people.

It is just as bad with the youth. Have you ever wondered why black young men are not in church? Well, they are on the street corner or in Islam saying, "Christianity is a white man's religion." And why do they think that way? Obviously, to them everybody in the Bible is white: God is white, Jesus is white, Gabriel is white, Adam and everybody of importance in the Bible, except the Devil, is white. So they figure the God of the Bible does not identify with Black people at all. Naturally, the impact is negative and detrimental. Beyond these conclusions the more serious implication is its challenge to the origin of the Black people. If the original people were all white, and if Adam and Eve were blue-eyed, blonde- haired, lily-white people, as painted on church walls, and as perpetuated by Hollywood theology, how did black folks come into existence?

Complicating the issue is the biological fact that genetically, the black gene is dominant and the white gene is recessive. I repeat for emphasis that two recessives cannot produce a dominant gene. Two white folks cannot produce black babies. Melanin makes the difference in skin color. The less melanin one has, the lighter one is and the more melanin one has the darker one's skin color. So, more melanin is needed to produce children with more melanin, that is, children with darker skin. It is impossible to produce children with more melanin if you didn't have more melanin in your genes. This means that you can't produce more (melanin) if you start with less. So how do you start with less melanin (white) and produce a black offspring with more melanin? The science doesn't match up on this point.

To elaborate, if a white couple cannot produce black children and the popular belief is that humanity started white, how then do you account for the origin and the existence of Black people in the world? How is it possible to get black folks from folks who could not produce black children? In short, how did we get here? Trying to resolve their toxic Hollywood theological confusion caused by the first lie, the peddlers of these lies have resorted to more lies. They tried amalgamation between man and beast, saying Black people came about as a result of a cross between humans and animals in the remotest past but that theory didn't work, because man's blood and beast's blood do not match. It is a scientific impossibility!

Another lie they concocted is that evil angels had babies with the daughters of men and produced mixed races of people. Reading between the lines you know whom they were talking about. If Satan's angels had babies with human beings and the devil is black, guess who their children would be? Well, this theory too did not hold because Jesus set them straight when he said angels neither marry nor are given in marriage (Matthew 22:30).

And when nothing seemed to work they grabbed at any straw they could find. They looked in the Bible and found Noah's curse and they concocted a theology of the "Curse of Ham," concluding that Black people were originally white and handsome and God's curse turned them black and ugly. For an explanation, read the following excerpt from Mormon Theology:

> "For behold they had hardened their hearts against him that they had become like flint; **wherefore as the y were wh ite and exceedingly fair and delightsome that they might not be enticing unto m y people, the L ord God did c ause a s kin of b lackness to come upon them** and cursed shall be the seed of him that mixeth with their seed; for they shall be cursed with the same cursing."[154]

Nobody may know the troubles we have seen, but don't we, at least, need to know the reason for the troubles we have seen? Lies are at the root of our oppression, suppression, and troubles around the world. The bottom line is that lies have been the basis on which oppressive societies have mistreated

---

[154] The Book of Mormons, II Nephi, Chap. 5, verses 21-23.

Black people. What is so distressing is that some of us believe in the lie and treat one another accordingly. Have we bought into the lies? Never forget that Satan lied and Adam fell and Satan took Adam's dominion, killed his dream and destroyed his destiny. Humanity fell because Adam bought into those lies.

The Third Chain of Lies:

The third lie that has been told to justify slavery is the lie that said Africa was a dark continent and pagan, its people subhuman, savage, bad, evil, and ugly. The European trader, envious of African wealth and eager to steal the natural resources—gold, bauxite, manganese and diamond, trumped up the need for Africa's children in the New World plantation economy, and lied to justify the enslavement of her people. There is nothing new under the sun, the Bible declares! To justify a war with Iraq many people lied, and most people unwittingly believed it. Here are those bent on forever trying to prove that point by putting negative images of dark hued people in general and Africans in particular on TV. You wonder why everything black is bad, and why Black people are hated and killed for nothing? Even world leaders subscribe to these, otherwise why would Mexico's President Vicente Fox say, "Mexicans are doing the work in America that even Black people would not do."

The slave master said Africa was a Dark Continent, pagan, evil and ugly and everybody said "Amen!" That's why everything black is bad and black music is not good enough in the church, black expressions are not sacred in the church, and black instruments are not holy enough in the church.

Can anyone explain why the use of drums in church is frowned upon, but the guitar is welcomed? The obvious question is: On what Biblical grounds do people make those judgments? Where in the Bible has God said He hates the drums but loves the guitar? There is no Biblical basis! Is it because drums came from Africa and the guitar came from Europe? Why are musical forms like Jazz, Reggae and Blues evil but Classical, Country and Brass Band holy? Sometimes we forget that Pathfinders play Brass Band with big drums all the time in our churches. It was the slave master, not God, who stigmatized everything African, calling it pagan, evil, and unworthy for holy use!

My research has uncovered that the Psalmist's word for drum (Timbrel, 150:4) in the Septuagint (Tumpano[155]) written in Egypt is not just an ordinary drum but a specific drum used in the ancient world which the Africans play in their royal gatherings today. The Akan people call it (Tumpan or Atumpan) with prefix. Encyclopedia Britannica's description is precise: "The *atumpan* talking drums of the Asante are barrel-shaped with a narrow,

---

[155]Sir Lancelot C. L. Benton, The Septuagint with Apocrypha: Greek and English, (Peabody, Massachusetts: Hendrickson Publishers, 1986,) 787.

cylindrical, open foot at the base."[156]   So it was with tumpan; timbrel (Psalm 150) that David called Israel to praise the Lord.

Atumpan - Ancient Royal Drum Played in Ghana

Here is the historical scenario behind the attitude. The slaves used the "Talking Drum" in and out of church to render praise to God and also to communicate amongst themselves their strategy for fighting or escaping. The slave master realized that whenever drums were sounded and the songs of Zion were sung somebody went missing and the slave master's kingdom shrunk. When the slave master could not control the drum, he banned its use, and branded it as a satanic instrument. He convinced others to believe that there was "evil in the drum" and since then that stigma has not been lifted. So, now even sophisticated blacks have come to believe that lie. Otherwise, how could church folks justify the evil of the drum and the holiness of the guitar, the organ or the keyboard? There is nothing inherently evil in an instrument. Rather, if there was any evil, it would be in the person playing the instrument! Instruments are not evil in and of themselves—they are neutral.

Who confers holiness on one instrument and not another, and who sanctions African instruments as evil but western instruments as holy? It certainly was not Jesus, the Holy Spirit, or the Father. It was the slave master. It was the slave master's theology, which has fostered such a depth of slave mentality within our ranks today to judge everything European as good and everything African as evil. For all it is worth, Euro-centricity is not Biblical Christianity. The fact is that God has not chosen European culture to represent His kingdom.

Instruments originating in Africa have been condemned not because they are intrinsically evil but because they are African. And some of us—because of our European sensibilities have become parties to our own victimization

---

[156] **"Atumpan."** Encyclopedia Britannica. 2010. Encyclopedia Britannica Online. 02 Jun. 2010 <http://www.britannica.com/EBchecked/topic/42352/atumpan>.

and destruction—rejecting our history, our roots, and our heritage in the name of bad racist theology without any Biblical foundation.

The Bible says, Praise God with cymbals—Praise Him in the Sanctuary with high-sounding cymbals, which are percussion musical instruments. God does not hate drums! It was the slave master who did. In Psalms 150, God through the songwriter David says "let (allow) everything that has breath, everything that can make sound, music, or can communicate, praise the Lord. Everything includes all musical instruments. God wants the whole orchestra, the string, the percussion, the wind, the voice, the hand and even the dance to praise His holy Name. That also includes the African drum. Let God be God to choose what God wants for His worship.

God wants authentic worship from all His creation. God does not expect red roses to turn lily white to give him glory. He doesn't want black folks sounding all white to be acceptable to Him. God wants our experience to inform our worship to be authentic. God loves the whole garden because He made the whole garden. He expects the whole garden— red, yellow, black and white—to give Him glory. He wants all people to be who they are and act like who He has made them to be in giving Him glory. God expects Black folks to give Him glory as Black folks can and white folks to do the same. God wants authentic worship. He knows Black people are an expressive people; we have spontaneous joy, and we can give Him ecstatic praise! And instead of giving God authentic praise—we rather argue about how to praise than to give Him the praise He deserves.

Too many of us are confused about our identity in God and somehow we seem to believe what the American children are saying about us: "If you are White, you are all right; if you are yellow, you can mellow; if you are brown, stick around, but if you are black, get back!." We don't have to get back for anybody. Blackness is not bad—God made us a strong people. Africa was not dark. The Holy Spirit was in Africa, and Africa knew God. The Slave master's lies won't stand forever. Truth cast to the ground will rise again.

The thief might have come to steal, to kill, and to destroy, by lies, deceptions and fraud, but I hear Jesus say; "I am come that they might have life, and have [it] more abundantly." Jesus also said, "You shall know the truth, and the truth shall set you free." We can be unshackled from the chains of Satan's lies! We can be unshackled from bad racist slave master's theology and mentality. We can be free from the bad press that has kept Black people back through the ages.

The Truth

So what is the truth to the lies that have shackled African lives for generations? Nobody is born racist to treat another human being with impunity. Racism therefore comes not by nature but by nurture. So the only way to remove racism, prejudice and bigotry is not only by legislation but by education, by telling the truth about our humanity to one another, to undo the lies that have nurtured society about other people, especially Black people for generations and all children will grow up with healthy attitudes toward others; children who will want to love and explore rather than to hate and destroy. When all societies stop feeding its people with lies about all others, prejudices will soon die out.

The Truth About African Paganism:

To the lie that says Africa was a dark continent before the arrival of the European missionaries – Here is the truth. Africa knew God before, not after, the arrival of the European missionaries set foot on the continent in 1471! Africans were not pagans in the same way the Jews were not pagans! Not knowing Jesus is not to be equated to not knowing God! The Jews were not pagans because they didn't know Jesus. They knew God. Africans did not know Jesus but they knew God. The Missionaries brought the Gospel of Jesus to Africa not the knowledge of God.

How could God manifest Himself on Mt. Sinai in Africa before the arrival of the missionaries and Africans not know Him until the time of the missionaries? How could Africans know God as the creator and worship Him before the arrival of the European missionaries if they were ignorant pagans?

Mark Finley who went to Ghana said that he was called Sunday white man and his interpreter explained that "Ghanaians from generation have known the God who made the world in six days, and rested on the seventh day and called Him 'The God of Saturday'. The missionaries came and changed it to Sunday. So the Akan people named the missionary after Sunday. When Mark Finley heard that, he protested to the Ghanaians saying, "I am not a Sunday white man, I am a Saturday white man." [157]

Africans might not have known Jesus but they surely knew the true God of creation, the God of Adam, Methuselah and the God of Noah and served Him before any European missionary got to the continent of Africa!

It was this God by His long Akan name, 'Onyankopon Twereduampon Kwame' that the slaves brought with them to the New World. The unconquered Maroons in Jamaica named their city "Accompong Town" after the God they knew in Africa!

"Bryan Edwards, in his brief outline of the religious beliefs of the Koromantyn slaves, asserts: They believe that Accompong, the God of the heavens, is the creator of all things; a Deity of infinite goodness.' In fact, we have in Jamaica today, in the Parish of St.

---

[157] Finley, Mark, *Testimony,* Northeastern Conference Commenting, 1999.

Elizabeth, a Maroon town called Accompong; which according to Cundall, the Island Historian, was so called after an Ashanti chief who featured in one of the early rebellions of the Island. One's first impression would be that this chief had arrogated to himself the title of Deity. But J. G. Christaller assures us that among the Ashanti the Divine Name was frequently given to a slave in acknowledgement of the help of God enabling the owner to buy the slave. The Supreme Being among the Ashanti is Nyame, whom we shall later try to identity with the Hebrew Yahweh. His primary title is Nyankopon, meaning Nyame, alone, great one. Accompong then, appears to be the white man's effort to express the spoken Nyankopon as heard from the early slaves.[158]

Accompong Town in Jamaica is a testimony to the knowledge of God in the African culture before missionaries got there. Thus, the African slaves did not have to adopt the religion of their captors as is erroneously purported but rather accepted the logic of their own indigenous religion. They accepted Christ as the logical conclusion of the African Akan culture, with its Biblical sacrificial system, the Sabbath concept, Yahweh's knowledge and blood atonement. Calvary was the best explanation or fulfillment for their sacrificial culture. The slaves accepted Christianity not because the slave master beat it into them but something rather in them agreed with it. It clicked and made sense to them and they were more than willing to embrace it regardless of the master's brutality. Africans knew God!

The Truth About The Original Man (Revisited):

To the lie that said humanity was originally white, what is the truth? Was man indeed created white? Did a curse turn us black? Here is what an inspired writer has to say:

> As Adam came forth from the hand of his Creator, he was of noble height, and of beautiful symmetry. He was more than twice as tall as men now living upon earth, and was well proportioned. His features were perfect and beautiful. His complexion was neither white, nor sallow, but ruddy, glowing with the rich tint of health.[159]

Adam was not white but ruddy and ruddy is "reddish brown." Brown is beautiful, not ugly! The thief came to steal and to destroy, but the truth has come to heal, and to set us free from the devil's lies!

---

[158] Joseph John. S.J. Williams, *Hebrewisms of West Africa, from Nile to Niger with the Jews* (New York: Biblo and Tannen, 1967), 16.
[159] Ellen White, *Spiritual Gift* 3 vol. 1864 (Battle Creek, MI: Seventh-day Adventist Publishing Association, 1945), 33. Also *The Spirit of Prophecy.* 3 vol. 1878.

I am not an afterthought in God's creation. I am not a product of evolution. I am no descendant of a monkey. I am a child of the king! I was made in the image of God. I am not the result of a curse; I came from the hand of my God. I am the crowning act of divine creation, made in the image of God! I am set free by the truth of Jesus. Unshackled! If Jesus sets you free you shall be free indeed!

The Truth About Human Origin:

To the lie that said humanity came in three distinct races of people, some superior and others inferior, what is the truth? Does the Bible support three distinct races of people? Not at all! In the beginning God made only one 'human family'! Adam and Eve were created in His image; not Negroid, Mongoloid and Caucasoid. In Genesis 10, Noah's sons were not three distinct species of humanity. Shem, Ham and Japheth were blood brothers, raised in the same home, nursed at the same breasts, ate the same bread, and had the same mother and the same father. They were one people of the same family.

In Acts 17:26 the Bible says God "hath made of one blood all nations of men for to dwell on all the face of the earth." So it is with all of us who are descendants of Shem, Ham, and Japheth. No matter what color we all are— red, yellow, black, and white, we are of one blood. There are no inferior or superior races. All are precious in His sight!

If the church had preached the oneness and equality of all humanity and rejected the lies of racism, bigotry would never have taken root in the world! We are all one race: the human race—in three families in God. We are one by creation and one by redemption. The ground is level at the cross. No one is inferior and no one is superior in God's creation!

God made us all in His image, so our souls are as precious as anybody's. Our bodies are as priceless as everyone else. Our children are as intelligent as anyone else; our women are as beautiful as beautiful women everywhere. Our hearts are as sacred as everyone else, our minds as keen as anybody's. "If it can be done we can do it!"

Only the Truth Shall Set All Free

Nobody should ever forget that black minds in ancient times built the pyramids that modern sophisticated people still can't fathom. Hollywood wants to rob us of our historic achievement, steal our ancestors' identities and attribute them to Europeans but it just won't happen. They can chip their noses but they can't chip their African names from History. African ancestors by their indigenous African names: Tutankhamen, Khuffu and Menes started ancient civilization.

110

How many Europeans do you know are called Tutu or Khuffu Menes or Amon? Show me one European Tutu and I will show you ten African Tutus, Khufus, Duffus, Manes and Amons. I will tell you about King Osei Tutu of the Ashantees in Ghana, Bishop Tutu of South Africa and a Duffu engaging you right now! We have done it before and we can do it now even better in Christ!

Instead of glorifying God for what He has given us. Too many of us are confused about who we are and who God has made us to be. Too many of us stew our hair, fry our heads and bleach our ebony skin. God made us a strong people—the very pigment of our skin is a sign of strength and not a sign of weakness. The ebony skin is as velvet of the night, dark and durable skin. Our hair is tough, motionless and obedient. It is hair that will lie where you put it until you move it. So don't you tell me my hair is bad! I have got good hair—hair that will not block my view, hair that will not stand in my way, hair that will rather disappear than block my progress! We are fearfully and wonderfully made!

In case you can't see it; you ought to get up early in the morning and look in the mirror and say, thank you Lord for me. I love me. God made me, Jesus saves me, and the Holy Spirit empowers me. Royal blood runs through my veins. I am a child of the king! I am somebody. Unshackled by Christ– I am free!

Jesus says, "The Spirit of the Lord is upon me, because he has anointed me to preach gospel to the poor, proclaim deliverance to the captives, heal the broken hearted, recovering of sight to the blind, and to set at liberty those who are oppressed. (Luke 4:18). Unshackled by Christ, we are free!

So on behalf of all oppressed people of the world, I reject all the devils lies about our history and our heritage and refuse to join the bandwagon to denigrate our humanity and destroy our destiny in the Lord!

We are unshackled to grow in Christ; unshackled to soar the sky, unshackled to serve the Lord, unshackled to praise the Lord. We are unshackled to worship the Lord, unshackled to love one another in Jesus! Salvation is a holistic experience! God doesn't merely want to set us free physically or socially! Almighty wants to set us free spiritually, mentally and psychologically as well!

The thief might have come to steal, to kill and to destroy, but Jesus has come to heal and to set us free. Therefore, by the authority of God's Truth, I challenge all our people to be unshackled! In the words of Dr. Martin Luther King, I claim the freedom. "Thank God Almighty, we are free at last." Unshackled in Jesus!

CHAPTER FIFTEEN

THE RISE AND FALL OF AFRICA!

Do not look where you fell, but where you slipped. (African proverbs)
He is a fool whose sheep runs away twice. (African proverbs)

Why and How did Africa Fall?

The Biblical (Prophetic) Reason

The earliest recorded civilization began with the kingdoms built by the descendants of Ham in what is called the Fertile Crescent in Mesopotamia, connecting westward to the Nile Valley in Egypt, and eastward to Euphrates Valley to the Persian Gulf. The Egyptian and the Babylonian or Sumerian civilizations were the oldest civilization in the world and they were all Hamitic. Historically, irrigation, writing, building, computation and science all began with Hamitic descendants either in Egypt or in Mesopotamia.

From *Black Spark White Fire* we read, "The Egyptian Pharaohs had been sitting on their thrones for at least two thousand years by the time Europe experienced its first major historical event—the Trojan War—sometime around 1250 B.C. As for the Romans, they arrived on the scene only yesterday. Rome had been founded a mere seven centuries before Caesar marched into Germany in 55 B.C."[160]

Egyptian Empire–Hamitic by Mizraim, a descendant of Ham! Babylonian Empire–Hamitic by Cush, also a descendant of Ham! Hamitic descendants were the first to build empires and to rule the world (Daniel 2:31-45). That same Biblical prophecy predicts that those empires would not last forever but will give way to empires from other nations. From Daniel's prophetic interpretation of history, we understand that though world domination would begin with Ham, it would not stay with Ham but move on through Shem and Japheth to Jesus at His Second Coming.

Medo-Persia under Cyrus, the Persian, overthrew the Babylonian kingdom under Belshazzar. Medo, Mede, Medes, Media, Median are Hebrew for "Maday." All refer to Madai, a people who descended from the son of

---

[160] Richard Poe, *Black Spark White Fire: Did African Explorers Civilize Ancient Europe?* (Lava Ridge Court, Roseville: Prima Publishing, 1999), 5.

Japheth. This people inhabited the land located in the northwest of Persia, south and southwest of the Caspian Sea, east of Armenia and Assyria, and west and northwest of the great salt desert of Iram."[161]

A Divine Panorama of World History

- *Ham Ruled The World: "Thou art the head of gold," Babylon ruled from (626-539 B.C.)*
- *Shem and Japheth Together Ruled the World: "After thee shall arise another kingdom": Medo-Persia ruled from (539-331 B.C.)*
- *Japheth Ruled the World: "A third kingdom of brass," Greece ruled from (331-168 B.C.)*
- *Japheth Continued to Rule the World: "Then the fourth kingdom of iron" Pagan Rome ruled from (168B.C. – A.D.476)*
- *Japheth Continued to Rule the World: "The little Horn," Papal Rome Ruled (A.D. 538 – 1798)*
- *Japheth Still Rules the World: "Mixture of Iron & Clay," Rome in her children (American iron and European clay) rules the world (from A.D. 1776) till the coming of the STONE KINGDOM of Jesus!)*

The Medo-Persian kingdom ruled for over two hundred years before succumbing to Alexander the Great of Greece. Greece was overthrown by Pagan Rome, which also fell in A.D.476. From that time onward there will be no Biblically legitimate World Empire although pretenders will seek to take power and dominate the world, but it will end in tragedy and disaster. The only legitimate World Empire yet to come is the kingdom of Christ represented in Daniel's stone that hits the image and smashes it into powder and brings earthly kingdoms to an end.

So Biblically, it was impossible for the Hamitic people to rule the world indefinitely. The dominion of this world was to move from one group to another until Jesus takes over and builds His everlasting kingdom. Prophetically then, as tragic as it might sound Hamitic descendants as a group

---

[161] *Logos Bible Dictionary* (Digital Edition).

113

do not have political dominance over this planet until we rule with Christ as kings and priests in His kingdom. Prophetically, the same decree goes for Shem as well. That means China will not rule the world, Japan will not rule the world, India will not rule the world, Pakistan will not rule the world, Arabia will not rule the world, Iran will not rule the world, Russia will not rule the world and Israel will not rule the world before Jesus comes, according to prophecy! And so prophetically, African Empires were not to last forever!

Why and How did Africa Fall?

The Historical Reason

Trans-Atlantic Slave Ship - Human Beings Packed Like Sardines

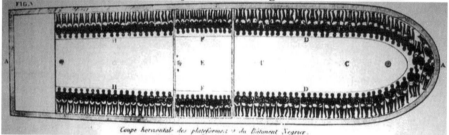

Coupe horizontale des plateformes du Bâtiment Negrier.

A.D. 1400-1600s was the weakest and lowest period in African history. After the fall of the Ethiopian, Babylonian and Egyptian Empires the last of which was in 331 B.C.. The Africans still tried to hang on to power until the fall of Cleopatra's Egypt into the hands of the Romans in the first century B.C..

> "When Alexander of Macedonia married many of his army generals into Egyptian royalty, he created the basis for Cleopatra's family still to come. She was of mixed Greek and Persian ancestry. If she lived today in the United States, she would probably be classified as a light-skinned African American. She was born in 69 B.C. on the eve of the Christian era. She was the seventh person to bear the name Cleopatra. She was an absolute ruler who tried to save Egypt from the worst aspect of Roman domination. She had African loyalties and political might, and by today's standard, she would be considered an African Nationalist. She was the last ruler of Egyptian birth and part African ancestry to rule Egypt before the emergence of Gamal Abdul Nasser some two thousand years later."[162]

---

[162] John Henrik Clarke, *African People in World History* (Baltimore, Maryland: Black Classic Press, 1993), 28.

114

After the fall of the Egyptian, and later the Carthaginian Empires - the last of the powerful Northern and Eastern African Empires, by the third Punic war of 146 B.C., the Western African Empires began to emerge. The first of these was the Ghana Empire. "Medieval Ghana (4th-13th Centuries): The Republic of Ghana is named after the medieval Ghana Empire of West Africa. The actual name of the Empire was Wagadugu. Ghana was the title of the kings who ruled the kingdom. It was controlled by Sundiata in A.D. 1240, and absorbed into the larger Mali Empire. (The Mali Empire reached its peak of success under Mansa Musa around A.D. 1307.)"[163]

The Mali Empire absorbed the Ghanaian Empire in the thirteenth Century and also gave way by A.D. 1645 to the Songhai Empire, which fell to a Moroccan Jihad.

"After Sundiata, the most famous ruler of the Mali Empire is Mansa Kankan Musa I, who came to power several decades after the death of his legendary predecessor. Musa was not the first emperor of Mali to embrace Islam; unlike the Soninke and the Soso, Mande royalty adopted the religion relatively early. However, Musa's *hajj* (pilgrimage to Mecca) of 1324–25 drew the attention of both the Islamic world and Europeans, who were unprepared for the lavish wealth and generosity that the Malian king displayed during his stopover in Egypt. Accompanied by an enormous entourage, Musa apparently dispensed so much gold in Cairo that the precious metal's value plummeted and did not recover for several years thereafter. The Mali Empire, previously little known beyond the western Sudan, now became legendary in the Islamic world and Europe. The image *of Mansa Musa bearing nuggets of gold* was subsequently commemorated in maps of the African continent."[164]

"The last of the African Empires was Songhai. "Songhai Empire was a black trading state in Africa that reached its peak during the 1400's and 1500's. Songhai began during the 700's, and by the 1400's had more power and wealth than any other West African empire. It extended from the central area of what is now Nigeria to the Atlantic coast and included parts of what are now Burkina Faso, Gambia, Guinea, Mali, Mauritania, Niger, and Senegal. Gao, the capital, stood on the Niger River.

Songhai became powerful chiefly by controlling trade across the Sahara. Most of Songhai people were farmers, fishers, or traders. The traders exchanged gold and other West African products for goods from Europe and the Middle East.

Two kings, Sunni Ali and Askia Muhammad, strengthened the empire more than any other rulers. Sunni Ali ruled from 1464 to 1492 and began a unified system of law and order, central government, and trade. His army conquered Timbuktu and Jenne,

---

[163] http://www.ghanaweb.com/GhanaHomePage/history, Posted 994-2005.
[164] http://www.metmuseum.org/toah/hd/ghan/hd_ghan.htm (Posted 2000 -2005.

two West African trading centers. Askia Muhammad, also known as Askia I or Askia the Great became king in 1493. Songhai reached its peak under his rule. Askia reorganized the government, expanded trade, and encouraged the people to practice Islam, the religion of the Muslims. His three sons deposed him in 1528. The empire ended in 1591 when a Moroccan army defeated Songhai in the Battle of Tondibi."[165]

It was around the fall of the last Western African Empire that the Trans-Atlantic Slave Trade began. Europe was just coming out of the Dark Ages and ironically studying what the Africans had developed in their universities to eventually exploit them.

> "Europe had lost the concepts of longitude and latitude. But they learned from the information gathered in Spain and preserved by the Africans and the Arabs, collectively called the Moors, at the University of Salamanca. There were only two great universities in the whole world at the time, Salamanca in Spain, and Sankore at Timbuktu. There was no Harvard, no Cambridge, no Oxford; none of these schools were in existence. Two universities in the world, one solely manned by Africans, Sankore at Timbuktu, one partly manned by Africans, Salamanca in Spain. They [were the] leading maritime nations of the world of that day. With maritime knowledge, the European goes out to sea."[166]

Africans did not have the time to catch their breath and regroup before the West exploited the Continent. The Akan people were trying to escape from the Moslem Jihad in the north. So they had no time to re-build and to be stable when the Europeans came to exploit the land of minerals, wealth, and people. And since the time of Slavery, there also has been exploitation, colonialism, imperialism, neo-colonialism and a continent bathed in foreign debt. It is hard to foresee when Africa is going to be left alone to regroup and to rebuild. Brother Clarke paints our demise in the following quote:

> "The nation-states of Europe stabilized themselves and developed their economy mainly at the expense of African people. Professor Boahen further tells us that: 'on balance then, politically, and socially, the European presence and activities in Africa during the second period were virtually an unmitigated disaster for the Africans. Earlier phase of exploration had turned sour. To borrow Basil Davidson's terms, Africa had by then turned into the "Black

[165]http://www.worldbook.com/wc/features/aajourney/html/aa_1_songhai.shtml (Posted 2004/Quoted 4/24/2005).
[166] John Henrik Clarke, *Christopher Columbus and the African Holocaust* (Brooklyn New York: A & B Publishers Group, 1993), 96.

Mother," producing slaves solely in the interest of the growing capitalist system in Europe and the New World and it was to do this for another hundred and fifty years. At the beginning of their contact, sub-Saharan Africa was politically, culturally, and artistically comparable to Europe. By 1700 Europe had leaped forward technologically and socially, but Africa and its Black peoples had become paralyzed and impoverished, a tragedy from which they still have not recovered.[167]

Unlike Africa, Europe had time to regroup after the fall of Rome. After the fall of Rome, Europe fell back into darkness in the period referred to as the Dark Ages. It took Europe more than a thousand years to get back into civilization referred to as the Renaissance. But they had time to get back on their feet – an opportunity Africa never had. So the fact of the matter is that since the fall of the western African Empires Ghana, Mali and Songhai, we have not had the luxury of regrouping and rebuilding. We have always had major troubles on our hands with no time to recuperate and regroup.

Another important phenomenon, which worked against Africa, was the drying up of the Sahara. "Sahara," or Wasteland, Chancellor Williams says, indicates what it became, not "what it was…But the Sahara, far bigger than the United States, was once a land of lakes, rivers, forest, green fields, farms, villages town and cites. Wildlife was abundant. Cattle grazed in meadows, and horse-drawn chariots sped over the highways. It was a great land, yet only a part of an ever – greater black world."[168] Can we do something about our plight? Sure we can do something about it if we knew what we are up against.

Why and How Did Africa Fall?

The Cultural Reason

In our relationship with the West, "our strengths became our weakness." The cultural reason for our fall can be attributed to the social graces we extend to others. We are a sociable and peaceful people. We are a people of kindness and are given to hospitality. We trust too quickly. I am inspired just by observing how President Obama keeps loving and smiling at America in the face of relentless attacks against him.

"Both the Africans and the Indigenous Americans befriended the Europeans at first, only to be rewarded by enslavement. They did not protect

---

[167] John Henrik Clarke, *Christopher Columbus and the African Holocaust* (Brooklyn New York: A & B Publishers Group, 1993), 48.

[168] Chancellor Williams, *Destruction of Black Civilization* (Chicago: Third World Press, 1956), 183.

themselves from the Europeans because they did not believe there was a need to."[169] Dr. Clarke points that out:

> "The main problem with the African, in dealing with the European during this early period, was the African's tragic naiveté. He had never dealt extensively with this kind of people. He came out of a society where nature was kind; nature furnished him enough food, enough land, enough of the basic things he needed to live a pretty good life. These old African societies were governed by honor and obligation. Land could neither be bought nor sold; there were no fights over ownership of land. The land belonged to everyone."[170]
>
> "The Europeans, coming from a society where nature was rather stingy and where he had to compete with his brother for his breakfast, his land, and his women, had acquired a competitive nature that the Africans could not deal with. In order to justify destruction of these African societies, a monster that still haunts our lives was created. This monster was racism. The slave trade and the colonial system that followed are the parents of this catastrophe."[171]

Europeans came to Africa with an agenda to take what the Africans had. Africans, with their inherent cultural hospitality, had no reason to be suspicious of the European. U.S. Secretary of State Condoleezza Rice demonstrated this strange African hospitality in April 2006, when she gave up her bed even though tired herself, for her counterpart, British Foreign Secretary Jack Straw on their way to Baghdad, Iraq. Europeans were driven by the prospect of money. "The basis for the European industrial revolution had already been established. They had already created an embryonic technology, including the gun. In the years that followed, they also used other advantages, mainly a large fleet of ships and rabble soldiers and sailors with no sentimental attachment to non-European people, to take over most of the world. In so doing, they destroyed large numbers of nations and civilizations that were older than any in Europe."[172] Dr. Clarke asks in his study why did that have to happen to Africans and replies "African people have always had and still have something that people want."[173]

---

[169] Chancellor Williams, *Destruction of Black Civilization* (Chicago: Third World Press, 1956), 183.

[170] Ibid,. 58.

[171] John Henrik Clarke, *Christopher Columbus and the African Holocaust* (Brooklyn New York: A & B Publishers Group, 1993), 58, 59.

[172] John Henrik Clarke, *Christopher Columbus and the African Holocaust* (Brooklyn New York: A & B Publishers Group, 1993), 58.

[173] Ibid., 13.

Bishop Tutu is quoted to have said that "when the white man came to Africa we had the land and they had the Bible and then they said let us pray. When we opened our eyes we had the Bible and they had the land." Well the same thing happened at the cross. Before we knew it, we were carrying the Cross to Calvary. And we have been carrying crosses ever since, but our God will not forget. Well, that's not gullibility, that's kindness! I have no problem with the cross; I will follow thee; my Savior! My problem is with the Euro-centricity we have accepted as gospel with institutionalized selfishness at the center and the collective European image that passed for us as the Christ. To this day, most of our people still do not know that Jesus of Nazareth was not a Caucasian and that the Caucasian divinity that is etched in our brain is a false representation of who Christ is.[174] This sustained falsehood about Christ is detrimental to the restoration and the empowerment of the oppressed.

Just as John Henrik Clarke writes:

> There was a man who stole a continent. Being cruel as well as greedy, and possessing power, *he en slaved twen ty million o f it s people,* sending them over the ocean – ten million to the Eastern Hemisphere and ten million to the Western Hemisphere. In the process of capturing the twenty million people whom he sold, eighty million others died – some during slave raids (for when a village was raided, often the very young and the very old and the sick were killed,) some from exposure, disease and grief during shipment abroad, and some by suicide at the water's edge or in transit. The sale of twenty million human beings as slaves gave the man hundreds of millions of treasure. But this was only the start of his enrichment. He and his children and grandchildren and those to whom they sold slaves received much, much more (many billions more) through the unpaid labor of whole generations of slaves. But this, too, was not at all the end of their enrichment.[175]

Notwithstanding, the naiveté on our part in our dealings with the Europeans, I think the most important virtue is our readiness to forgive. Chancellor Williams put his finger on the strange African forgiveness that we still practice when he said: "For they were, as a race, too ready to forgive and forget past evils committed by foreigners; whereas, on the other hand, a fellow African tribe could easily become a "traditional enemy" and continue as such for so many generations that no one could remember what the original quarrel was all about."[176] Rwanda was a case in point. Strange indeed!

---

[174] "Real Face of Jesus," *Popular Mechanics,* December 2002.
[175] Clarke, 49.
[176] Chancellor Williams, *Destruction of Black Civilization* (Chicago: Third World Press, 1956), 67.

However, it does not negate the fact that this culture of hospitality was led to our downfall. But that same weakness will become our strength when we have an encounter with the Man who is the Way, the Truth and the Life and put our trust in the right personalities. These trusted and trustworthy personalities are: Our Father which art in Heaven, Jesus the only begotten Son, and the Sweet Holy Spirit.

We African s have been kind in   sharing with everybody but everybody did not treat   us   with ki ndness. Our forefather s (Afri can Republics) b orrowed f rom their fath ers (Colonial Masters) who now say we ow e th em. Th eir an cestors (Slave Maste rs) borrowed gol d, diamond, oil, timber,   land and   people and no one remembers this huge indebtedness to African children! Whatever happened to   restitution! Time should have been m   ade to   relieve both the European and the African debt. But no! Time relieved one and not the other.

We took them in, warmed them up and fed them only for them to turn around and kick us in the face as payment for our kindness and hospitality. They took advantage of African hospitality, waged their cold war in proxy on our continent, dumped their old weapons, ammunitions and nuclear waste and polluted our soil, killed our leaders, retarded our economy and disrupted our progress. Most European nations: Great Britain, France, Germany, Portugal, Spain, and Italy, and also the United States of America, benefited from the exploitation of Africa. The West was built on the backs of Blacks!

Our African wealth built and now maintains the Western civilization. That's why it is necessary for African children born and unborn to demand payment for the damages to Africa caused by the West. African children are impoverished today not because they are inferior but because they have been exploited. We therefore, call for a lawsuit against the Western governments for their exploitation of Our Motherland.

We have about 15 million Africans in America. Don't we deserve a little recognition and why not? For example; we have China town, little Italy and Jerusalem Boulevard, where is Africa town or Ghana village or Nigeria Boulevard? African Children have come to cash the overdue check!

How Long Must Mother Africa Pay for her Kindness?

120

When is Mother Africa Going to Finish Paying her Debt to the West and Start Taking Care of her own Chidden?

The debt question is a theological issue and the church cannot stand idly by and allow injustice to flourish. Interestingly, most of the people calling for justice in debt forgiveness are the so-called secularist. Europeans got rich on the backs of African and now they say we owe them and the church seem to be silent.

Beside other things, Europeans got hold of the collective wisdom of our forefathers and turned that information against us. John Henrik Clark speaks for mother Africa when he writes:

> The Europeans would now use that information and turn on the people who had preserved it. No one has ever sent us a thank-you note for anything we ever did for them, which makes a totally unobligated people. We owe no one anything, politically left or right. Everybody who has come among us has taken away more than they brought, and more than they gave. We have been humane to all the people we have met. No one ever fought their way into Africa. They came as guests and stayed as conquerors or Slave traders.
>
> With Europeans beginning to see the light, they start looking for something to replenish their empty bowls. They are coming out of the lethargy of the Middle Ages. They have survived famines and plagues and lost one-third of their population. They are looking for the spices and sweets of the East. They were not looking for Africa at first. They were looking for something to put on that [...] food so they could eat it, and they discovered Africa, en route to Asia. They discovered a richer prize while seeking a route to the east, and they captured this prize instead of pursuing the route to Asia.

They would get to Asia and find Asia more politically sophisticated because the Asians were accustomed to conquerors and visitors with no good intentions. Europe would have to deal with Asians in a different way. The Asians would have invited them to dinner, but they would have watched them through the dinner and if they suspected that they had evil intentions, they might have slipped something into the food. But the Africans were generous and that's why they were trapped.[177]

Looking at the prospects prophetically, historically and culturally the odds are not promising. It doesn't look like Africa will regain any political dominance before the coming of Jesus. Our hope should be invested in the kingdom of God, which is the last kingdom to rule the world. "Our hope is built on nothing less than Jesus' blood and righteousness. We dare not trust the sweetest frame, but wholly lean on Jesus name. On Christ the solid Rock we stand; all other ground is sinking sand!"[178]

There was a time when African leaders were capable, willing and debt free to build Africa. There was a time when men like Kwame Nkrumah of Ghana, Lumumba of Congo, Jomo Kenyatta of Kenya, Julius Nyerere of Tanzania, Samora Marshall of Mozambique, Haile Selasssie of Ethiopia, Kenneth Kaunda of Zambia, Joshua Nkomo of Zimbabwe, Nelson Mandela of South Africa, Sekou Toure of Guinea, Houphouet Boigny of Ivory Coast and others could have built an economically viable Africa if left alone. But what happened to them – almost all of these were assassinated, imprisoned, destroyed or scarred for life by Western imperialism backed by African puppets. Which other African star did they not destroy? It wasn't only in Africa where black leaders were destroyed. It happened also in the Diaspora – we can think of Martin Luther King Jr., Malcolm X and Marcus Garvey, just to name a few. We hope the new generation of African leaders would be spared the sword, so they can lead in the re-building of the Motherland.

Africa still suffers at the hands of oppression. If it wasn't slavery, it was exploitation or colonialism or imperialism or neo-colonialism, and now brain drain – these and others are the reasons Africa has not been able to stand on her feet. If Africa is ever going to succeed all the African brains must go home to help rebuild. As such native Africans must make it easier for all Diaspora Africans to go home to help. Custom and economic laws ought to be made flexible to attract Africans abroad to return home to help develop the continent.

---

[177] John Henrik Clarke, *Christopher Columbus and the African Holocaust* (Brooklyn New York: A & B Publishers Group, 1993), 97.

[178] The Advent Hymnal (Washington, DC: Review and Herald Publishing Association, 1985) Hymn # 522.

<u>__Here is a   warning and a prom ise:__</u> Africa could be enslaved or colonized again if she does not stop begging and start building. How long must it take for Africa to recognize that nothing the West gives is free and that sooner or later she would be made to pay by any means necessary? If time should last, the only economic hope is going to be by educating her children in the use of modern technology to create industries that the rest of the world would need. If this happens Africa will become the next booming economy in the world. After Europe has used up her land and America has exhausted her labor force, Africa will still be a virgin by virtue of her vast land and new labor force and would be the prime location for business outsourcing. However, Africa must strategize her economy and industry to meet that demand. She must invest in her people to take advantage of the Green Revolution that is upon us. Africa must be a supplier and not just a consumer in this new emerging market economy.

Meanwhile, we must deal with the past honestly if we are all going to succeed in the future together. We must all succeed together as brothers and sisters or we will perish separately as fools. The choice is ours! But the tragic history of man's inhumanity to man must not be repeated!

On a Sober Note:

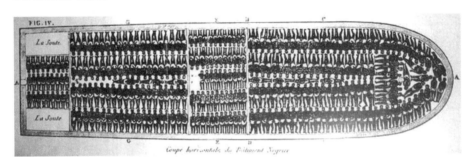

A Call to Mourn the Dead and Defend the Weak

The living shall have no psychological rest until the dead are put to rest by proper burial with formal ceremony. We seem to be doing fine psychologically when we don't have to think about the death of the innocent. There are numerous dead that have not been recognized and formally funeralized. Fifty to eighty million in the Middle Passage, six million in the Holocaust, Fifty million in the Dark Ages, and who knows how many Indians died as a result of Columbus' voyage to the Americas. Countless other millions have perished in countless revolutions, genocides, and ethnic cleansings, racial and hate crimes around the world.

On behalf of all those who have died because of man's inhumanity to man not receiving a proper funeral ceremony, I declare a global week of mourning to put their memory to rest. Together, all humanity must join hands and hearts in this global mourning and a covenant in the end, never again to be initiators, participants, collaborators or spectators to any genocide in this world. We need to join hearts and hands and pledge that together we shall defend the vulnerable.

The Reader's Response

I take the bold stand of affirming my "Heritage in Africa" in God and celebrate my "Destiny in God" and I break free from the myths and fictions designed to keep me captive and I rise by the power of God to a new creation in truth, faith, hope, love, righteousness and glory of the Lord in response to the knowledge and the truth of my ancestry that have been revealed to me. I shall no longer accept the untruths about Africa that have been used to keep Black people in the shadows for generations.

In the meantime while we wait for true justice to emerge on the horizon, Chancellor Williams suggests that Africans can do something. "The African people are highly spiritual. A truly higher civilization can develop only from such a spiritual-minded foundation. Africans already possess the kind of spirit that should permeate their educational system, govern their economic activities, and guide their political actions. In practical everyday living this would mean *actualizing* brotherhood and sisterhood through an each-for-all and all-for-each way of life, especially in economic activities."[179]   In view of all that is said, let us team up together for the collective good for future generations and never again succumb to slavery!

---

[179] Chancellor Williams, *The Rebirth of African Civilization* (Chicago: Third World Press, 1987), 15.

PART 3

PROPHETIC
AFRICA

Prophetic Observation About The Motherland

CHAPTER SIXTEEN

PROPHETIC HISTORY OF THE KINGDOMS OF THE WORLD

Peace is costly but it is worth the price. (African Proverb)

One Race - Three Families

We will start this message by clearing some popular myths regarding the concept of race. If all people came from Adam and Eve how could there be three races of people? If we believe that we are all the children of one original man and woman then what's all this confusion about races? Where did this idea of three races of people come from? Not from God, for sure!

The idea of three distinct races of people is not only incompatible with theology; it's also contradictory to the concept of creation. One cannot believe in the idea of three distinct races of people and the Biblical concept of creation. The concept of multiple races is an evolutionary one. It is a belief that is based on the outward biological differences of man and seeks to place human origins in different categories and locations of the earth and in different evolutionary stages. The concept of three races of man is not Biblical, it's evolutionary and it's the basis of the sinister concept of inferior and superior races.

**Ham, Shem and Japheth are blood
Brothers at the Flood and at the Cross**

**The Three Sons of Noah represented at the Cross!
All are Adams's Children!
One Family – Three Brothers!
Or One Race – Three Families!**

We are all Adam's children before the flood and Noah's children after the flood. Created in the image of God, we are all the children of God both by creation and by redemption. In the beginning God made only one race of humanity. As such we don't have three races of people as society promotes. Biblically, every one of us comes from Noah's three children, and are descendants of Shem, Ham and Japheth "Now these are the generations of the sons of Noah, Shem, Ham, and Japheth: and unto them were sons born after the flood" (Genesis 10:1). The descendants of these sons of Noah populated the whole world.

The Semitic (or Shemitic)

The Semites

The Hebrews and other Semitic tribes trace their roots to Shem the son of Noah. That's why they call themselves Semitic people which means they came from Shem. *"Unto Shem also, the father of all the children of Eber, the brother of Japheth the elder, even to him were [children] born. The children of Shem; El am, and Asshur, an d Arph axad, and Lu d, and Aram" (Genesis 10:21)*. The Jews claim Semitic roots. The Arabians are partly Ham by virtue of Hagar and Keturah and Shem by virtue of Abraham.

Japhetic

Europeans trace their roots to Japheth whose descendants after the flood settled on the Caucasus Mountains in Southern Russia and thus acquired the name Caucasians. *"The sons of Japheth; Gomer, and Magog, and Madai, and Javan, and Tubal, a nd M eshech, and Tiras. And the sons of Gomer; Ashkenaz, and Riphath, and Togarmah. And the sons of Javan; Elishah, and Tarshish, Kit tim, and Dodanim. By these were the isles of t he Gentiles divided in their lands; every one after hi s tongue, after their families, in their nations" (Genesis 10:2-5)*. Interestingly enough, the first usage of the term Gentiles was applied to Japheth who from all the Biblical account separated himself from the rest of his brothers and went to live where the Bible calls the Isles of the Gentiles. The Isles of the Gentiles were north of Ararat where the Ark rested. That's why the prophet Ezekiel referred to Gog, the chief prince of Meshech and Tubal, as descendants of Japheth, coming from the north" (Ezekiel 38: 1, 15).

Isaiah also p rophesied ab out the chil dren of Japhet h, And I will set a sign among t hem, and I will send those that escape of them unto the nations, [to] Tarshish, Pul, and Lu d, th at draw the bow, [to] Tubal, a nd Javan, [to] the isles afar off, that have not heard my fam e, neit her have seen my glory; and they shall declare my glory among the Gentiles. (Isaiah 66:19).

127

Furthermore, the Caucasus Mountains are found north of Ararat in southern Russia where most of the descendants of Japheth multiplied and divided. "The Japhethites lived generally north and west of Palestine in Eurasia. *"Gomer"*- The people of Gomer (the later Cimmerrians) and related nations (see vs.3) lived near the Black Sea. *"Magog,"* possibly the father of a Scythian people who inhabited the Caucasus and adjacent regions southeast of the Black Sea."[180]

The Caucasus Mountains are a chain of high mountains between the Black Sea and Caspian Sea separating the Republic of Georgia from Russia.

This mountainous range forms the conventional geographic border between Asia and Europe. Richard Poe gives us a historical account:

> For all that, Europe's most dangerous predators were not animals, but men . . . Perhaps the fiercest barbarians were the Celts . . . . The Gauls of France were great enthusiasts of human sacrifice, which carried out by holy men called Druids. . . Nearly as disagreeable as the Celts were the Scythians, who roamed the vast grasslands of Southern Russia. . . Warlike peoples are often called bloodthirsty. But rarely is the term as literally accurate as when applied to the Scythians, who customarily drunk the blood of the first man they slew in Battle.. . . For their most hated foes, they reserved a special humiliation. They would turn their enemies' skulls into drinking cups.[181]

The *Logos Bible Dictionary* sums up the points thus: *"Japheth as the 3rd son of Noah whose descendants after the Flood settled on the coastal lands of the Mediterranean spreading north into Europe and parts of Asia."*[182]

> At a time when barbarism engulfed all of Europe, Greece alone rose to take its place among the literate and industrious nations of the Mediterranean "pond." For a thousand years, the Greeks alone knew the use of books, mathematics, architecture, and stonemasonry, while the rest of Europe slept. Whatever we mean when we speak of "European civilization," we find its first and purest expression in Greece...Europe, as we have seen, was the last of the great Mediterranean region to acquire civilization.[183]

History affirms what prophecy says concerning world political dominations. It starts with Ham and ends with Japheth.

---

[180] NIV Study Bible, (Margin), 20.

[181] Richard Poe, *Black Spark White Fire: Did African Explorers Civilize Ancient Europe?* (Lava Ridge Court, Roseville: Prima Publishing, 1999), 7.

[182] Logos Bible Dictionary (Digital Edition).

[183] Richard Poe, *Black Spark White Fire: Did African Explorers Civilize Ancient Europe?* (Lava Ridge Court, Roseville: Prima Publishing, 1999), 8, 9.

World Political Dominance

Hamitic

Black People Trace Their Roots to Ham and Therefore are Hamitic

The following is the Biblical account as depicted in Genesis 10:6-20:

"And the sons of Ham; Cush, and Mizraim, and Phut, and Canaan. And the sons of Cush; Seba, and Havilah, and Sabtah, and Raamah, and Sabtecha: and the sons of Raamah; Sheba, and Dedan. And Cush begat Nimrod: he began to be a mighty one in the earth. He was a mighty hunter before the Lord: wherefore it is said, Even as Nimrod the mighty hunter before the Lord. And the beginning of his kingdom was Babel, and Erech, and Accad, and Calneh, in the land of Shinar. Out of that land went forth Asshur, and builded Nineveh, and the city Rehoboth, and Calah, And Resen between Nineveh and Calah: the same [is] a great city. And Mizraim begat Ludim, and Anamim, and Lehabim, and Naphtuhim, And Pathrusim, and Casluhim, (out of whom came Philistim,) and Caphtorim. And Canaan begat Sidon his firstborn, and Heth, And the Jebusite, and the Amorite, and the Girgasite, And the Hivite, and the Arkite, and the Sinite, And the Arvadite, and the Zemarite, and the Hamathite: and afterward were the families of the Canaanites spread abroad. And the border of the Canaanites was from Sidon, as thou comest to Gerar, unto Gaza; as thou goest, unto Sodom, and Gomorrah, and Admah, and Zeboim, even unto Lasha. These [are] the sons of Ham, after their families, after their tongues, in their countries, [and] in their nation."

Just as the Jews call themselves Semitic because they are descendants of Shem, Black people are Hamitic because they are children of Ham. Africa, as a name, was an imposition by the Roman hegemony, in the days of the Punic wars, after the fall of Carthage. It was a name of a tiny city in the north of what was called the Western Sudan where present Tunisia is located. We dwell on the continent called Africa but we are of Hamitic decent.

129

The Modern world is populated with the descendants of Noah through his three children. We all came from one or combination of these three brothers; Shem, Ham or Japheth and not from three distinct so called "*Homo-Erectus or Apes*" of different orders. As such there is only one human race of three families, not three races of people. The concept of racism therefore has no basis in theology and is dangerous where entertained. We believe it to our own demise! For God *"...hath made of one blood all nations of men for to dwell on all the face of the earth, and hath determined the ti mes before appointed, and the bounds of their habitation"* (Act 17:26).

Now that we have cleared that issue, let us address our mission. Biblical records show that all the three children of Noah have had the chance or the opportunity to do ministry for the Lord. We shall examine how they shouldered the responsibility.

God Used Ham First

Ham, Noah's last son, was the father of Cush, Mizraim, Phut and Canaan. Three of Ham's children migrated to the continent of Africa, which was referred to as the "Tabernacles", or the dwelling places of Ham. Mizraim occupied both Upper and Lower Egypt on the African Continent. "And smote all the firstborn in Egypt; the chief of [their] strength in the tabernacles of Ham" (Psalms 78:51) or simply the "Land of Ham." *Israel also came into Egypt; and J acob sojourn ed in the land of Ham" (* Psalms 105:23). Africa was the land of Ham.

Cush means Ethiopia. Cush was his Biblical name, Ethiopia was a term used by the Greeks to refer to Ethiopians' black beautiful skin, which was like the velvet in the night. Blackness was celebrated in the ancient world as beautiful, a sentiment which was echoed by the Shulamite woman in the Song of Solomon: *"I am black, but comely, O ye daught ers of Jerusalem, as th e tents of Kedar, as the curtains of Solomon" (Song of Solomon 1:5).*

Curiously enough, in the Septuagint, the Greek does not have "but comely" rather "kai" which is commonly rendered as "and." The translation would then be **"I am black and comely"** from (Μέλαινά είμι έγω καί καλή); as it is written in Greek. The former rendering makes it appear that beauty and blackness are strangers. The Black should not change his skin to be beautiful or acceptable. God made us all beautiful and does not intend for any of His children to become like the other to please him. It is an insult to God and therefore an abomination for Black people to bleach their skin to look attractive. For one thing, you can't improve on God's work, and secondly, you end up destroying the natural beauty God gave you. Ponder over Jeremiah question; *"Can the Ethio pian chan ge his sk in or the leopard his spots?"* (Jeremiah 13: 23).

130

Ham's third son Phut was the one Bible students call Put. He settled either in Somalia in the east or Libya in North Africa. His descendants spread over both regions! Unlike his other brothers, Canaan occupied the whole of Palestine. Out of Canaan came the Jebusites, from whom came the greatest descendant of Ham, a man named Melchizedek. Melchizedek was a Jebusite king, a descendant of Canaan who was the last-born of Ham, the father of Black people. This Melchizedek was the king of Salem, and the priest of the Most High God.

The land of Canaan refers to the land occupied by the Canaanites. It was that land which flowed with milk and honey. The land of Canaan was the land occupied by the Canaanites out of whom came the Jebusites the royal high priest Melchizedek, king of Salem, dwelling in *Jebus-Salem* which became Jerusalem. This was the land given to the Israelites under Joshua after the death of Moses. *"As for the Jebusites the inhabitants of Jerusalem, the children of Judah cou ld not drive them out: but the Jebusites dwell with the children of Judah at Jerusalem unto this day" Joshua 15:63.*

Melchizedek was a Jebusite king, a descendant of Canaan, son of Ham, father of Black people. Melchizedek was a non-Hebrew worshipper of the true God and that's also the reason the Hebrews could not account for his genealogy. However, he recognized Abraham the moment he saw him. He was the high priest chosen to bless Abraham the father of the promise. *"And Melchizedek king of S alem brought f orth bread an d wine: and he [was] the priest of the most high God"* (Genesis 14:18).

"For this Me lchisedek, king of Salem, priest of the m ost high God, who met Abraham returning from the slaughter of the kings, and blessed him; To whom also A braham g ave a tenth part of all; first being by i nterpretation King of right eousness, and after that also King of Salem, which is, King of peace" (Hebrews 7:1, 2).

Melchizedek was the king of Salem, which was the capital city of the Jebusites. The Jebusites were the descendants of Canaan. And Canaan was the last born of Ham, the father of all Black people. So Melchizedek, the first high priest of the Most High recorded in the Bible was a black man and a descendant of Ham. The Bible does not shy away from his greatness:

> "Now consider how great this man [was], unto whom even the patriarch Abraham gave the tenth of the spoils. And verily they that are of the sons of Levi, who receive the office of the priesthood, have a commandment to take tithes of the people according to the law, that is, of their brethren, though they come out of the loins of Abraham: But <u>he whose descent is not counted from them</u> received tithes of Abraham, and blessed him that had the promises. And without all contradiction the less is blessed of the better" (Hebrew 7:4-6).

131

The Biblical logic is that the Melchizedekian ministry was superior to Aaronic ministry because among other reasons, Aaron, the priest was a descendant of Abraham (in Abraham's genes). Abraham gave tithe to Melchizedek who in return blessed him (Abraham). Biblically, it takes the greater to bless the lesser.

Melchizedek was greater than Abraham, however, most importantly, he was so faithful that God Almighty swore an oath to make him a model for Jesus. Jesus' ministry would not be patterned after Aaron, but after Melchizedek. *"The Lord hath sworn, and will not repent; Thou [art] a priest forever after the order of Melchizedek"* (Psalms 110:4).

Prophetic History of the World

Priesthood and Government

Ham in Babylon

Ham First

Politically, Ham was given the power of world dominance first. Right after the Flood, Nimrod, which means "the valiant", described in the Bible as a "mighty hunter before the Lord;" the son of Cush, grandson of Ham, established an empire in Babylon and Assyria. So it is likely that Nimrod, the Cushite, was the father of both the Sumerian and the Babylonian Empires founded in Mesopotamia.

Along with the Mesopotamian Empires founded by the Cushite descendants of Ham in the east, were also the African Empires founded by the Hamites in the West. In western Sudan both the Ethiopians and Egyptians controlled the longest-lasting empire in history. The Egyptian Empire lasted from Menes the Ethiopian who founded Memphis and united the two kingdoms of Upper and Lower Egypt into the Egyptian Empire (historians say took place around 3100 B.C.?). It finally succumbed to defeat by Alexander in 332 B.C..

132

CHAPTER SEVENTEEN

HAM RULED THE WORLD

The Dream That Unfolded History

When mahogany falls Pawpaw takes the throne.(African proverb)

Here is the Prophet Daniel's presentation of the succession of world-dominated kingdoms from the beginning to the end. King Nebuchadnezzar of Babylon dreamed a dream that troubled his mind. Fearing the implications of the dream for his kingdom, he called for his wise men to recall the dream, which was vague in his mind and then also to interpret for him. None of the wise men in Babylon were able to perform such a task, so Daniel the Hebrew slave was brought in to interpret. Daniel attributed his ability to interpret the dream to the God of Heaven and asked for time out to pray for wisdom. God revealed the dream and the interpretation to him. The Dream deals with the kingdoms of this world down through the ages starting from Babylon. Daniel recounted:

"Thou, O king, sawest, and behold a great image. This great image, whose brightness [was] excellent, stood before thee; and the form thereof [was] terrible. This image's head [was] of fine gold, his breast and his arms of silver, his belly and his thighs of brass, his legs of iron, his feet part of iron and part of clay. Thou sawest till that a stone was cut out without hands, which smote the image upon his feet [that were] of iron and clay, and brake them to pieces" (Daniel 2:31-34).

That was the dream. Daniels' interpretation follows: "Thou, O king, [art] a king of kings: for the God of heaven hath given thee a kingdom, power, and strength, and glory. And wheresoever the children of men dwell, the beasts of the field and the fowls of the heaven hath he given into thine hand, and hath made thee ruler over them all. **Thou [art] this head of gold**" (Daniel 2:37, 38)! The Scripture says God appointed king Nebuchadnezzar to lead in the succession of kingdoms, which would reach down to the end of time.

Ham Ruled the World First

Babylon - The Head Of God

Babylon under King Nebuchadnezzar was the head of gold among the kingdoms. God chose a descendant of Ham to lead the world in politics. Although Nebuchadnezzar's relationship with God had a rocky start, it ended on a positive note and Nebuchadnezzar repented and made his calling and election sure before dying. He may have a bad rap now because of bad theology but we can expect him in heaven because when confronted by God he submitted.

The Babylonian Empire fell in 538 BC to Cyrus when Nebuchadnezzar's later successor Belshazzar, a grandson, plunged the Empire into the sin of idolatry, insulted and blasphemed God. When grandfather Nebuchadnezzar served the Lord, his kingdom was preserved, but when grandson Belshazzar departed from the Lord with impunity, God took it from him (Ham), and gave it to the United Kingdom of the Medes and Persians which were a combination of Shem and Japheth.

Media or Medes came from Madai a son of Japheth; and Persians came from Shem. *"The sons of Japheth; Gomer, and M   agog, and   Madai, and Javan, an d Tubal, and Meshech, and Ti ras"* (Genesis 10:2) *"And after thee shall arise another kingd om inferior to thee, and   another third kingdom of brass, which shall bear rule over all the earth"* (Daniel 2:39).

Medo-Persia

134

The second kingdom; a joint empire of Japheth and Shem; Media and Persia ruled from 539 B.C. to 331 B.C. and yielded to Alexander the Great the Grecian.

Greece

From the Grecian Empire 331 B.C. to 161 B.C. onward until Christ, Japheth would dominate the political world.

"And the fourth kingdom shall be strong as iron: forasmuch as iron breaketh in pieces and subdueth all [things]: and as iron that breaketh all these, shall it break in pieces and bruise. And whereas thou sawest the feet and toes, part of potters' clay, and part of iron, the kingdom shall be divided; but there shall be in it of the strength of the iron, forasmuch as thou sawest the iron mixed with miry clay. And [as] the toes of the feet [were] part of iron, and part of clay, [so] the kingdom shall be partly strong, and partly broken. And whereas thou sawest iron mixed with miry clay, they shall mingle themselves with the seed of men: but they shall not cleave one to another, even as iron is not mixed with clay" (Daniel 2:40-43).

Rome

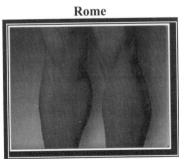

From Greece, the Biblical Javan in Genesis 10:2 to Rome all the way to its break up in AD 476, into the ten divisions of Europe to America, until the coming and the establishment of the kingdom of Christ, Japheth would rule the world. Japheth's temptation would be to try to consolidate his powers to build a counterfeit everlasting world empire. Like Nebuchadnezzar, his goal will be to prevent the kingdom of Christ from coming.

Divided Europe

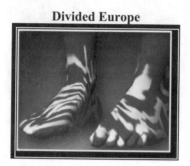

Church and state would unite to suppress the voice of dissent and silence all opposition in hopes of establishing a kingdom that will last forever without a rival and without a challenge.

America in Prophecy

"And in t he days of the   se kings shall the God   of heaven set up a kingdom, which shall never be destroyed: and t he kingdom shall not be left to other people, [but] it shall break in pieces and consume all these kingdoms, and it shall stand for ever" (Daniel 2:44).

In the Days of these kings!

Jesus Comes

But the point is that Ham dominated world politics first and his kingdom came to an end as predicted by the prophet Daniel. Shall not all other predictions associated with the prophecy come to pass?

Ham, Shem and Japheth:

Prophetic Reasons for Some Existing Conditions

- Japheth's domination of the modern political scene – is prophetic! Cornelius' horn or Roman iron, rules the world, that's why it was Japheth who introduced politics into the modern church weakening its spirituality.
- Shem wields economic power. She still enjoys the result of Abraham's tithe to Melchizedek.
- Ham still carries crosses! Ham inherited the cross by virtue of Simon of Cyrene. It's our spiritual power if we can see Christ's victory in it and be faithful and humble like Job to be vindicated at the end. Take up thy Cross and Follow Me, I hear the Savior call! How can I do any less when Jesus gave His all!

Spiritually, Ham Was First To Lead the World and Became the Envy of the World in the Ancient Times

Interestingly, Ham was not only first and foremost in politics but also first in the old time religion. Just as the kingdoms of the world, Daniels's image moves from Ham to Shem and then to Japheth, so also did the ancient ministry move in the same direction. It started with Ham through Melchizedek to Shem through Abraham and then to Japheth through Cornelius.

In the Bible inheritance gets transferred from one patriarch to the next. Abraham blessed Isaac; Isaac blessed Jacob and Jacob blessed Israel. As such, the blessing of the Lord moved from one generation to another. And with the blessing also come spiritual inheritance and Divine promise, responsibility and destiny. But it always carries with it the call to the ministry of calling the world to God.

So when Melchizedek blessed Abraham, the ministry was officially but potentially transferred from Ham to Shem in Abraham. But it would take effect at a later date when the conditions were right. Shem's ministry would be effective when the sins of the Amorites filled their cup of iniquity. Ham was under probation and the clock was ticking. It would be only a matter of time for the Divine clock to strike midnight. Only faithfulness and righteousness would delay the hand of time.

Abraham and his descendants were told to wait till the probation of the inhabitants was closed.

And he said unto Abram, Know of a surety that thy seed shall be a stranger in a land [that is] not theirs, and shall serve them; and they shall afflict them four hundred years; And also that nation, whom they shall serve, will I judge: and afterward shall they come out with great substance. And thou shalt go to thy fathers in peace; thou shalt be buried in a good old age. But in the fourth generation they shall come hither again: **for the iniquity of the Amorites [is] not yet full (Genesis 15:13-16).**

The iniquity of the Amorites is a euphemism for the disobedience of the dwellers of the region of Canaan. And these were the "Tabernacles of Ham." The iniquity of the Amorites or Canaanites would cause Ham to lose to Shem both the ministry and the land in which to do the ministry.

When Melchizedek was faithful, Canaan was blessed until a successor whose unfaithfulness propelled the Canaanites into apostasy, the result of which was the forfeiture of both the ministry and the land in which to do ministry. Not only was Melchizedek faithful, Ham's religiosity was renowned and unmatched. In the ancient world, the Greeks literally envied the Egyptians for their spirituality and boasted about having Ethiopians as their teachers.

When Canaan departed from the principles of the Lord, the Land of Canaan would be taken away from them and given to the Hebrews, children of Abraham, and descendants of Shem! The transfer would be effective.

Curiously enough, politically and spiritually, in both cases, the patriarchs seemed to be more faithful than the descendants. On the political front, the patriarch Nebuchadnezzar was more faithful than Belshazzar, the descendant who lost the kingdom. And on the spiritual front Melchizedek was far more faithful than his later successor Adonizedek who also lost the ministry. So because of unfaithfulness Ham lost the power and God handed it over to Shem. However, God had used Hamitic people—Black people, in the past.

The Disobedience of Canaan

Ham's Apostasy

Ham's Melchizedekian ministry would come to an end when Adonizedek, later successor of Melchizedek failed to follow his footsteps and instead rebelled against God by seeking to wipe out the children of Abraham according to Joshua 10. Finally, the conditions were fulfilled. The sins of the Amorites had reached up to heaven and God was about to give the Land of Canaan to the Hebrews. Four hundred and thirty years (Galatians 3:17) after Joseph went to Egypt Yahweh came down to deliver the Children of Israel

138

from captivity to lead them to the Promised Land— the Land of Canaan. *"And I am come down to deliver them out of the hand of the Egyptians, and to bring them u p out of th at land unto a good lan d a nd a l arge, u nto a l and flowing wit h milk and h oney; unto t he place of the Cana anites, and t he Hittites, and the Amorites, and the Perizzites, a nd the Hivites, and the Jebusites" (Exodus 3:8).*

The Transfer of Ministry and Power

In the fullness of time as He had promised Abraham, God fulfilled His word by delivering Israel from Egypt. He gave them the Land of Canaan in which to continue the ministry heretofore entrusted to Melchizedek. *"Now therefore, if ye will obey my voice indeed, and keep my covenant, then ye shall be a peculiar treasure unto me above all people: for all the earth [is] mine: And ye shall be unto me a kingdom of priests, and an holy natio n" (Exodus 19:5-6).*

The important lesson to learn here is that apart from being a promise, carrying out the ministry for the Lord was conditional upon obedience. Israel was to obey the Lord and be used by the Messiah to spread the gospel. The other option was to disobey and be rejected.

Ham's disobedience almost led to his destruction. The dumb pride of Pharaoh led to a severe devastation of Egypt, the death of their first-born and the destruction of the Egyptian army in the Red sea on one side and the overthrow of Canaan for departing from righteousness on the other side. Ham's probationary time for holy living and ministry was up, and his power was relinquished. He had forfeited the option to keep the power.

So Israel got the ministry and the land in which to do the ministry. But just as Ham's descendants were given time to repent, Shem was also given a probationary time in which to get it right through obedience. After many failed attempts at righteousness, when judges and prophets could not help Israel, God finally sent them again into captivity in Babylon. Here is why:

> "And they caused their sons and their daughters to pass through the fire, and used divination and enchantments, and sold themselves to do evil in the sight of the Lord, to provoke him to anger. Therefore the Lord was very angry with Israel, and removed them out of his sight: there was none left but the tribe of Judah only. Also Judah kept not the commandments of the Lord their God, but walked in the statutes of Israel which they made. And the Lord rejected all the seed of Israel, and afflicted them, and delivered them into the hand of spoilers, until he had cast them out of his sight" 2 Kings: 17:17-20.

There in Babylon, the Lord gave them their final probation.

Seventy Weeks for Israel to Repent

"*Seventy weeks are det ermined upon t hy people and upon thy holy city, to finish the transgression, and to m ake an end of sins, and to make reconciliation for ini quity, and to bring in everlasting righteousness, and to seal up the vi sion and prophecy, and t o anoint the most Holy" (Daniel 9:24.)* (Prophetically, a day equals a year – Ezekiel 4:6). *Seventy* weeks, therefore is calculated (70 X 7) as 490 literal years.

So, Israel was given 490 years starting from the Persian decree to repent and to rebuild Jerusalem that was ruined from the Babylonian invasion. "*Know therefore and understand, [that   ] from t he going forth of the commandment to restore and to buil d Jerusalem unt o the Messiah the Prince [shall be] seven weeks, and threescore and two weeks: the street shall be built again, and the wall, even in troublous times (Daniel 9:25).*

The decree became effective in 457 B.C. when Artaxerxes made the final law to free Israel from Babylonian captivity. "Moreover I make a decree what ye shall do to the elders of these Jews for the building of this house of God: that of the king's goods, [even] of the tribute beyond the river, forthwith expenses be given unto these men, that they be not hindered" Ezra 6:8.

Artaxerxes, king of kings, unto Ezra the priest, a scribe of the law of the God of heaven, perfect [peace], and at such a time. I make a decree, that all they of the people of Israel, and [of] his priests and Levites, in my realm, which are minded of their own freewill to go up to Jerusalem, go with thee" (Ezra 7:12-13).

The Hebrew's seventy weeks' probation would reach all the way to the first coming of Christ to the stoning of Stephen which would seal their fate as a chosen nation. Should they refuse to accept the Messiah's salvation in A. D. 34, the Romans would come and destroy Jerusalem again as a sign.

AD 27
7 weeks = 49 years; 3 score and 2 weeks = 62 weeks = 483 years which brings us to AD 27

Jesus the Messiah showed up exactly as prophesized. In AD 27 Jesus was baptized in the Jordan River by John the Baptist and was anointed by the Holy Spirit to begin His ministry. "*The Spirit of the Lord [is] upo n me, because he hath a nointed me to preach the gospel t o the p oor; h e hath sent me to heal the brokenhearted, to pr   each deliverance to the captives, and recovering of sight to the blind, to set at liberty them that are bruised" (Luke 4:18).*

In AD 27 God anointed Jesus with Holy Spirit to usher Him into His ministry. "*How God anointed Jesus of Nazareth with the Holy Ghost and with*

140

power: who went about doing good, and healing all that were o ppressed of the devil; for God was with Him (Acts 10:38).

Jesus ministered from AD 27 to AD 31 and was cut off, that is, killed/crucified in the middle of the last prophetic week of seven years, which is the final segment of the 490 years allotted to the Jews as probationary time. Jesus made that ultimate sacrifice, not because of his own sins, for he was wounded for our transgressions, bruised for our iniquities and the chastisement of our peace [was] upon Him and with His stripes we are healed.

"And after threescore and two weeks shall Messiah be cut off, but not for himself: and the people of the prince that shall come shall destroy the city and the sanctuary; and the end thereof [shall be] with a flood, and unto the end of the war deso lations are determined. So the Bible says Jesus must die in the middle of the week. "Saying, the Son of man must be delivered into the hands of sinful men, and be crucified and the third day rise again" (Luke 24:7). Just as the Bible predicted, it came to pass. We can trust the Word of God!

Crucified in the Midst of the Week

Now one prophetic week is left for the Jewish nation before their probation runs out. *"And he shall conf irm the covenant with ma ny for one week: and in the midst of the week he shall cause the sacrif ice and the oblation to c ease,* and for the overspreading of abominations he shall make [it] desolate, even until the consummation, and that determined shall be poured upon the desolate (*Daniel 9:26-27).*

The last of the 70 Prophetic Weeks was seven literal years. Since the 70 weeks began in B.C. 457, the 70th week takes us to AD 34. The last prophetic week would be the 7 years between AD 27 and AD 34. The middle of the week therefore was the middle of AD 31, the time that Jesus was crucified on the cross.

In the Midst of the Week

The Jewish Rejection of Christ:

Shem's Apostasy

Before Jesus died, He had pleaded with the Jewish nation to repent, believe the gospel and be saved. All His pleadings however, amounted to nothing. At last He cried, *"O Jerusalem, Jerusalem, [thou] that killest the prophets, and stonest them which are sent unt o thee, how often would I have gathered thy children toge ther, even as a hen gat hereth her chickens under [her] wings, and ye would not! Behold, your house is left unto you desolate"* (Matthew 23:37-38).

141

Before this time, He had claimed Jerusalem to be His "Father's House" (Why do you make my Father's house a den of thieves?). But after they had rejected Him, He referred to it as "your house left unto you desolate." Nevertheless, Israel's "cup of iniquity would not be full" until AD 34, the end of the 70th week of their probationary time.

End of 70th Week: Close of Probation

Israel had been given every opportunity to repent and be used by Jesus as God's chosen vessels in Jerusalem for the salvation of humanity. That was why God called Abraham to leave Ur of the Chaldees, and planted him at the crossroads of the continents of Africa, Asia, and Europe, so that Israel could fulfill their mission as His preacher nation, but instead they apostatized. Each time God sent them messengers they mistreated them and in some instances killed them. Israel finally rejected the Lord of life, betrayed Him, wrongfully accused Him, and crucified Him. But Jesus was not through with them yet. He was to confirm the Covenant with them for one week, literally seven years. Since He died to ratify the covenant in the midst of the Week, there was yet 31/2 years left for the confirmation of the covenant.

At the fullness, that is the end of the 70 weeks or 490 years, the Jews sealed their rejection of Jesus by stoning Stephen while he was preaching the gospel for their repentance and salvation. *"Then they cried out with a loud voice, and stopped their ears, and ran upon him with one accord, And cast [him] out of the city, and stoned [him]: and the witnesses laid down their clothes at a young man's feet, whose name was Saul. And they stoned Stephen, calling upon [God], and saying, Lord Jesus, receive my spirit"* (Acts 7:57-59).

Jesus started His ministry in AD 27. He died in the middle of the week, which was AD 31. Therefore the Week ended in AD 34, corresponding with the stoning of Stephen and the spreading of the message and the ministry to the Gentiles. Prior to the stoning of Stephen and as part of confirming the covenant with Israel, Jesus had instructed the disciples to refrain from going to preach among the Gentiles.

"These twelve Jesus sent forth, and commanded them, saying, Go not into the way of the Gentiles and into [any] city of the Samaritans enter ye not" (Matthew 10:5). But now after the three and a half years of confirming the covenant with the House of Israel and because of their persistent refusal to obey the covenant, the way was open to the Gentiles. So right after the stoning of Stephen, the door was opened to the Gentile Ministry.

Pride and unbelief were the twin causes of the fall of Ham – Pharaoh's pride and Canaan's unbelief caused the demise of Ham. Sadly the same was true with the House of Israel – Spiritual pride and unbelief was Shem's

142

undoing. The ministry would be transferred to Japheth who was "first among the Gentiles" to see what he should do.

Probation Closes for Jewish Nation as the Chosen Instrument for the Salvation of the World

Paul calls Israel's sins that led to her demise "unbelief and high-mindedness," which is the same as pride and unbelief. *"Well because of unbelief they were broken off.., and thou standest by faith. Be not highminded, but fear"* (Romans 11:20).

So in AD 34, at the end of 70 prophetic weeks, when the house of Israel failed to heed the final call to repent and to accept the Messiah, God dismissed them as a viable instrument, His preacher nation of His salvation to the world. Their role as a chosen nation came to an end. They would soon lose the ministry and the land. The land was given for the ministry. To fail to do the ministry is to forfeit the land. As predicted by Daniel and emphasized by Jesus, the Romans came in and destroyed the Temple and also Jerusalem.

The Fall of Jerusalem

After the destruction of the Temple, Israel would go into exile for a very long time. Israel had been chosen to be the instrument in God's hand for the salvation of the world. When she failed to fulfill her Ministry, she was cut off and the Gentiles were adopted. The transfer from Shem to Japheth would soon take place. But the challenge to the Gentiles was to be careful not to fall into the same sins of unbelief and pride:

"And if some of the branches be broken off, and thou, being a wild olive tree, wert grafted in among them, and with them partaketh of the root and fatness of the olive tree. Boast not against the branches. But if thou boast, thou bearest not the root, but the root thee" (Romans 11:17-18).

143

And just as Joshua, from the loins of Shem, led in the overthrow of Ham in Canaan, so also Titus, the Roman, from the loins of Japheth led the overthrow of Shem when the time was right.

> "When the Jewish people rejected Christ, the Prince of life, He took from them the kingdom of God and gave it unto the Gentiles. God will continue to work on this principle with every branch of His work. When a church proves unfaithful to the word of the Lord, whatever their position may be, however high and sacred their calling, the Lord can no longer work with them. Others are then chosen to bear important responsibilities. But if these in turn do not purify their lives from every wrong action; if they do not establish pure and holy principles in all their borders, then the Lord will grievously afflict and humble them, and, unless they repent, will remove them from their place and make them a reproach."[184]

Shem is broken off for Japheth to come in. It is Gentiles' time now.

> "Ancient Israel suffered calamities on account of their unsanctified hearts and unsubmitted wills. Their final rejection as a nation was a result of their own unbelief, self-confidence, impenitence, blindness of mind, and hardness of hearts. In their history we have a danger signal lifted before us." [185]

---

[184] Ellen White, Instruction for Men in Positions of Responsibility, Manuscript Releases Volume 14, 1903), 102.
[185] Ellen White, Letter 30, 1895.

CHAPTER EIGHTEEN

THE GENTILES GRAFTED

You do not laugh at your neighbor when you see his beard on fire. Get water by yours. (African proverb)

The first use of the word Gentiles was used to refer to the children of Japheth. "By these were the isles of the Gentiles divided in their lands; every one after his tongue, after their families, in their nations" (Genesis 10:5). Though the term "Gentiles" generally refers to the rest of the world, it specifically refers to Japheth, the ruling kingdom of our time.

Prophetically also "Gentiles Times" refers to Roman domination of Christendom or Papal supremacy in the Dark Ages. *"But the court which is without the temple leave   out, an d measure it not; for it is given unto the Gentiles: and the   holy c ity shall t hey tread un der foot forty [and] two months" (Revelation 11:2).*   Politically, the Romans destroyed the temple and controlled Jerusalem. Spiritually they trampled upon God's truth throughout the Dark Ages.

Forty-two prophetic (Jewish) months which calculates to 1260 literal years, spanned the entire prophetic period of the Dark Ages from AD 538 to 1798. In AD 538 the "Holy Roman Empire" officially gained ascendancy in Europe and dominated its life. As such, the Romans persecuted the Remnant—"righteous rebels," the "faithful dissenters" or the "so-called heretics" until 1798 when Napoleon's French Revolution finally broke the power of the Papacy.

The Blessing Passes to Japheth via Cornelius to the Gentiles

It was the Gentiles turn to carry on the work and Cornelius was ready for the blessing. The ministry was to be transferred gentiles but the Jews were not sure. So God had to give Peter, one of the leaders of the apostles, a vision to confirm the transfer. Right after the vision the Bible says:

> "There was a certain man in Caesarea called Cornelius, a centurion of the band called the Italian [band], [A] devout [man], and one that **feared God with all his house**, which gave much alms to the people, and prayed to God alway. He saw in a vision

evidently about the ninth hour of the day an angel of God coming in to him, and saying unto him, Cornelius. And now send men to Joppa, and call for [one] Simon, whose surname is Peter." (Acts 10:1-5) (Bold mine).

Compton's Bible dictionary renders Cornelius as belonging to a horn. "CORNELIUS (of a horn) Roman centurion stationed at Caesarea and the first Gentile convert"[186] (Acts 10:1). His name is of Latin origin meaning "of a horn" or belonging to a horn. Regardless of how we look at his name a "horn" comes out of it.

Horn means strength; either of the people by numbers; *"Then said I, What come these to do? And he spake, saying, These [are] the horns which have scattered Judah, so that no man did lift up his head: but these are come to fray them, to cast out the horns of the Gentiles, which lifted up [their] horn over the land of Judah to scatter it"* (Zachariah 1:21).

Horn can also signify the power of God on behalf of His people; *"The Lord [is] my rock, and my fortress, and my deliverer; my God, my strength, in whom I will trust; my buckler, and the horn of my salvation, [and] my high tower"* (Psalms 18:2). Horn can also mean a brutish power in general: *"I beheld, and the same horn made war with the saints, and prevailed against them"* (Daniel 7:21).

Cornelius would be the forerunner of Japheth's Christianity. His name "of a horn" would have prophetic significance for generations to come. Either they would throw their lot with God and rely on His strength for salvation or rely on their own power to lead them into apostasy. So the horn could eventually go either way for Japheth.

In short, the significance of "the horn" would work out for better or for worse. It could be prophetic of salvation or apostasy. Japheth could rely on his own power or the power of God to do the ministry of the Lord. Japheth had the power to choose his prophetic destiny but the prophetic forecast did not look promising because of the lust for power on Japheth's horizon.

If he indeed was the first official Gentile convert, then that also made him the first Roman convert. Cornelius therefore became the forerunner of Gentile Christianity. "One that feared God with all his house" would make him like Abraham of whom it was said, *"For I know him, that he will command his children and his household after him, and they shall keep the way of the Lord, to do justice and judgment; that the Lord may bring upon Abraham that which he hath spoken of him"* (Genesis 18:19). Therefore, because of his faithfulness, Cornelius was a perfect choice, and just as Melchizedek; a God-ordained high priest blessed Abraham, so Peter, a God-ordained Apostle, would bless Cornelius to effect the transfer.

---

[186] *Compton's Interactive Bible NIV.*, (SoftKey Multimedia Inc. 1996).

Peter's defense for going to bless Cornelius was that God orchestrated the whole thing and that he could not disobey the heavenly vision. God was about to do a new thing and Peter had to learn to obey. *"And he said unto them, Ye know how that it is an unlawful thing for a man that is a Jew to keep company, or come unto one of another nation; but God hath shewed me that I should not call any man common or unclean" (Acts 10:28).*

Peter had learned a valuable lesson from the vision the Lord sent him. Peter learned that the blessing of the Lord comes to the faithful and the obedient. Also that this had nothing to do with status or ethnicity. So Peter was moved to confess before them all.

> Then Peter opened [his] mouth, and said, Of a truth I perceive that God is no respecter of persons: But in every nation he that feareth him, and worketh righteousness, is accepted with him. While Peter yet spake these words, the Holy Ghost fell on all them which heard the word. And they of the circumcision which believed were astonished, as many as came with Peter, because that **on the Gentiles also was poured out the gift of the Holy Ghost.** (Acts 10: 34-35, 44-45)

"And the apostles and brethren that were in Judaea heard that the Gentiles had also received the word of God" (Acts 11:1). Transfer effected!

Japheth's 1260 Years of Probation

At the beginning of the ministry of Japheth, the firstborn son of Noah, he started out as well as his other two brothers before him. However, he too became spiritually corrupt. The church in Rome in the beginning was as faithful as the other churches of the first century. It was to that church, that the Apostle Paul sent the Roman Epistle. The Roman Church was obedient until Constantine came on the scene of action and created the union of church and state. This process brought about an amalgamation of secular religions, which eventually resulted in the formation of the Papacy. The Papacy in a nutshell is the union of the Christian Church and the Roman state, hence the term "Holy Roman Empire".

Prophecy saw it coming when Daniel commented on the Pagan Roman Empire which was also the kingdom of Japheth, *"Thus he said, The fourth beast shall be the fourth kingdom upon earth, which shall be diverse from all kingdoms, and shall devour the whole earth, and shall tread it down, and break it in pieces (Daniel 7:2).*

The fourth prophetic kingdom of Daniel – Rome which succeeded Greece, would produce ten kings or kingdoms. This was a reference to the breaking up or division of the Roman Empire in AD 476 which resulted in the formation of the ten European kingdoms. These were the Franks – France;

147

the Alemanni – Germany; the Burgundians – Switzerland; the Suevi – Portugal; the Vandals – northern Africa; the Visigoths – Spain; the Anglo – Saxons – England; the Ostrogoths – Italy; the Lombards – part of Italy and the Heruli – the other part of Italy.

The Ten Divisions of Rome

The Scriptures say more about these kingdoms, *"And the ten horns out of this kingdom [are] ten kings [that] sh all arise: and <u>anot her</u> shall rise after them; and he shall be diverse from the first, and he shall subdue three kings" (Daniel 7:24).*

Among the ten political divisions of Rome would come a diverse or a different power unlike the rest, which had gone before. It would be different in one crucial respect. Apart from subduing three kings or kingdoms, which was fulfilled in the destruction of the three Gothic kingdoms before the Papacy gained complete control of Europe; it was diverse because this "horn" would be a Religio–political power. This power would persecute the Saints and seek to distort the will of God and confuse the way of salvation.

"And he shall speak [great] words against the most High, and shall wear out the saints of the most High, an d think to change times and laws: and they shall be given into his hand until a time and times and the divi ding of time" (Daniel 7:25).

John, in the book of Revelation, also picks up the theme where Daniel left off and predicted the abuses of the descendants of Japheth in the Temple of God. The same time period or probation of forty-two prophetic months is mentioned again in connection with the papal beast.

148

The Beast from the Sea

> And I stood upon the sand of the sea, and saw a beast rise up out of the sea, having seven heads and ten horns, and upon his horns ten crowns, and upon his heads the name of blasphemy. And the beast which I saw was like unto a leopard, and his feet were as [the feet] of a bear, and his mouth as the mouth of a lion: and the dragon gave him his power, and his seat, and great authority. And I saw one of his heads as it were wounded to death; and his deadly wound was healed: and all the world wondered after the beast. And they worshipped the dragon which gave power unto the beast: and they worshipped the beast, saying, Who [is] like unto the beast? who is able to make war with him? And there was given unto him a mouth speaking great things and blasphemies; and power was given unto him to continue forty [and] two months." (Revelation 13:1-5)

For forty and two months or 1260 literal years, Japheth's descendants terrorized the Church in the name of God. The "horn" of Cornelius and the strength of Japheth were used to wear out the saints of the Most High. It is believed that more than 50 million Christians, "heretics (so called)," were put to death. The Saints of the Most High were also the objects of the Dragon's attack in Revelation 12:17 as well as the Saints in Revelation 14:12; which says, *"Here is the patience of the sain   ts: here [are] they that keep the commandments of God, and the fait h of Jesus."* Unfortunately the prophetic direction of Japheth's "horn" did not look right. Even though Japheth sought to control the pleasant land, God had moved the headquarters of the ministry from earthly Jerusalem to the heavenly Jerusalem after the death of Jesus.

Whereas his brothers before him sought to use Jerusalem as their base for their Ministry, Japheth, despite his control of earthly Jerusalem, had his eyes focused beyond the earthly to the heavenly. He sought after the prophetic Jerusalem. The horn of Japheth would push in all directions especially toward the Pleasant Land. *"And out of one of them came f orth a little horn, whic h waxed exceeding great, toward the south, and toward the east, and toward the pleasant land" (Daniel 8:9).*

149

Japheth's aim was not only to control the world, the saints of the Most High God, but also to take over Mount Zion; the Heavenly Jerusalem, the Church of the Firstborn which is written in Heaven. Paul, reading Daniel, says there would be apostasy among Japheth's descendants before the second coming of the Son of God. *"Let no man deceive you by any means: for [that day shall not come], except there come a falling away first, and that man of sin be revealed, the son of perdition;   Who opposeth and exalteth himself above all that is called God, or that is worshipped; so that he as God sitteth in the temple of God, shewing himself that he is God" (2 Thessalonians 2:3, 4).*

The Apostasy of Japheth

Ham indulged in pride, Shem indulged in Pride, but Japheth's pride excelled them all! Japheth elevated pride to the highest order by attempting to exalt himself above God. He sat in the temple of God to show himself as God. One of the major claims of the Papacy in the Dark Ages was that of the infallibility of the Pope and that he was verily God. "In a passage which is included in the Roman Catholic Canon Law, or *Corpus Juris Canonici,* Pope Innocent III declares that the Roman Pontiff is "the Vicegerent upon earth, not of a mere man, but of very God;" and in a glossary on the passage, it is explained that this is because he is the Vicegerent of Christ, who is "very God and very Man."[187]

The Gentiles' Abuses: Japheth's Apostasy

The Little Horn

So Japheth engaged in self-exaltation, spiritually claiming to be God on earth and socially claiming to be superior to all of his brothers! And from this philosophy has transpired the worse abuses humanity has seen in history.

---

[187] *Decretals of the Lord Pope Gregory IX,* (Decretales Domini Gregorii Papae IX).

Untold atrocities have been wrought on the basis of these assumptions. Numerous lives were taken at the hands of the Papal church. Persecution in the Dark Ages resulted in the massacre of more than 50 million Christians.

Apart from that, Japheth was also responsible for the deaths of millions of his brothers' children. Millions of Shem's children, the Jews, died as a result of the twin evils of racial and spiritual superiority. Millions of Ham's children, Black people, died as a result of the same twin evils of racial and spiritual superiority claimed by Japheth. Many crimes, even in our times, are still motivated by these twin evils of racial and spiritual superiority. Western triumphalism is at the heart of ecclesiastical and racial divisions in this world.

From this same spiritual pride came the concept that the church is given the authority to change even God's laws and times. So the Sabbath was changed from the original day of worship immortalized by Jesus' example to Sunday the "venerable day of the sun;" the day on which the Romans worshiped the sun god. This too, was perpetuated by the papacy, who claimed to have the authority to make these changes.

So, Japheth's corruption includes the introduction of Sunday sacredness, the pagan origin of Christmas and falsity of December 25th as the day of the Savior's birth. It was also responsible for the introduction of image worship in the church and the following:

- The practices of the indulgences and penance
- The practice of confession to the priest instead of to Christ
- The interception of Christ's Ministry in the Heavenly Sanctuary
- The Papal blasphemy of absolution; a man presuming to forgive sins
- The change of the salvation message by faith to salvation by works
- The change of the name of Christ (Yehshua to Jesus)
- The change of all the "Y" sounds in the Hebrew Bible into a "J" sound in the English Bible. How did Yehshua become Joshua, Yerushalaim become Jerusalem and Halleluyah become Hallelujah?
- The change of the ethnic features of Biblical characters (ruddy; reddish-brown or brownish to white European?)
- The change of God's laws and times: Including the Sabbath day from Saturday to Sunday

What does Santa Claus have to do with Christmas? Why is Mary still a virgin and how did she become a Mediatrix? What does an Easter egg and bunny rabbit have to do with Christ? All these things raise serious questions – is Japheth's Jesus the real Christ of the Bible at all? How disappointed some would be when the real Jesus comes back!

This European Jesus (image) whom so many worship may one day appear to be an imposter or a fabrication of the West. The real Jesus was not white European male who kept Sunday for Sabbath but a Semitic commandment keeping, Saturday–Sabbath–observing Jew. "Salvation is of the Jews" not of the Gentiles (Europeans). The Savior was Jewish! This European Jesus who is only merciful, who has managed to abolish the law, who is half way lawless, who has changed God's Sabbath, who is not Semitic— could he be Yehshua at all? Here is another question to ponder: Why is everybody following Japheth's version of Christianity uncritically? What if Japheth is wrong? What then? Think about the damage done in the name of the Lord! Chancellor Williams shows the historical damage done by European Christianity to people of color, He stated:

> Now 'black' was the badge of evil, all that was bad – even bad luck. To make a white man look evil you had to dress him in black; life's final tragedy, death, called for mourning in black; happy events, such as baptisms and weddings, required the wearing of white. God Himself, being white, had cursed the Blacks and made them "servants of man" – man being white man, for was not he made in the "image of God?" To worship God, in effect was to worship the white man. A volume could be written on the scores of these little psychological gimmicks that are now so deeply embedded in cultural thought that they are taken as a simple matter of course and require no comment. Yet they are the subtle weapons, which have been more devastating in conquering the Blacks, and reducing them to an inferior status than armed might. Caucasian victory was complete and seemingly permanent when the Blacks throughout the world joined the whites in glorifying all things white and condemning all things black or even tinged with black, including themselves. Here we are at the very heart of the "race problem," this self-abnegation, self-effacement, the loss of self-identity by cutting their roots with the past and thereby losing the very links with their history from which a people draw strength and inspiration to move forward to even higher ground and, in fact, the reason for being.[188]

There is a common Ghanaian adage that says, "When you are going to church and you meet a white man on the way, go back home for you have seen God." And this concept did not emerge in a vacuum. It came about as a result of portraying Biblical characters and especially Jesus as white European people to the Africans. Now, apart from its idolatrous and blasphemous implications, such a belief is both spiritually and psychologically detrimental to those who hold it. And until Africans dismantle the Caucasian image of God (set up by Papacy) in the high places of their souls, they will not prosper.

---

[188] Chancellor Williams, *Destruction of Black Civilization* (Chicago: Third World Press, 1956), 250.

However, it seems as though the whole world is practicing some kind of "Simon-says-religion." But, inevitably, Simon-says-religion leads to Zombie theology which creates worshipers with hearts only but not heads, where the blind leads the blind without a question and loving it. No wonder the "whole world will worship the beast" (Revelation 13:3 & 4). Simon says the dead goes straight up to heaven and everybody around the world says the dead are happy in heaven. Simon says God changed His day of worship from Saturday to Sunday and everybody around the world says the day of worship is changed to Sunday. Simon says Church can't do business and everybody around the world says church can't do business so we suffer. Simon says-no clapping in church and everybody around the world says no clapping in church. Simons says no drums in church and everybody around the world says no drumming in church even though Psalms 150 calls for it. Simon says indigenous polygamists should divorce their wives and everybody around the world says they should divorce their wives even though God says I hate divorce. Simon says original Biblical people were Caucasians and everybody around the world says they were Caucasians and deck their Churches with Caucasian images of Biblical characters. Simon says Jesus was a Caucasian man and everybody around the world says He was a white Caucasian male. We have far too many Simon says-Christians but our time demands a "Thus saith the Lord-Christianity!"

The Papacy

Well, we know that the Papacy was the union of church and state symbolically depicted in the compromise between "the Woman and the Beast' as portrayed by John: "So he carried me away in the spirit into the wilderness: and I saw a woman sit upon a scarlet coloured beast, full of names of blasphemy, having seven heads and ten horns" (Revelation 17:3). And the same compromise is also portrayed as fornication between the woman and kings of the earth: "With whom the kings of the earth have committed fornication, and the inhabitants of the earth have been made drunk with the wine of her fornication" (Revelation 17:2). Simply put, therefore the remnant or the faithful church would be all those who refused to submit to the corrupt teachings and the abusive authority of the Papacy, those who keep the commandments of God together with the faith of Jesus, (Revelation 14:12).

The commandments manifested in the Ten could also be summarized into Two. In Matthew 22:40, Jesus said all the commandments hang or anchored on love to God and love to man. So in the Dark Ages all those who maintained a supreme love for God and unselfish love for their fellow men; and held on to the faith of Jesus were numbered among the remnant. That would include the Waldenses, the Albegenses, the Huguenots, the Coptics, the

Abyssinians and many countless others who remained faithful to the light they knew in spite of apostasy:

> Such examples are not found in the Bible only. They abound in every record of human progress. The Vaudois and the Huguenots, Wycliffe and Huss, Jerome and Luther, Tyndale and Knox, Zinzendorf and Wesley, with multitudes of others have witnessed to the power of God's word against human power and policy in support of evil. These are the world's true nobility. This is its royal line. In this line the youth of today are called to take their places."[189]

The Deadly Wound

As The Pope Is Led Into Captivity

But as with all things human, a day of reckoning was coming and Japheth would be made to know that he was not God. What he did to others would be done to him. In 1798, at the end of the prophetic 1260 years, Japheth's pride was broken. Pope Pius VI was carried captive from Rome to Valence in France to die in captivity, thus fulfilling the prophecy; *"He that leadeth into captivity shall go into captivity: he that killeth with the sword must be killed with the sword. Here is the patience and the faith of the saints" (Revelation 13:10).*

Japheth was knocked down but not out. He would not bow out easily: His deadly wound would be healed! The Bible says "his deadly wound was healed" (Revelation 13:1). Japheth is coming back stronger than before but this time to go into perdition. "The beast that thou sawest was, and is not; and shall ascend out of the bottomless pit, and go into perdition: and they that

---

[189]Ellen White, Education. (Mountain View, CA: Pacific Press Publishing Association, 1952), 254

dwell on the earth shall wonder, whose names were not written in the book of life from the foundation of the world, when they behold the beast that was, and is not, and yet is," (Revelation 17:8).

Only the coming of the Stone will break the evil horn of Japheth. Only the armies of the east could break the powers of the beast. *"An d the sixth angel poured out his vial upon t he great river Eu phrates; and the water thereof was dried up, that the way of the <u>kings of the east</u> might be prepared,"* (Revelation 16:12). While Japheth would be consolidating his power to deal a deathblow to the Saints of the Most High, he is perplexed by the news from the East.

From here-on Japheth, by the instigation of the Devil, will organize all other members of the family to fight against even the Lord to maintain power. *"And I saw three unclean spirits like frogs [come] out of the m outh of the dragon, and out of the mo uth of the be ast, and out of the mout h of the false prophet. For they are the spirits of dev ils, working miracles, [which] go forth unto the kings of the earth and of the whole world, to gather them to the battle of that great day of God Almighty" (Revelation 16:13-14).*

The Final Fall

The news or tidings from the east is said to be the cause of the destruction of the "man of sin" while he is trying to complete an unfinished business of taking over the throne of God. In Daniel we read: *"But tidings out of the east and out of the north shall trouble him: therefore he sha ll go forth with great fury to destroy and utterly to take away many. And he shall plant the tabernacles of his pala ce between the seas in the glorious holy mountain; yet he shall come to his end, and none shall help him" (Daniel 11:44, 45).* Yet he, the Papacy, the visible representation of that wicked one shall be destroyed. Euphrates of earthly support will dry up and so no one will help him.

So from a political and spiritual standpoint, Japheth's life would be prolonged until the day of the final judgment when his apostate children would be destroyed under a symbolic name of Babylon, in a symbolic place called Armageddon. Yet, although Japheth would lose his divine authority, he would still carry on with business as usual. He would not yield the battle without a struggle until Heaven transfers both the political and spiritual dominion to Christ. And Christ in turn gives it to the saints.

Europe and America are first cousins. The New World is an extension of the Old and in time both will come to realize their common destiny to rule the world. No obstacle will be allowed to stand in the way; even the United States Constitution will be altered, to the point of repudiation to accommodate the lure of global control.

155

The day is coming when Europe will cave in to Americas' pressure and America will cave in to Papal pressure; and things will go from bad to worse for the entire world. It is just a matter of time! In addition nature will react. Calamity after calamity will cause the Right to react to the Left with moral solutions resulting in a new political moral code for this nation pushing the church/state union to the edge for the devil to take advantage of it and shake the foundations of the republic. There will be troubles of international proportions on every side.

The Locusts of Arabia or the Desert locusts (Rev. 9:1-3) would be fully unleashed on the West and the West will not know what to do. To kill them or to leave them; that will be the question! The more they kill the more and harder they will come! And the world would be thrown into chaos and there will be confusion on every side. The moral clock of the world would strike midnight.

It is there that the devil will impersonate Christ, appearing in the handsome portrait of the Jesus we have on our walls—he will come and endorse the new polices of the world to fix the crisis and introduce some agenda of his own. He will purport to have changed "his laws" and that all must cooperate. Evil spirits will be discharged to convince the world to accept Satan's rule. And those who disobey this pseudo Jesus will be blamed for the troubles of the world and persecution will be unleashed on the righteous.

You can unmask the anti-Christ by realizing that the historical Jesus was a Semitic man, not a European man. The historical Jesus would never change God's laws and also that in His Second Coming, His feet will not touch the ground. In the same way the Jews missed their Messiah, most Christians will accept an imposter in place of the real. What a tragedy!

Well, the locusts of Arabia by the great river are already tormenting the "dwellers of the earth" (Revelation 9 & 13). The Eagle is not only frustrated but desperate. Is there a way out of the desert dilemma? You be the judge. For me, it's Checkmate! However, in the end the Eagle backed by the "horn" will prevail; the king of the north will prevail over the king of the south until the Kings of East take over the kingdoms of the world (Daniel 11:40-45, Revelation 16:12). So fear not! The STONE is coming!

> *"As concerning the rest of the beasts, they had their dominion taken away: yet their lives were prolonged for a season and time. I saw in the night visions, and, behold, one like the Son of man came with the clouds of heaven, and came to the Ancient of days, and they brought him near before him. And there was given him dominion, and glory, and a kingdom, that all people, nations, and languages, should serve him: his dominion [is] an everlasting dominion, which shall not pass away, and his kingdom that which shall not be destroyed" (Daniel 7:12-14).*

CHAPTER NINETEEN

JESUS TAKES OVER THE KINGDOMS

When your neighbor's horse falls into a pit, you should not rejoice at it, for your own child may fall into it too. Simply put, what goes around comes around!(African proverb)

"But thou, Bethlehem Ephratah, [though] thou be little among the thousands of Judah, [yet] out of thee shall he come forth unto me [that is] to be ruler in Israel; whose goings forth [have been] from of old, from everlasting" (Micah 5:2).

THE STONE COMETH!

Herein is the final transfer of Power as the Stone comes to smash all earthly kingdoms to establish an everlasting kingdom for God. Both the Political Kingdom and the Ministerial Priesthood will finally fall into the hands of Christ. His will be the everlasting Royal Priesthood. The dominion of this world goes to Jesus, the righteous King who will rule in the New Jerusalem. Jesus is the anticipated King of Salem, the High Priest of the Most High God.

The Last Kingdom to Rule the Earth

The Overthrow of Japheth: The Establishment of God's Everlasting Kingdom

The kingdoms of the world come to an end under Japheth's watch. No one nation would be given the right to dominate this world from then on until the Kingdom of the Stone comes. God will set up His kingdom in the days when the strong and weak kingdoms of this world are trying to consolidate their power by uniting. These attempts to unite in this era of "clay and iron" of weak and strong nations or of churches and states will be futile says the Word. *"And whereas thou sawest iron mixed with miry clay, they shall mingle themselves with the seed of men: but they shall not cleave one to another, even as iron is not mixed with clay" (Daniel 2:43).*

Clay and iron represent Japheth and spring from the 10 divisions of Rome. They are products of Rome trying to mingle or join back together, but they will not cleave or stay with one another just as clay and iron are not mixed together. In a general sense, it also represents powerful nations of the earth trying to take advantage of the weaker nations. Why do you think a little iron controls so much clay—a little European Iron controls a world of clay? Prophecy! But Japheth will presume to think he rules the world forever and would try to exercise global domination. So his seed would still be holding on to world power at the time the Stone hits the image. *"And in the days of these kings s hall the God of heaven set up a kingdom, which shall never b e destroyed: and the kin gdom shall n ot be left to other people, [but] it shal l break in pieces and consume all thes e kingdoms, and it shall stand for ever"* (Daniel 2: 44).

This cosmic transfer of the kingdom comes about when Japheth still rules politically and spiritually albeit falsely. And he would do anything to maintain power. But when God's clock strikes midnight, no power can stop it. God will overthrow Japheth politically and transfer the kingdom to the saints of the Most High. God is about to take the kingdom from Japheth, but Japheth is not ready to give it up, so Japheth is going to fight until it is taken by force.

And John referring to that time says:

> And he gathered them together into a place called in the Hebrew tongue Armageddon. And the seventh angel poured out his vial into the air; and there came a great voice out of the temple of heaven, from the throne, saying, It is done. And there were voices, and thunders, and lightnings; and there was a great earthquake, such as was not since men were upon the earth, so mighty an earthquake, [and] so great. And the great city was divided into three parts, and the cities of the nations fell: and great Babylon came in remembrance before God, to give unto her the cup of the wine of the fierceness of his wrath. (Revelation 16:16-19)

And like the Canaanites and the Israelites; Ham and Shem before him, Japheth's cup of iniquity is full and his kingdom would be taken and given to the Saints who will reign with Christ in righteousness forever. The final

158

transfer goes this way; *"And the kingdom and dominion, and the greatness of the kingdom under the whole heaven, shall be given to the people of the saints of the most   High, whose kingdom [is] an everla sting kingdom, and all dominions shall serve and obey him" (Daniel 7:27).*

The same condition that befell Ham and Shem has overtaken Japheth. He is fallen and God is calling his faithful children out. *"And I hea rd another voice from heaven, sayin g, Come out of her, my people, that   ye be not partakers of her sins and t hat ye receive not of her plagues. For her sins have reached unto heaven and God hath remembered her iniquities" (Rev. 18:4-5).*

Interestingly enough, Babylon out of which God is calling His children is the prophetic Roman system. Peter in Rome referred to it as Babylon. "The church that is at Babylon, elected together with [you], saluteth you; and [so doth] Marcus my son" (1Peter 5:13). Peter understood the prophetic role of Rome as Babylon referred to in Revelation. Here is where Harold Camping (Family Radio open forum Bible talk show preacher) went wrong calling out Christians from every church saying, "The church-age is over" and predicting the coming of Jesus on May 21, 2011. Jesus never said the church age will be over. In fact, Jesus assured His church, "The gates of hell shall not prevail against the church" and he promised, "And I will pray the Father, and he shall give you another Comforter that he may abide with you for ever" (John 14:16). The Comforter will be with the church till the end of the age. The church age is not over. It is Babylon; Japheth's apostate Christianity that is being disqualified and not the True Church of the Living God. God is calling His children out of Babylon into his true church (the One Fold) to be prepared for the coming of Jesus.

Also concerning His coming, Jesus said, "But of that day and hour knoweth no *man*, no, not the angels of heaven, but my <u>Father only</u>" (Matthew 24:36). No man knows except the father, so Camping cannot know and to continue to set dates and call Christians out of Christ's Church is making Jesus a liar and that is presumptuous; borderline blasphemous! So upon the authority of the Word of God, I declare Camping's predictions false and call on those deceived by Camping and other false prophets to look for the Remnant Church of Revelation 14:12, "Here is the patience of the saints: here *are* they that keep the Commandments of God, and the faith of Jesus," and prepare for the soon coming of Jesus.

Japheth's Kingdom

- The Beast from the sky (the dragon) Roman paganism – Japheth's kingdom (Revelation. 12)
- The Beast from the Sea with the woman – Papacy – Japheth's Christianity (Revelation 13/17) Woman on the beast is the apostate European Christianity

159

sitting on a corrupt European political system to sway the world to Satan.
- The Beast from the Land—America (Japheth's military power) (Revelation. 13)

As recorded in Revelation 18:8, all these symbolic powers team up in the end to fight the saints of the Most High. Curiously enough, after the Millennium, the Devil gathers the nations which are in the four quarters of the earth to fight against God. He uses Gog which was the prophetic prince of Meshech together with Tubal, and Magog. All these were the children of Japheth. Magog was a direct descendant of Japheth! *"Son of man, set thy face against Gog, the land of Magog, the chief prince of Meshech and Tubal, and prophesy against him" (Ezekiel 38:2).*

The Final Battle before the Final Transfer

CHAPTER TWENTY

END TIME SCENARIO

Words are spoken in their shells; it is the wise man's duty to find the kernel (African proverb)

There are two strong distinguishing features that stand out for the descendants of Japheth, namely, economy and power. It is the devil's plan to complicate and confuse the world's economy to the extent that many will find it difficult to survive in the last days. One solution will be to work on Sabbath. The Christian world and other religions would not mind endorsing the law mandating all to work Saturdays and resting on Sunday.

While the church compromises with the state on this point, United States Constitution and the Truth will be sacrificed. The US Constitution will be severely altered to fix the world's economy. The faithful (believers) who hold closely to God's directive as stated in the Bible will stand in the way by their refusal to compromise. These will be persecuted for the good of the economy and for the life of the world. "And that no man might buy or sell, save he that had the mark, or the name of the beast, or the number of his name" (Revelation 13:17). Make no mistake about this! This persecution is not far into the future.

And in the crisis, Satan will impersonate Christ resembling very much the European Christ of Michael Angelo's imagination. His purpose will be to endorse the unification of church and state to solve the problems of the world and condone the persecution of those religious dissidents.

Japheth's Legacy-Spiritual and Socio-Cultural Superiority

As the author of this book, I challenge the church to rid itself of colonial and imperial theology that condones the social and spiritual superiority and take up the humility of Christ. We ought to steer clear of perpetuating the belief that one person is better than the other, on the basis of race, degree, pedigree, class, knowledge, political party or church affiliation. Could it be that all the brouhaha over music, dress, marriage and others have nothing much to do with the global Church and all to do with the European Church? Could it really be about how they ought or ought not to be done in the

European church and not in other ethnic churches? Could it be that these things are culture sanctified by theology, and not theological per se and that indigenous theologians, not foreigners be the ones to contextualize what can and should be done in the indigenous church?

Europeans would not know what music is appropriate and what is not in the African, Chinese or Indian context. For one thing they are clueless about indigenous culture and history. Africans, Chinese and Indian theologians must be allowed to contextualize theology for their people since they are the ones who understand their people's culture and the way of life in the context of the Word of God. Failure to recognize this simple fact has created Euro-centric churches all around the world. European culture is mistaken for Christianity the world over. In many places wearing of the suit and tie has become not only standard but sacred Christian dress. No one dares go to the pulpit without them. And yet God admonishes us not to minister before Him wearing "anything that causes sweat" Ezekiel 44:18.

In short, all of Noah's children have had their turn with the divine Ministry and all have failed miserably. The Gospel would be taken and given to the nation that will bring forth its fruits. Jesus said, *"Therefore say I unto you, The kingdom of God shall be taken from yo   u, and given to a nation bringing forth the fruits thereof" (Matthew 21:43).*

Love to God and to man is a requirement for the proclamation of the gospel. Those to whom the ministry is granted ought to learn to love all God's people. The gospel cannot be preached if the bearers do not accept the people for whom the message is directed. After all, the gospel is about people! *"And he said unto me, Thou must prophesy again before many peoples, and nations, and tongues, and kings" Revelation 10:11* . Simply put, the qualification for the proclamation of the gospel is love for God and love for people.

Ham, Shem, and Japheth: Acknowledgements and Credits

Ham gave us Monotheism. Shem gave us Exclusive Monotheism (Deuteronomy 6:4). And Japheth gave us Triune-Monotheism. In his *Egyptian Religion*, Sir Wallis Budge, a renowned Egyptologist, describes Egyptian Monotheism:

A study of ancient Egyptian religious texts will convince the reader that the Egyptians believed in One God, who was self-existed, immortal, invisible, eternal, omniscient, almighty, and inscrutable, the maker of heavens, earth and underworld, the creator of the sky and the sea, men and women, animals, and birds, fish and creeping things, trees and plants, and the incorporeal beings who were the messengers that fulfilled his wish and word.[190]

- Ham gave us the art of writing, Shem wrote the "Books of the Bible," and Japheth used the principles of the Books for his Constitution.
- Ham in Africa preserved Saturday as God's Memorial Day of Creation in the Akan oral tradition.
- Shem in Israel observed Saturday as God's Memorial Day of Creation from the Hebrew Biblical tradition.
- Japheth in Rome authorized Sunday; the venerable day of the sun as God's Day from the Roman pagan tradition.
- Ham discovered the atom, Shem split the atom and Japheth made the atom bomb.
  - Egyptians discovered the secret of the Atom and they were filled with reverence. {Scholars say relationship exits "between Atum (Atom) of the Egyptian sun god and the atom of the modern science."[191]
  - Einstein discovered the secret of splitting the Atom and he was filled with awe.
  - America discovered the secret of the split Atom and she was filled with remorse.

Three Ways Japheth May Lose His Freedoms

Japheth gave his children freedoms of speech, of choice, of assembly, and of governance and the world is better off because of that. But they won't last forever. There will be an end to freedom! First, the fear of "locust" will cause Japheth to give up Constitutional freedoms for security.

The Second threat occurs when rights carried to the extreme will be the negation of itself. So when individual rights become a license to indulge the self to death, freedom will lead to the bondage of an unrestrained self and will make one a slave of an uncontrolled will. There will be an end to freedom as we know it. "While they promise them liberty, they themselves are the servants of corruption: for of whom a man is overcome, of the same is he brought in bondage" (II Peter 2:19).

The third threat will come when individual rights will collide with community rights and cause a reaction from politicians to impose morality to curb individual rights and freedoms. At that time religion will be married to the state to ensure compliance of religious dogmas to cause suppression and oppression which will inevitably result in the end of freedom as we know it.

---

[190] Sir Wallis Budge, Egyptian Religion (Bell: New York 1959), 17. Sir Wallis Budge, Egyptian Religion (Bell: New York 1959), 17.
[191] George G. M. James, *Stolen Legacy* (Chicago, Illinois: African American Images, 2002), 147.

CHAPTER TWENTY-ONE

MODERN STEWARDSHIP

Ashes fly back into the face of him who throws them. (African proverb)

"Indigenity" Against Modernity

Indigenous Stewardship Versus the Modern Stewardship

And It Was Good!

"Aborigines' and "Indigenous" have been ascribed negative connotation, but the words simply mean "original" and "authentic" respectively. The knowledge of God has always been present in the cultures of the so-called indigenous peoples. The God who does not discriminate made sure His gems of truth would be scattered abroad and disseminate among all people, including indigenous people. And it was this awareness of the divine in the culture that made them good stewards of nature

It was the genius of the indigenous people to protect the earth and its ecology, the source of human sustenance for a very long time that modern people are sustained today. By simply obeying taboos—their unwritten laws—the indigenous preserved the earth in a pristine condition. The West calls them primitive and yet their stewardship was impeccable. Under their watch the ecosystem, water, vegetation, air and the whole environment remained viable and healthy. If the essence of civilization is to use available tools to protect life and to preserve the environment that supports life, then modern man with the best tools has done poorly.

Sadly, with all the modern technology, with tremendous advances in agriculture, communication, ecology, engineering, genetics, medicine, and space exploration, Japheth's seed has done far more damage to the environment than Ham and Shem combined. With all their so-called "superstitions," the Native Americans preserved the environment in an impeccable condition, a far better job than modern sophisticated technology has done.

Indigenous people with all their "superstition" gave us a better world than moderns with all our technology are able to leave for our children. What does it profit our civilization if we should split the atom, travel to space and in the end die in the smog of pollution? Go to the moon but lose the world in a miasma of our own garbage? What is the real benefit to mankind to make "Nukes" to protect ourselves and in the end, die as a result of its radiation emissions?

The height of stupidity and insanity is wasting oneself to satisfy oneself. The absurdity of it all is killing self with your eyes wide open and feeling helpless to stop it or having no desire to halt it. That's the mark of our age. It feels like a global drug addiction. Corporate pollution of the environment for financial gain is like a person shooting drugs into his system for an emotional high. They are both drunk with the power of permanent self-destruction for a quick temporary high.

The heart of this irony is the selfishness of Japheth seeking to control the riches of the whole world, all for himself. If it's not in his interest, he will not do right. Japheth's corporatocracy is directly responsible for the "Globacide" we are all experiencing today: unnatural environmental disasters and industrial pollution of global proportions. Yet the same Japheth, unlike his brothers would travel the world to bind the wounds of the world's poor. That's awesome and we need to celebrate that spirit. So on behalf of Ham and Shem I salute you Japheth! However, to minimize the contradiction, surely, Japheth can also learn from Ham and Shem in the care of the environment if we all are going to survive together in this cosmic dance of death.

Judgment

Nevertheless, there was a reason Ham was the object of Divine judgment in the Old Testament at the time of *Yehshua;* pronounced as Joshua, and Shem the object of the same in the New Testament in the time of *Yehshua;* Jesus Christ. There will be similar reason for the judgment of Japheth at the Second Coming of *Yehshua* at the end of time. There is time and season of judgment for each one of them.

What do these people have in common? They were and are guilty of idolatry! Materialism with its worship of mammon and self in our day, (which deprives people of essential time with the Lord) is no different from idol worship of the past which robbed the ancients of their relationship with the true God. They were idolaters and all nations have been found guilty of the same.

The Spiritual Corruption of Ham and its Corresponding Judgment

- Spiritual pride and abuse of power in Babylon and Egypt
- The pride of Pharaoh and the hardness of his heart that led to the overthrow of his Egyptian government
- The pride of Nebuchadnezzar and his punishment to dwell in the wilderness for seven years
- The arrogance of Belshazzar and the overthrow of his Babylonian government
- The temptation of Black people in yielding to inferiority complex is as sinful as the sin of pride

Spiritual Corruption in Shem and His judgment

The following is the picture painted by Jesus of "Shem" in his corrupt state of hypocrisy:

> Then spake Jesus to the multitude, and to his disciples, Saying, The Scribes and the Pharisees sit in Moses' seat: All therefore whatsoever they bid you observe, [that] observe and do; but do not ye after their works: for they say, and do not. . . . But woe unto you, scribes and Pharisees, hypocrites! for ye shut up the kingdom of heaven against men: for ye neither go in [yourselves], neither suffer ye them that are entering to go in. Woe unto you, scribes and Pharisees, hypocrites! for ye devour widows' houses, and for a pretence make long prayer: therefore ye shall receive the greater damnation. Woe unto you, scribes and Pharisees, hypocrites! for ye compass sea and land to make one proselyte, and when he is made, ye make him twofold more the child of hell than yourselves. . . .
>
> Woe unto you, scribes and Pharisees, hypocrites! for ye pay tithe of mint and anise and cummin, and have omitted the weightier [matters] of the law, judgment, mercy, and faith: these ought ye to have done, and not to leave the other undone. [Ye] blind guides, which strain at a gnat, and swallow a camel. Woe unto you, scribes and Pharisees, hypocrites! for ye make clean the outside of the cup and of the platter, but within they are full of extortion and excess. [Thou] blind Pharisee; cleanse first that

166

[which is] within the cup and platter that the outside of them may be clean also.

Woe unto you, scribes and Pharisees, hypocrites! for ye are like unto whited sepulchers, which indeed appear beautiful outward, but are within full of dead [men's] bones, and of all uncleanness. Even so ye also outwardly appear righteous unto men, but within ye are full of hypocrisy and iniquity. Woe unto you, scribes and Pharisees, hypocrites! because ye build the tombs of the prophets, and garnish the sepulchres of the righteous,

And say, If we had been in the days of our fathers, we would not have been partakers with them in the blood of the prophets. Wherefore ye be witnesses unto yourselves, that ye are the children of them which killed the prophets. Fill ye up then the measure of your fathers. [Ye] serpents, [ye] generation of vipers, how can ye escape the damnation of hell? Wherefore, behold, I send unto you prophets, and wise men, and scribes: and [some] of them ye shall kill and crucify; and [some] of them shall ye scourge in your synagogues, and persecute [them] from city to city: That upon you may come all the righteous blood shed upon the earth, from the blood of righteous Abel unto the blood of Zacharias son of Barachias, whom ye slew between the temple and the altar. Verily I say unto you, All these things shall come upon this generation (*Matthew 23:1-36*).

Shem was full of exclusivism, disobedience, spiritual pride, and persecution.

Spiritual Corruption Found in Japheth and his Judgment: Revelation 18

Here follows the picture of Japheth's corruption as painted by the Lord in the book of Revelation:

And after these things I saw another angel come down from heaven, having great power; and the earth was lightened with his glory. And he cried mightily with a strong voice, saying, Babylon the great is fallen, is fallen, and is become the habitation of devils, and the hold of every foul spirit, and a cage of every unclean and hateful bird. For all nations have drunk of the wine of the wrath of her fornication, and the kings of the earth have committed fornication with her, and the merchants of the earth are waxed rich through the abundance of her delicacies.

And I heard another voice from heaven, saying, Come out of her, my people, that ye be not partakers of her sins, and that ye receive not of her plagues. For her sins have reached unto heaven, and God hath remembered her iniquities. Reward her even as she rewarded you, and double unto her double according to her works:

167

in the cup which she hath filled fill to her double. How much she hath glorified herself, and lived deliciously, so much torment and sorrow give her: for she saith in her heart, I sit a queen, and am no widow, and shall see no sorrow. Therefore shall her plagues come in one day, death, and mourning, and famine; and she shall be utterly burned with fire: for strong [is] the Lord God who judgeth her. And the kings of the earth, who have committed fornication and lived deliciously with her, shall bewail her, and lament for her, when they shall see the smoke of her burning, Standing afar off for the fear of her torment, saying, Alas, alas, that great city Babylon, that mighty city! for in one hour is thy judgment come. And the merchants of the earth shall weep and mourn over her; for no man buyeth their merchandise any more:

The merchandise of gold, and silver, and precious stones, and of pearls, and fine linen, and purple, and silk, and scarlet, and all thyine wood, and all manner vessels of ivory, and all manner vessels of most precious wood, and of brass, and iron, and marble, And cinnamon, and odours, and ointments, and frankincense, and wine, and oil, and fine flour, and wheat, and beasts, and sheep, and horses, and chariots, and slaves, and souls of men. And the fruits that thy soul lusted after are departed from thee, and all things which were dainty and goodly are departed from thee, and thou shalt find them no more at all. The merchants of these things, which were made rich by her, shall stand afar off for the fear of her torment, weeping and wailing, And saying, Alas, alas, that great city, that was clothed in fine linen, and purple, and scarlet, and decked with gold, and precious stones, and pearls!

For in one hour so great riches is come to nought. And every shipmaster, and all the company in ships, and sailors, and as many as trade by sea, stood afar off, And cried when they saw the smoke of her burning, saying, What [city is] like unto this great city! And they cast dust on their heads, and cried, weeping and wailing, saying, Alas, alas, that great city, wherein were made rich all that had ships in the sea by reason of her costliness! for in one hour is she made desolate. (Revelation 18:1-19)

Among other things we see from the scriptures there are also such things as: secularization, exploitation, materialism, pollution, spiritism, racism, apostasy and persecution are the causes of the downfall of Japheth.

However, one thing is clear, all the sons of Ham have been tried and tested and all have been found wanting. The Cycle is completed!

CHAPTER TWENTY-TWO

WHO WILL BE NEXT?

He who fights and runs away lives to fight another day. (African proverbs)

The leadership establishment of Japheth at this time is losing its spiritual authority because of its continuous condoning of racism, modeling a type of selfishness that is couched in individualism, importing worldly politics into the business of the Lord, and the abuse and misuse of power for selfish gains. Japheth may be in power, but spiritually not in charge. Japheth's leadership is becoming a ghost of a leadership. His glory is almost departed and the kingdom of God is about to be given to a nation that will bring forth its fruits.

The day when worldly politics and the spirit of racism seeps into the soul of the leadership of the church, that is the day God disqualifies them. Just as God disqualified Ahab and Caiaphas from leadership, God will disqualify corrupt leadership and appoint the leadership of His own choosing, leaders who in the spirit of Elijah (like John the Baptist) will lead His people, to prepare the way of the Lord and to finish the work! The following is a passage that should be considered seriously. *"And now also the **axe** is laid unto the root of the trees: ever y tree therefore which bringeth not forth good fruit is hewn down, and cast into the fire"* (Luke 3:9).

John cautions, *"Bring forth therefore fruits worthy of repentance, and begin not to say within yourselves, we have Abraham to [our] father: for I say unto you, that God is able of these stones to raise up children unto Abraham"* (Luke 3:8, 9).

This may well be a period of transition, from Saul's kind of leadership, to David's, a man after God's own heart. This is a transition time illustrated by the period between Malachi and Matthew; an Inter-Testamental time dominated by conservative Pharisees and the liberal Sadducees, a time ruled by the Sanhedrin. It is a time of "a form of godliness" and powerlessness in the spiritual life.

God is looking for a nation that will bring forth fruits that accurately represents his kingdom. He is looking for a people to preach the kingdom message. God is looking for preachers worldwide who will transcend racism, sexism, and classism. God needs leaders who love all nations, kindred, tongue and people, and are willing and able to work with all the so-called races, genders, classes and cultures, to lead in preaching the final message of mercy to a dying world. *"And I saw another angel fly in the midst of heaven, having the everlasting gospel to preach unto them that dwell on the earth, and to every nation, and kindred, and to ngue, and people" (Revelat ion 14: 6).* Angels flying in the midst of Heaven preaching the everlasting gospel signifies the universality of the message, the messengers and the object of the message. People everywhere are the target of the gospel and those who would preach it cannot harbor hatred for one another. For this gospel is to lead humanity to accept Jesus, (God's gift of supreme love).

The madness of the hegemony of men to think that God cannot or should not or will not use women as equally and as effectively as men implies they know the mind of God. Do they know the mind of God? Can they command God to follow their reasoning? Whenever human beings have become comfortable with the status quo, believing it was ordained by God, and tried to preserve it out of self-interest under the pretense of preserving God's interest, God has always surprised them. Just as God rejected Jewish prejudice of the first century and brought the Gentiles into the ministry (Acts 10); rejected the racial prejudice of the nineteenth century and brought Black people into the ministry, so will He destroy male chauvinism of our time to bring women into the ministry! All barriers and partitions will be broken down, and all God's people will be brought to the table to finish the work of the ministry of saving souls for whom our Savior died. God will soon overthrow the hegemony of men, take their office and give it to others who will follow His leadings and promptings.

Spiritual and social superiority manifesting itself in racism and prejudice are obstacles to the efforts of Japheth's ministry. European Christianity can never rise higher than it has been in ministry to the world as long as she holds on, albeit tacitly to the doctrine of inferior and superior races and condone racism albeit in the soul. Right now European Christianity is destitute of life and vitality. It has plenty of wealth and political power but is short on life and spiritual power. Just as the Pope once said, *"The Church can no longer say silver and gold have we none, but the old preacher said, neither can she say in the name of Jesus rise up and walk"*

God is looking for a people, a "nation" that will be faithful in carrying forth the global ministry that will mark the end time. God is counting on the nation that Jesus prophesied about to receive the kingdom. *"Therefore say I unto you, The kingdom of God shall be taken from yo u, and given to a nation bringing forth the fruits thereof"(Matthew 21:43).*

The term "n ation" can refer to any group of people with something in common. In this context, faithfulness is what is common to them –at the core of their being is their obedience to God. Peter says the nation must show the praises of God to the world. *"But ye [are] a chosen generation, a royal priesthood, an holy nati on, a peculiar people; that ye should shew forth the*

170

praises of him who hath c alled you out of darkness into his marvellous light" *(1Peter 2:9).* Simply put, that means to demonstrate God's power and His attributes of love and grace to all God's children.

There are several qualifications to God's Prophetic nation. This nation must show the praises or virtues of God. This means she must show love to God and to all humanity. This nation must be infused with the spirit of Christ to preach to all without discrimination. God's prophetic nation must embrace all humanity as God's purchased possession. They cannot have a Babylonian spirit, be part of Babylon or be in Babylon. This separation enables this people to preach the message *"come o ut of her my people."* The spirit of Babylon is the spirit of spiritual pride, resulting in social and racial superiority. Racial superiority, a fruit of spiritual exaltation, produces racism. Therefore the prejudice of racism disqualifies a people from fulfilling this role. No one can uphold racism and preach the Everlasting Message! I say again, end-time global preachers must love all people and treat them equally and fairly.

God wants all of Noah's children to participate in this end time global mission. However many are called but few are chosen. Therefore, any people who will be allowed to participate in this everlasting ministry must reflect the attitude of Christ.

America, therefore, must repent of racism and hypocrisy if she will have the privilege of participating in the final lap of the relay race that the church has been running. She must show forth fruits of repentance by ceasing to treat some groups better than others because of trite reasons. This attitude was demonstrated in her response to the Balkans while abandoning Rwanda, Sudan, Congo and Chad to genocide.

All nations have some repentance to do before they can be used of God. Arabia must repent from trying to play God. She must depart from the theology of violence of killing anyone who does not share their beliefs! China must repent of persecuting dissenters if China wants to participate in God's agenda! Africa must repent from begging the West for food and train its citizens to be creative and productive self-sufficient citizens of God's Kingdom on earth. It is acceptable to borrow, but by all means borrow the equipments that can be used to produce your own food.

It was the old time theology of racism that has now produced discrimination and inter-racial hatred of the modern times. The powerful must understand that God gives power for the benefit of all his people especially for the protection of the vulnerable. God will not entertain abusive and discriminatory use of power.

God expected Nebuchadnezzar to bless all with the exercise of God's entrusted power. On that matter, Daniel described God's expectation in these symbolic terms. *"The tree that tho u sawest, which grew, and was strong, whose height reached unto the heaven, and the sight thereof to all the earth;*

171

Whose leaves [were] fair, and the fruit thereof much, and in it [was] meat for all; under which the beast s of the field dwelt, and upon whose branches the fowls of th e heaven had their h abitation" (Daniel 4:2 0, 21) . In acknowledgement of the power that is God's to give, all those who hold this honor must recognize the need for the beasts of the field and the birds of the air to lodge or perch in their branches.

God reserves the right to punish any kingdom for the abuses of its power. Babylon, Egypt, Rome and even Israel were punished for political abuses and persecution.

From the sons of Noah—Shem, Ham, and Japheth, Daniel's image revealed that Ham would be the head of gold, Shem and Japheth the breast and arms of silver, also Japheth the thighs of brass, legs of iron and the feet part of the mixture of iron and clay. The kingdom of God would come in the days of Japheth's kingdom. But the ministry will be given to a holy nation that will bring forth its fruit to finish the work. It will be a nation that is faithful to the Gospel ministry itself to reach out to all God's people everywhere.

AFRICA'S TIME TO BLESS AGAIN!

From Melchizedek to Abraham to Cornelius

The Cycle is Complete

When the drumbeat changes the dance changes. (African proverb)

"Therefore say I unto you, the kingdom of God shall be taken from you, and given to a nation bringing forth the fruits thereof" Matthew 21:43.

Who would God send and who will go for Him?
Who will be obedient to the requirements of the gospel?
Who will be merciful, fair and loving to do the work?
Who will do away with racism in order to save souls for God?

"Princes shall come out of Egypt; Ethiopia shall soon stretch out her hands unto God." (Psalms 68:32)

Our time has come to bless. But we can only bless without harboring prejudice and racism! Are we ready?

172

As discussed in previous chapters, all of Noah's children have had their chance. The ministry has gone from Ham to Shem and to Japheth. Where is the ministry going now? Is it going to complete the cycle? It is the belief of this author that the time of Ham has returned. God is looking for obedience.

The gospel is available but who will carry the mantle? Which nation is willing to bring forth its fruits? Which prophetic or literal nation will accept the call? Who will form the core of the nation we are reminded of – that peculiar people willing to show forth His praises, virtues or character to the world? *"But ye [are] a chosen generation, a royal priesthood, an holy nation, a peculiar people; that ye should shew forth the praises of hi m who hath called you out of darkness into his marvelous light"* (1Peter 2:9).

The ministry of the end time will be the same as the original ancient ministry modeled by Melchizedek; it will be a royal ministry. The ministry of Melchizedek was both royal and priestly. Jesus' ministry was a Royal Priesthood. Levitical ministry was supposed to be a Kingdom of Priests. Papal ministry perverted the Royal Priesthood. In the end, we will return to the original ministry after the order of Melchizedek.

It is to this ministry, a Royal Priesthood, that Jesus calls us. Princes from Egypt depict royalty and Ethiopia's outstretched hands to God is a priestly posture of confession and intercession. So in the prophecy of Egyptian princes responding to God's call and Ethiopian priests performing their priestly duties in the last days is the restoration of Ham's ministry. Ham, through his children, will stretch out his hands to God and reach out to all mankind (as Melchizedek reached out to Abraham) in order to prepare a people for the coming of Jesus.

The Gospel Moves

The gospel, like civilization, political power, wealth, status or position changes hands. No condition is ever permanent. When the gospel comes your way and you do not grasp it and keep it faithfully, it will move. It moved from Ham to Shem then to Japheth. From Melchizedek it went to Abraham and to his children.

The Hebrews received the Gospel in Palestine during the time of Jesus, through apostolic preaching, but because of unbelief, it moved. The Greeks had their time. Paul went to the Greeks to present the gospel. The book of Revelation was first sent to the people of Ephesus, Smyrna, Pergamos, Thyatira, Sardis, Philadelphia and Laodicea in Asia Minor. Where was the Jerusalem church? The gospel has always been on the move!

The humanistic philosophy that consumed and distracted the thinking of the Greeks caused the Good News of the crucified Christ to move on. Rome was given the opportunity to be ministers but because of paganism in the form of Sun worship enforced by Constantine's decree, it had to move. Europe received the gospel during the Reformation through such leaders as Martin Luther, John Wesley, Charles Wesley, John Calvin and others. However, because of Darwinian atheistic philosophy and papal supremacy that invaded Europe, it had to move.

The Pilgrim Fathers of America also had opportunities to share it in the New World but now because of materialism, racism and spiritual pride, the gospel is moving away from the very people who started the Advent Movement in America. The presentation of the gospel will continue to move until it gets to a people who will bring forth its fruits.

Africa, No Longer a Minority in the Remnant Movement

"General Conference Membership Distribution Pie as of 2008"[192]

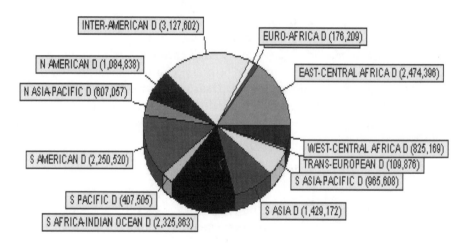

General Conference - Membership Distribution

INTER-AMERICAN D (3,127,802)
EURO-AFRICA D (176,209)
N AMERICAN D (1,084,838)
EAST-CENTRAL AFRICA D (2,474,396)
N ASIA-PACIFIC D (607,057)
WEST-CENTRAL AFRICA D (825,169)
TRANS-EUROPEAN D (109,876)
S AMERICAN D (2,250,520)
S ASIA-PACIFIC D (965,608)
S PACIFIC D (407,505)
S ASIA D (1,429,172)
S AFRICA-INDIAN OCEAN D (2,325,863)

African's Mission to the World

Have prophetic Ethiopians realized that they are no longer a minority in the Remnant Church, a movement that will give the last message of mercy to mankind? The total membership of the Remnant church in 2008 was 15,921,408 and out of that number over ten million are Black people. What does this mean to us? What are you doing about it? The Gospel message moved from Ham to Shem and then to Japheth. It has completed its cycle and

---

[192]http://www.adventiststatistics.org/view_Summary.asp?FieldID=G10001&Year=2010&submit=Change#AnnualStats

now is coming back to Ham! We are not there in the kingdoms of Daniel chapter 2, wielding power in the last days! But we are there in the New Testament taking up the cross and following Jesus. We are there in the preaching of the gospel to a dying world till Jesus comes! What we have is a fortune in the midst of misfortunes!

All Noah's children and their progeny made poor choices, and failed in their mission however, in spite of all this, God has continued to bless us all. The people of Shem were blessed with oil and money in Arabia. Aaron still enjoys the blessings of Abraham's tithe paid to Melchizedek. Japheth still enjoys the legacy of Roman political power and money that accrued from colonization. Ham may have neither power nor wealth. But Ham does have power and wealth of the Cross. Does anybody want the cross? There seem to be no volunteers. Do Black people want to take up the challenge of the cross?

Take up the Cross and Follow! On the day of Christ's crucifixion who comes running for it? Simon of Cyrene, a black man from Libya. That's another way of seeing Ethiopia stretching her hand unto God! So what is left is suffering! The suffering, inherited from the cross. Not only are we to take up our crosses, we are also chosen to take up His Cross. In this world until Jesus comes back we carry double crosses. But taking them with dignity and carrying them in faithfulness, is our opportunity. Our time has come to bless!

However, if Africans fail to carry the cross to the end, somebody else will carry it, and we loose out on the greatest of all prizes-eternal life, because where there is no cross there will be no crown! *Therefore say I unto you, The kingdom of God shall be taken from you, and given to a nation bringing forth the fruits thereof (Matthew 21:43).*

The gospel has moved around and is returning to where it began. Business cannot be carried on as usual. The gospel keeps moving! It's not enough to go to church and say Lord, Lord—the Gospel Moves! Are we just benchwarmers in this Christian Movement? Watch out, the Gospel Moves! Are we just going and coming to church without witnessing about Jesus? Inadequate! The Gospel Moves! Are we waiting for Jesus in name only or in deed also? Watch out for the Gospel Moves!

Listen to me today, your time has come to bless. These are the last days. Expect God to use you, descendants of Africa, and children of Ham. Oh, child of the king, your roots are in God and now is the time to bring forth fruits to God's glory. Can God depend on you, children of Africa? May we abide in the True Vine, so that we may bring forth much fruit! May God help us all! So I say, "back to our roots we go forward with our fruits in God," for the Gospel Moves!

"Princes shall come out of Egypt, Ethiopia shall soon stretch her hands unto God," This means confession and intercession in the context of royal ministry! Like Melchizedek, our royal ancestor, our heritage is that of a Royal Priesthood, a holy nation, a blessed community, a peculiar people, we have been called out of darkness into His marvelous light that we might represent Him to a world still in darkness.

Like Melchizedek, and like Jesus Christ, we are given this blessed ministry in these last days to help the weak, to heal the sick, to preach the gospel to the poor, to preach deliverance to the captives, to set at liberty those that are oppressed. We are charged to preach the acceptable year of the Lord, telling the whole world that Jesus is coming again! Children of Africa, are you going to be a blessing to humanity in these last days? The ministry has completed its cycle and its being returned to Ham. The largest membership of Christianity is in the third world especially Africa. It is Ham's time to bless!

So God is calling you: Princes of Egypt, priests of Ethiopia – it is time to stretch out your hands unto God. The call goes out to Nubia, Abyssinia, Algeria, Angola, Benin, Botswana, Burkina Faso, Burundi, Cameroon, Cape Verde, Central African Republic, Egypt, Chad, Congo Democratic Republic, Congo (Zaire), Djibouti, Equatorial Guinea, Eritrea, Ethiopia, Gabon, Gambia, Ghana, Guinea Bissau, Guinea, Ivory Coast, Kenya, Lesotho, Liberia, Libya, Madagascar, Malawi, Mali, Mauritania, Mauritius, Morocco, Mozambique, Namibia, Niger, Nigeria, Reunion, Rwanda, Senegal, Seychelles, Sierra Leone, Somalia, South Africa, Sudan, Swaziland, Tanzania, Togo, Tunisia, Uganda, Zambia, Zanzibar and Zimbabwe!

Princes of Egypt, priests of Ethiopia, it is time to stretch out your hands unto God. Anguilla, Antigua and Barbuda. The Antilles, Aruba, Bahamas, Barbados, British Virgin Islands, Cayman Islands, Cuba, Dominica, Dominican Republic, Grenada, Guadeloupe, Guyana, Haiti, Jamaica, Martinique, Montserrat, St. Kitts and Nevis, Puerto Rico, St. Lucia, St. Vincent, Trinidad and Tobago, US Virgin Islands! The call goes out to all of you! Africans in Antarctica, Asia, Australia, Europe, North America and South America and on the Continent of Africa, your time has come to bless!

Africa! Lift up the trumpets and loud let them ring. Jesus is coming again. Let them resound with the message that Jesus is coming. Let It Ring! Africans, like the Jews who knew the true God of creation and preserved His knowledge in their historical, cultural and religious records. Now it is our time to preach it to the whole world.

The knowledge of the God of creation is deeply embedded in Africa. It is difficult to hear Black people say that Christianity is a white man's religion. When Black people accept Islam over Christianity they ought not to do so on the premise that Islam was the authentic indigenous religion of Africa. The Indigenous religion of Africa was the Old Testament religion practiced as a culture preserved in the Oral Tradition. So in a sense Africans knew Christ in the symbol of the sacrificial lamb before Islam was introduced and certainly before the missionaries came. The old time religion was neither white nor Islamic. Islam was founded around A.D. 622 and arrived in Africa around A.D. 800. However, the knowledge of the true God had been on the continent

176

of Africa for over 4000 years, since the time of Noah precisely when Ham's children settled on the African continent.

Until the "Islamization" of North Africa, the concept of God in that part of Africa was either indigenous, consistent with the Old Testament Bible or Christian of the Coptic order. Remember, indigenous Africans fled to the interior of Africa from the north because of Islamic Jihad of the medieval years. Akan people of Ghana who are mostly Christians now would have been subjected to Islam and made Moslems by force had not our ancestors fled around the time of the fall of Timbuktu in the Middle Ages.

So, remember Africa! Our ancestors knew God, and that is not all. We also know that God knew Africa. We are children of the King. And He is calling us back to Himself. So, now Africa your time has come to bless! Be a blessing to the whole world!

No Condition is Permanent

Africa, Your Time Has Come To Bless! Do Not Waste It.

CHAPTER TWENTY-THREE

BLACK MAN'S REDEMPTION

It is the fool's sheep that break loose twice. (African proverb)

Eternal Lessons Black People Must Learn From Slavery Past

Black People must find Theological Answers to the Following Questions if we should Never Again Submit to Servitude.

Questions!
Why did Black People go into Captivity?
Why did Europeans Make Black People Slaves?

God allowed Black people to suffer enslavement for the same reason He suffered Joseph and Israel to go into captivity, not because he hated them but because He loved them and wanted them to learn some eternal principles of life! "Those I love," He says, "I rebuke and chasten" Revelation 3:19. Even Jesus had to learn obedience by the things He suffered" Hebrews 5:8, 9.

There are some lessons you learn only by experience—you have to go through something to learn something. There are some things you learn only after you have gone through some memorable experience. You are not learning anything until you begin to sing, "Nobody knows the trouble I've seen." You are learning something when you are singing, "Sometimes, I feel like a motherless child away from home." You have learnt your lessons when you are singing, "How I made it over" and "Victory is mine." So, God allowed Black people to go into slavery that they might learn to sing the Lord's song in a strange land. Like the children of Israel, Africans too went into captivity for five major reasons:

1. To learn, to know, to remember, to love and serve God alone. That after we have eaten and are fed, that we do not forget God. (Deuteronomy 5:6-21. Deuteronomy 6:4-25. Deuteronomy 6:4-12)

2. To learn to cherish, remember, and respect freedom and liberty for all. After

all, what does God require of thee oh man—but "to love mercy, to do justly and to walk humbly with your God?" God requires of Black people, by virtue of their suffering, to make it a mission to pursue justice and to protest all injustices not only done against them but also against all people.

3. To become compassionate and merciful toward the down trodden because we have also been in captivity and God has shown mercy to us. We ought to have mercy on the stranger, the orphan, the widow, the children, the sick, and the oppressed; and to be the voice of the voiceless, feet of the cripple, hands of the handless, friends of the captive, and the advocate of the accused. We ought to be our brothers' keepers.

4. To appreciate the Rest that only God can give. One major reason for the deliverance of Israel was that they would have the freedom to worship their creator. Pharaoh was to "let my people go so they may sacrifice unto God" (Exodus 3:18/Deuteronomy 5:6, 12). They were delivered to worship the creator by observing the Sabbath. The Sabbath rest therefore, becomes a symbol of God's freedom over and against Pharaoh's bondage symbolized in Papal religion signified by Sunday sacredness!

5. To never again surrender to slavery. Never again should we go back to any form of slavery, whether it is physical, spiritual, social, psychological, economic, or chemical- (of drugs, alcohol) or sexual. Our ancestors experienced slavery so their children should never again go into servitude. We should learn to develop the sense of abhorrence to sin and shun slavery in all its forms.

So the Lord suffered Black people to go into slavery not because we were under Noah's curse but so that we may learn to love God, to cherish liberty, to become compassionate and to appreciate God's rest in Christ.

We suffered, so that, like Jesus, we would be touched with the feelings of the infirmities of the poor, the oppressed and the dispossessed. Our brother, Simon of Cyrene, the black man from Libya, was forced to carry the cross – he did not volunteer – so it is with us, we did not choose to suffer – but now that providence has chosen suffering for us; we must suffer with dignity and with God's help turn our disadvantages into opportunities for service for the Divine.

We have suffered injustice so we may be provoked to stand for justice and protect the civil liberty of all humanity: to stand for holiness and righteousness; to stand up for the oppressed and the marginalized; to fight none-violently against discrimination, segregation, oppression, racism, apartheid, colonialism and bigotry.

179

"Unblack Behavior"

By virtue of our suffering as Black people in the world, and because we understand what it means to suffer, and are able to sympathize with those who suffer, we can be used by God to intercede on behalf of all the suffering masses of the world. Providence through redemptive suffering has called us to "stand in the gap" for the vulnerable across the globe. It is therefore; "unblack" to be unmoved about the plight of the suffering neighbor. "Unblack" to sit idly-by unmoved to watch Islamic extremists chase indigenous Africans across the continent. Unblack to team up with any oppressor to oppress the vulnerable among us.

Immigration Debate - Theological Matter!

God Cares about the Stranger

God cares about the stranger or the foreigner and He included him or her in the Covenant blessings of Israel. He commanded Israel saying: "Six days shalt thou labor, and do all thy work but the Seventh day is the Sabbath of the LORD thy God: in it thou shalt not do any work, thou, nor thy son, nor thy daughter, thy manservant, nor thy maidservant, nor thy cattle, nor thy stranger that is within thy gates" (Exodus 20:9, 10). If the stranger "within thy gates" must share in the obedience to the Covenant of the God of Israel, then the stranger within thy gates must also share in the blessings of the covenant of the God of Israel. God expects that one law be applied to all! In Exodus 12:49 we read, "One law shall be to him that is homeborn, and unto the stranger that sojourneth among you". Therefore the stranger within our gates (borders) must share in the blessings God brings through our gates.

God cares about the stranger and He admonishes His children: "Be not forgetful to entertain strangers: for thereby some have entertained angels unawares" (Hebrews 13:2).

God cares about the stranger. Jesus said; "I was a stranger, and ye took me not in: naked, and ye clothed me not: sick, and in prison, and ye visited me not (Matthew 25:43). Understand, that "what you did for the least of this my brethren you did for me, Jesus says! (Matthew 25:40).

God cares about the stranger, and if we are children of God, we can't help but to care for the stranger in our midst or within our gates. Immigration debate is a theological matter. God's word is clear: "Love ye therefore the stranger: for ye were strangers in the land of Egypt" (Deuteronomy 10:19). This admonition agrees with the Golden Rule for all: "Do unto others what you want others to do unto you" (Luke 6:31). Therefore, let us be merciful to the stranger or the immigrant for it is the will of God. Truth be told, we are all

180

strangers here. Heaven is our home. So, while here, let's show mercy to one another, especially, the strangers among us.

To Be Black In The Americas!

To be Black in America by virtue of our suffering is to understand the suffering of the poor, the dispossessed, the oppressed, marginalized, stigmatized, the voiceless, the disabled, the captives and the outcasts. To be black is to be concerned enough to care about all life.

To be a black person in America is not about color or a curse but a calling born out of our suffering – it's a calling; a calling to dream of equality and bring it to reality, a calling to stand for justice though the heavens fall, a calling to fight for the poor masses of the world.

It's a calling to dream not just the American dream but also the African American Dream of seeing to it that men and women are not judged by the color of their skin, but by the content of their characters.

It's a calling, which runs deep down in Martin Luther King's soul when he burst out with those prophetic words "I have a dream."

It's a calling, which troubled Colin Powell's spirit to cause him to resign from the Bush Administration than to defile his soul in perpetuating a lie to defeat an enemy.

It's a calling, which Jessie Jackson has sought to follow on behalf of the poor all his life albeit imperfectly.

It's a calling which Al Sharpton tries to answer albeit controversially. Being black in America is a calling born out of suffering to stand for truth, and righteousness, freedom and justice, mercy and forgiveness and above all faith and love to the glory of the God of our weary years and our silent tears.

Therefore, like Joseph, we too have learned to say concerning the black experience that, "the devil meant it for evil but God meant it for our good – I was brought here before you to preserve your lives." God's fires of affliction have purified my soul of bitterness. "I am not under a curse but under a blessing."

Have we learned from suffering yet? Well, then answer the call to your name and serve the Lord alone, be compassionate to others, celebrate your liberty symbolized by the Sabbath and never again surrender to any form of slavery. Until a man has found a cause for which to die, he is not fit to live. And that's the essence of our calling!

CHAPTER TWENTY-FOUR

AFRICA'S TIME TO BLESS!

A child whose hand is clean may eat with the elders. (African proverb)

Of all that we have discussed so far, here is the summary: Africa's Time has come to bless! The Ministry baton is passed on to Africa to finish the race. But before we nail that point, let's go back to the records in Genesis Chapter 10 for a quick review of some salient points. Our human origin after the flood goes back to Shem, Ham and Japheth.

Semitic people trace their roots to father Shem, that's why anti Jews are called anti-Semitic; it really means you are against the children of Shem. Europeans trace their roots to father Japheth who migrated northward with his family after the flood to the Caucuses Mountain in Southern Russia where they multiplied and acquired their name Caucasians.

Black People trace their roots to father Ham whose sons, Cush, Mizraim and Phut settled in Egypt and Ethiopia and Libya all the way to Timbuktu in Africa. The last son Canaan, settled in Palestine by which acquired the name, 'the land of Canaan'

Every one of the sons of Noah was given opportunity to bless the world in ministry and in civilization. However, Ham first ruled the world, in the Sumerian Empire, in the Acadian Empire, in the Cushite Empire, in the Egyptian Empire and in the Babylonian Empire. Ham through Nebuchadnezzar was the head of gold (Daniel Chapter 2) of the prophetic kingdoms of the world, after which came Medo-Persia (of Shem and Japheth), and then Greece (of Japheth) and then Rome (of Japheth) to the divided kingdoms of the last days of our time, to the coming of the Lord.

Spiritually too - Ham first blessed the world in the Ministry of Melchizedek. Melchizedek, a descendant of Ham, was the first recorded High Priest of the Most High God. And who was this Melchizedek? The Bible calls him King of Salem, now Jerusalem which then was the capital city of the Jebusites, descendants of Canaan, son of Ham (Judges 19:10, 1Ch 11:4, and Genesis 14:18)

And who was this Melchizedek? Melki-zedek means king of righteousness and Salem (shalom) means peace (Heb 7:1). So you put his name and title together you get his character; the righteous King of peace.

Melchizedek was a Jebusite king of Salem, descendant of Ham, a true worshiper of Elohim, a faithful servant of Yahweh, and a diligent Minister of the Most High God. It was through Melchizedek, that God blessed Abraham. God used Ham first to bless the world.

However, there were two conditions for dwelling in the land of Canaan, as they are in being a Christian, namely: faithfulness to God and mission to the world. You lived in Jerusalem to obey God and to do His ministry. And as long as Canaanite dwellers of Canaan were faithful to God, they prospered until even their land became the land flowing with milk and honey.

The Principle of the condition was simple "If ye be willing and obedient, ye shall eat the good of the land: But if ye refuse and rebel, ye shall be devoured with the sword: for the mouth of the Lord hath spoken [it]" (Isaiah 1:19 - 20). For "righteousness exalts a nation but sin is a reproach to any people." However, a new generation of the Canaanites emerged that rebelled against God and closed their docket of probation and left God with no choice than to remove them from the land. "Therefore say I unto you, the kingdom of God shall be taken from you, and given to a nation bringing forth the fruits thereof" (Matthew 21:43). Ham blessed the world but Shem's time had come! So Ham was broken off and Shem was grafted in. It was Shem's Time to bless the world! Shem's time had come to bless!

By blessing Abraham, Melchizedek had symbolically transferred the ministry to Abraham. But his children would not possess the land until the iniquity of the Amorites was full and the probation of the Canaanites was closed. After 400 years of Egyptian captivity, the time came when Moses and later Joshua led Israel to overthrow the Canaanites and to posses the land flowing with milk and honey.

So it was Shem's time to bless. Through Abraham and his descendants, God blessed the world. Prophets of Israel prophesized of the coming Messiah, a child was to be born, a son was to be given. "But thou, Bethlehem Ephratah, [though] thou be little among the thousands of Judah, [yet] out of thee shall he come forth unto me [that is] to be ruler in Israel; whose goings forth [have been] from of old, from everlasting" (Micah 5:2), whose government shall be upon his shoulder: and his name shall be called Wonderful, Counsellor, The mighty God, The everlasting Father, The Prince of Peace (Isaiah. 9:6). He would be born of the Seed of Abraham, to be the lion of the tribe of Judah, root of David, of the lineage of Shem. Through Judah salvation would come to the world. Thus "salvation" Jesus said "is of the Jews" (John 4:22). Shem blessed the world with the Savior (Luke 2:11)!

But the same conditions applied to all. "If ye be willing and obedient, ye shall eat the good of the land: But if ye refuse and rebel, ye shall be devoured with the sword: for the mouth of the Lord hath spoken [it] (Isaiah 1:19, 20).

So, Seventy weeks, (Daniel 9:24), were determined upon thy people (Israel), and upon thy holy city, to finish the transgression, and to make an end of sins, and to make reconciliation for iniquity, and to bring in everlasting righteousness, and to seal up the vision and prophecy, and to anoint the most Holy.

Seventy weeks, which means 490 years of probationary time was decreed, or given to Israel to repent, forsake their sins, accept the Messiah and prosper, or rebel and the gentiles would come and overthrow them from the land, occupy the City and destroy the Temple.

Sure enough, Jesus came to his own, but his own received him not. So, looking through the corridors of time and seeing the fulfillment of prophecy, Jesus cried out (Matthew 23:37-38) "O Jerusalem, Jerusalem, [thou] that killest the prophets, and stonest them which are sent unto thee, how often would I have gathered thy children together, even as a hen gathereth her chickens under [her] wings, and ye would not! Behold, your house is left unto you desolate." Then comes the Divine decree, "Therefore say I unto you, the kingdom of God shall be taken from you, and given to a nation bringing forth the fruits thereof. (Matthew 21:43). Now behold Shem's time ended – now was the time of the gentiles (Revelation 11:12).

Japheth's time had come to bless the world: In his frustration with the children of Israel and the hardness of their heart, the apostle Paul and Barnabas lamented, (Acts 13:46) "It was necessary that the word of God should first have been spoken to you: but seeing ye put it from you, (rejected it) and judge yourselves unworthy of everlasting life, lo, we turn to the Gentiles."

Prior, to this, Jesus had commanded the disciples not to go to the Gentiles, but rather to the lost sheep of the house of Israel to preach the gospel, (because it was not the gentile's time yet.) (Matthew 10:5)

But now because of unbelief and spiritual pride, Israel, like an olive branch, was broken off, and the gentiles were grafted in. God gives Peter a vision to bless Cornelius, a Roman and a descendant of Japheth. So from Shem the ministry moved to Japheth for the same condition applies: "If ye be willing and obedient, ye shall eat the good of the land: But if ye refuse and rebel, ye shall be devoured with the sword: for the mouth of the Lord hath spoken [it]" (Isaiah 1:19, 20). Yes, Japheth blessed the world in his missions to the world and in his ministry of reformation of the Christian church.

However, it was Japheth descendants who ushered the world into the apostasy of 1260 years of spiritual darkness, and the persecution of millions of Christians, and into the mystery of iniquity; of the man sin sitting in the Temple of God showing himself that he is God; of a man claiming to be God in God's Temple, and of the sin of slavery which the prophet calls the sin of the deepest dye, and of commercializing the gospel (Revelation. 18:13) and blurring the lines between Church and state, and of persecuting the saints of the Most High God. Remember, all this was done in the name of the Lord!

184

Luke 21:24 warns us that many shall fall by the edge of the sword, and shall be led away captive into all nations: and Jerusalem shall be trodden down of the Gentiles, until the times of the Gentiles be fulfilled. How long was to be the gentile's times?

Here is their prophecy: "But the court which is without the temple leave out, and measure it not; for it is given unto the Gentiles: and the holy city shall they tread under foot forty [and] two months" (Revelation 11:2). Papacy trampled upon God's law and persecuted the saints of God for 1260 years- (A.D. 538-1798) during the Dark Ages.

The Gentile's time has been served. Their probationary time has expired, and Japheth is being disqualified for Moral Corruption, Spiritual Pride and Racial Prejudice. How can anyone be qualified to preach to every nation, kindred, tongue and people if he or she can't discriminate against God's Children?

Revelation 14:8 handed down the sentence this way: "And there followed another angel, saying, Babylon is fallen, is fallen, that great city, because she made all nations drink of the wine of the wrath of her fornication." And in Revelation 18:3-5 For all nations have drunk of the wine of the wrath of her fornication, and the kings of the earth have committed fornication with her, and the merchants of the earth are waxed rich through the abundance of her delicacies. "And I heard another voice from heaven, saying, Come out of her, my people, that ye be not partakers of her sins, and that ye receive not of her plagues for her sins have reached unto heaven, and God hath remembered her iniquities."

The Gentile spiritual leadership has unraveled. Japheth has been disqualified! The Divine Decree comes down again in unmistakable tones. "Therefore I say unto you, The kingdom of God shall be taken from you, and given to a nation bringing forth the fruits thereof" (Matthew 21:43).

The ministry has made its rounds. The cycle is complete. It has gone from Ham to Shem and from Shem to Japheth, and it is coming back to Ham again for what may be the last lap of this relay race. Time is running out for planet earth, Jesus is coming soon; the whole earth must be full of the glory of His ministry, His message, His gospel as the waters cover the sea. Africa! Prepare yourself for end time ministry for Jesus! For your time has come to bless! Africa's time has come to bless the world. African children, rise and shine for your light is come and the glory of the Lord is risen upon you.

Why do you think the spirit of prophecy was first given to a Black man in America, even when Black people did not have civil rights? Because your light is come and the glory of the Lord is risen upon you. It is time for princes to come out of Egypt and Ethiopia to stretch out her hands unto God to perform royal ministry.

Why do you think Black people are a majority in the church and in the remnant movement in the last days, a movement that will soon finish the work

185

and usher in the second coming of Jesus? Because your light is come and the glory of the Lord is risen upon you.

Why do you think a number of European mainline congregations are coming under African leadership? Because your light is come and the glory of the Lord is risen upon you.

Why do you think African-Americans are said to surpass other ethnic groups in religiosity in America according to the Pew Research Center reported by the Review and Herald Publishing Association, 2009?[193] Because your light is come and the glory of the Lord is risen upon you.

And why do you think a black man is the President of this United States of America at such a time as this? Because your light is come and glory of the Lord is risen upon you.

Gentile time is up, Ham's time is now! Now is Africa's time to bless the world. The Gospel has gone around full circle and has come back to Ham. "But ye [are] a chosen generation, a royal priesthood, an holy nation, a peculiar people; that ye should shew forth the praises of him who hath called you out of darkness into his marvellous light" (1Peter 2:9).

As I ponder over these facts I realize that the Jews have money – a blessing accruing from father Abraham's tithe to Melchizedek. Europeans will maintain political power according to Daniel to the very end until the stone hits the image and God's everlasting kingdom is established.

And I wonder what Africans have! Africans! You don't have money! You don't have power! So what then do you Black people have to offer the world? Well consider this, when the Jews had condemned Jesus and the Romans made Him a heavy cross, who came to his rescue? Simon of Cyrene, a black man from Libya, an African, he carried his cross. What do we have? Answer! The Cross!

So, Africa, never mind that the Jews have money and Europeans have power, we've received the cross and in the cross of Jesus is our wealth and power and victory and our glory, for the cross is the symbol of the gospel of Jesus; the power of God unto salvation!

So, Africa, stay with the cross, cherish the cross, go on and carry his cross faithfully, (take up your cross and follow me, says the Lord), and then with the cross rise up and shine for your light is come and glory of the Lord is risen upon you.

> So, I'll cherish the old rugged cross
> Till my trophies at last I lay down
> I will cling to the old rugged cross
> And exchange it some day for a crown

---

[193] Banks, M. Adelle, Religion News Service, 2009 (Review and Herald) 2009.

To the old rugged cross I will ever be true
It's shame and reproach gladly bear
Then he'll call me someday to my home far away
Where his glory forever I'll share

So I'll cherish the old rugged cross
Till my trophies at last I lay down
I will cling to the old rugged cross
And exchange it some day for a crown

How long? Not long! For the trumpet shall sound and the dead in Christ shall rise, and we shall be changed, this mortal shall put on immortality, this corruptible shall put on incorruption. When we shall see Him we shall be like Him and we shall be caught up to meet the Lord in the air – so shall we ever be with the Lord. How long? Not long!

For "At that time gifts will be brought to the Lord of hosts from a people tall and smooth, from a people feared near and far, a nation mighty and conquering, whose land the rivers divide, to Mount Zion, the place of the name of the Lord of hosts." (Isaiah 18:7). You ask how long? I say, not long!

Because, "In that day shall Israel be the third with Egypt and with Assyria, [even] a blessing in the midst of the land: whom the Lord of hosts has blessed, saying, "Blessed be Egypt my people, and Assyria the work of my hands, and Israel my heritage." (Isaiah 19:24) Praise the Lord, Halleluiah Amen! Redeemed how I love to proclaim it!

So Africa, by all means "Arise, shine; for your light has come, and the glory of the Lord has risen upon you. For behold, darkness shall cover the earth, and thick darkness the peoples; but the Lord will arise upon you and his glory will be seen upon you. And nations shall come to your light, and kings to the brightness of your rising. Lift up your eyes round about, and see as they all gather together to come to you (Isaiah 60:1-4).

The Latter rain will come with the restoration of the royal priesthood, the gift of prophecy, the power of healing and our ministry of the last days will be more glorious! Rise up and shine! AFRICA, YOUR TIME HAS COME TO BLESS THE WORLD AND TO FINISH THE WORK!

The Jews did not finish it, Europeans could not finish it! Now it's your turn, Africa to hear the call of God and answer to your name and run the race to the finish line for the eyes of the universe are upon you!

Your Ministry is the last lap in the relay race after which the Exodus will be Completed and God's people shall be ushered into the kingdom of glory and all God's children shall be "Home at Last" in the Promised Land. So run in such a way that you may get to the finish line and finish Hard!

CHAPTER TWENTY-FIVE

AFRICA ON MOUNT ZION WITH GIFTS

God Has Always Involved Africans In His Divine Plans!

Let's Look at the Role Each Son of Noah Played at Jesus' Birth

All Noah's sons – Shem, Ham, and Japheth were there at His birth.
Some came with their gold, incense and myrrh. Others with the sword!

Wise Men from the East and the Three Sons of Noah

Here is the Involvement of the three Sons of Noah in the life of Christ at his birth! Matthew says, *"Now when Jesus was born in Bethlehem of Judea in the days of Herod the king, behold, there came wise m en from the east to Jerusalem. . . . And when t hey were co me into the h ouse, they sa w the young child with Mary his moth er, and fell down, and wo rshipped him: and when they had opened their t reasures, they presented unto him gifts; gold, and frankincense, and myrrh"* (Matthew 2:11).

Japheth through the Roman power tried to kill Him, Shem through the Temple priests failed to recognize Him. But Ham through the Spirit gave gifts, worshipped, and protected Him. Yes indeed, all of Noah's sons were present at His birth.

The Psalmist's Account

The prophecy of Ps alms 72 t alks about Jesus' messiahship, the extent of Hi s dominion, and those that will co me to worship. Most of these a re fo und in Genesis under the list of nations representing the three sons of Noah.

"He shall have dominion also from sea to sea, and from the river unto the ends of the earth. They that dwell in the wilderness shall bow before him; and his enemies shall lick the dust" (Psalms 72:8). This part of the prophecy points to those who dwell in Arabia, the people of the desert.

In verse 10 of Psalms 72, it goes on to talk about those who would come to visit. "The kings of Tarshish and of the isles shall bring presents." Here we are dealing with Japheth. "Tarshish" and "Isles"; the descendants of Japheth, would come bringing their presents.

Ham also is present in two of his descendants. Again verse 10 says, "the kings of Sheba and Seba shall offer gifts." Verse 11 presents the universal worship that will

188

be accorded the King "Yea, all kings shall fall down before him: all nations shall serve him." So here in Psalms 72 the three sons of Noah are represented at the birth of Jesus.

Isaiah's Account

Isaiah 60 is specific and gives us details of the <u>nature of presents each one (Sons of Noah) would bring.</u>

Again the first part deals with the <u>Arabs from the lineage of Abraham and Keturah</u>, *"The multitude of camel s shall cover thee, the dromedaries of Midian and Ephah"* (Vs. 6). So the Arabs out of the loins of Abraham and Keturah of both Shem and Ham are present.

Isaiah identifies <u>Sheba from the lineage of Ham</u>, "all they from Sheba shall come: they shall **bring gold and incense**; and they shall show forth the praises of the Lord." Ham comes not with empty hands but with ***gold and frankincense***. Ham recognizes Him as both King and Priest and His gifts attest to His royal ministry.

Isaiah says Ishmael would be there. "All the flocks of <u>Kedar</u> shall be gathered together unto thee, the rams of Nebaioth shall minister unto thee: they shall come up with acceptance on mine altar, and I will glorify the house of my glory" (Isaiah 60:7). Kedar, meaning "dark", was a son of Ishmael.

Isaiah says <u>Japheth also would come in Tarshish:</u> "Who [are] these [that] fly as a cloud and as the doves to their windows? Surely the <u>isles shall wait for me, and the ships of Tarshish</u> first, to bring thy sons from far, <u>their silver and their gold with them</u>, unto the name of the Lord thy God, and to the Holy One of Israel, because he hath glorified thee" (verses. 8, 9).

We cannot be sure whether Japheth parted with his silver, since the New Testament does not mention silver in the gifts. The Gospel writers did not account for Japheth's silver! So where is the silver? What happened to the silver is open to speculation. One thing is sure; Jesus might not have been so poor if Japheth had given his silver and maybe his gold as well. It is also not certain who gave the myrrh, which signified His death. Since gold and incense were presented to the Savior, we can be certain that Ham parted with his gold and incense.

The Role of Each Son at Jesus' Death

Shem Betrayed Him
Japheth Crucified Him
Ham Carried His Cross

Ham was there at His birth! Jesus was taken to Africa for protection from the Roman "FBI" which was on His trail. By killing all children under the age of two, the Roman rulers demonstrated that they were dead serious! And

God must be also serious about hiding and protecting His 'Only One-of-His-Kind' Son from destruction. And there was no better place to protect a dark-skinned baby than Egypt. Herodotus had already established that Egyptians as well as the Ethiopians were black with thick lips, broad nose, and wooly hair and burnt of skin.

Nevertheless! We were there at His birth! We were there in His ministry! We were there at His death!

He called our ancestors, some of the Wise Men from the east to bring gifts at the birth of Jesus. The ASV renders Isaiah 60:6 this way: "The multitude of camels shall cover thee, the dromedaries of *Midian and Eph ah*; all they *from Sheba* shall come; they shall bring *gold and frankincense, and shall proclaim the praises of the Lord."*

Is it not exciting to know that African gold built the Temple of Solomon, decorated the Wilderness Sanctuary and most importantly sponsored Jesus flight to Africa? (1 Kings 10:1, 10-11; 1 Chronicles 29:4, 2 Chronicles 8:18 & 9:1, 9). Black people have been involved in the work of God for many generations.

Matthew also says one of the twelve Apostles was a Canaanite. He was called Simon the Canaanite, (Matthew 10:4) which would make him a descendant of Ham." God called our ancestor from Libya to carry Jesus' cross to Calvary at His death. We were there at His birth, in His ministry, and at His death.

At The Welcome Table!

Now the question is: Will we be there at the welcome table, in the sweet by and by, in the Kingdom of Glory? Do we have an official invitation to appear before His Majesty in Heaven, and how? We certainly do. Consider the following: "At that time gifts will be brought to the Lord of hosts from a people tall and smooth, from a people feared near and far, a nation mighty and conquering, whose land the rivers divide, to Mount Zion, the place of the name of the Lord of hosts" (Isaiah 18:7 RSV).

The Nile is the river referred to here. The land is the land of Cush. Remember, Ethiopia in verse one, means black. So the prophecy is calling African people to bring gifts to Jesus when He sits on Mount Zion to rule. What kinds of gifts are these? This time the gifts are not gifts of gold and frankincense but the gifts of souls in Righteousness. And Mount Zion is not earthly, but heavenly; Mount Zion is in the kingdom of Glory. The writer of the Hebrews says, "But ye are come unto Mount Zion, and unto the city of the living God, the heavenly Jerusalem, and to an innumerable company of angels" (Hebrews 12:22).

In the last days Africans are called to present the gifts of souls to the kingdom of God. The wise, again are to present their gifts. "The wise will

190

turn many to righteousness and shall shine as the stars of the firmament" (Daniel. 12:3). In heaven there will be a roll call! Each child of Ham will be asked to present his or her stewardship of souls to God.

Just as, on certain occasions in the United Nations or especially at the General Conference convocations when people from all nations in their colorful garments march in the auditorium with their flags to the stage to present their personal ministry reports, so all will be asked to give their reports to His Majesty, the King of kings and the Lord of lords. Every nation, kindred, tongue and people will be present and Africans from all over will be there with their gifts to the Lord as well. The role call may go something like this: **Priests of Ethiopia/Patriarch of Abyssinia turn in your gifts? Princes of Egypt turn in your gifts! Nubian, Som   alia, Libya, Gam bia, Nigeria, Ghana, Congo, Sudan,   Afro-Caribbean, Canadian, North   American Africans, E uropean Af ricans, Aust ralian Afric ans, Africa- Americans, Alabama, Mississippi and Georgia turn in your gifts! Afri ca! Where are your gifts for the Lord on Mount Zion?**

Then Jesus Himself will place on each one of the heads of the faithful, a crown of gold with stars representing the souls they brought to Mount Zion, to the Kingdom of God. 'And behold, there shall be no starless crown.' Oh what shall I render unto the Lord for all His benefits of redemption? (Psalms 116:12). Now is the time for the smooth-skinned people across the river to make their offering ready! Everybody is expected to play a part. So, "Lift up the trumpet and loud let it ring; for it won't be long before Jesus comes again."

Ham, through his descendant, Melchizedek was doing his priestly duties when blessings were pronounced on Abraham. Ham's descendants were also present at Jesus' birth when, through Sheba, gifts were brought to Jesus. Likewise, we expect that in the closing of the gospel ministry, Ham's line will again stand up and be counted. "In that day shall Israel be the third with Egypt and with Assyria, [even] a blessing in the midst of the land: Whom the Lord of hosts shall bless, saying, Blessed [be] Egypt my people, and Assyria the work of my hands, and Israel mine inheritance" (Isaiah 19:24).

In the mean-time, the truth, the whole truth and nothing but the truth ought to be told regarding how God has always involved Africans in His plans and how He desires to use us in the last days. Oh that our children will answer when He calls! So, remember, Africa, our people knew God, and that's not all. God knew Africa. We are blessed children of the King. We are rooted in God! We are counted first among the blessed.

In conclusion, as I look at the records, I must ask, is it any wonder that the Akan people of Africa kept many Biblical truths in their culture. Any wonder Africans kept the original name of God: Yah, Yahweh, Yahmeh (Akan) and practiced the sacrificial system with its blood atonement. Is it any wonder that they have known Yahmeh as the Creator, whose Memorial Day of creation is Saturday? Any wonder that they called Him Onyame Kwame, which literary means "the God of Saturday."

Finally, is it any wonder therefore that somehow, Saturday in the Akan language means I AM THAT I AM'S DAY? No Sir! Why not? God and Africa have always been intimate – worked together in the past! Yahmeh in the Akan linguistics also means "satisfied when found." He is God, the end of our discovery. He is the One by whom we are satisfied when we finally connect with Him. The Hebrew rendering is similar. "I AM THAT I AM," the root of Yahweh, denotes fullness. To have Him is to have all things because He can be whatever He wants to be. He is all and in all. To find Him is to find satisfaction and fullness.

We become forgetful of whom we are when we allow ourselves to forget the rich heritage that forms our collective identity. The core of history, though contrary to popular stereotype, is that we as a people are firmly rooted in the God of creation. My belief is that our collective identity needs to be repaired and our rightful image restored before our collective mission can be accomplished. So repeat to yourself:

"I Am A Child Of The King, A Prince Or Princess Of Africa And I Am
Bound For Success!
I Accept my Heritage In Which I am a Prince or a Princess Of Africa. I am a
Child Of The King Of The Universe! Africa Is In God And God Is In Africa!
Amen!

**I recommend the Following Song to those
Engaged in "Diaspora Evangelism."
Find it a Blessing as you seek to bless others.**

O'er The Waves

Verse 1
O'er the waves a call is wafted
In the stillness of the night;
'Tis the cry of unsaved millions
Who are longing for the light,
From the island shores of Haiti,
To Aruba and Bonaire;
From Jamaica to Honduras
Let us answer them out there

Verse 3
Costa Rica and Chiapas,
Venezuela, Bogota,
Nicaragua, Guatemala,

192

Yucatan, and Panama;
Trinidad, Belize, and Saint Kitts
Oh, the workers are so few;
Let us rise and answer quickly,
"We are sending help to you!"

Verse 4
Suriname and then Guyana
Need the Gospel, like the rest.
Martinique and Guadeloupe
Call on you to give your best.
Long the island fields have waited;
So has fruitful Mexico.
There's a call for every member
To awake, to give, to go.

Verse 5
Dominica and Saint Lucia
Antigua and Barbados
Africa, Philippines, India
Montserrat and Carriacou
Oh the Continents and Islands
Get to them where'er they be
They are yearning for the Savior
Who had died for them and me.

Verse 6
Puerto Rico and Saint Vincent
St Martin, Bermuda, St Croix
Cuba, St Thomas, Bahamas
All shall rise and shout for joy.
Let us lift their every burden
Open blinded eyes to see
Tell them of the blessed Savior
Light their world and set them free. [194]

---

[194] Diaspora Song Composed by a Member of the First SDA Church of Teaneck, Teaneck NJ, 2009. For a tune use "Hark! The Voice Jesus is calling"- Adventist Hymnal 359

CHAPTER TWENTY-SIX

THE EXODUS IS COMPLETED

Home At Last

Even the mightiest eagle comes down to the tree tops to rest. (African proverbs)

Glory to the God of Our Weary Years and of Our Silent Tears!

In spite of the stony road we have trod and the bitter chastening rod we felt in the days when hope was unborn, though not always true to our God and our Native Land, we never forgot our Motherland. And we never forgot the God of our weary years and of our silent tears! From the place where our fathers sighed, over the way bedewed with tears, treading through the blood of the slaughtered, we have come, finally out from the gloomy past, now standing in the light, in the Promised Land, on Mount Zion with our gifts of souls and praise to the King of Kings. So:

> **Lift ev'ry voice and sing, Till earth and heaven ring.**
> **Ring with the harmonies of Liberty;**
> **Let our rejoicing rise, High as the list'ning skies,**
> **Let it resound loud as the rolling sea.**
>
> **We have come, over a way that with tears has been watered,**
> **We have come, treading our path through the blood of the slaughtered,**
> **Out from the gloomy past, Till now we stand at last,**
> **Where the white gleam of our bright star is cast.**
>
> **God of our weary years, God of our silent tears,**
> **Thou who has brought us thus far on the way;**
> **Thou who has by thy might, Led us into the light,**
> **Keep us forever in the path, we pray.**
>
> **Lest our feet stray from the places, our God, where we met Thee,**
> **Lest our hearts, drunk with wine of the world, we forget Thee,**
> **Shadowed beneath thy hand, May we forever stand,**
> <u>**True to our God True to our native land.**</u>"[195]

---

[195] James Weldon Johnson

EPILOGUE

RISE, AFRICA RISE!

Smooth seas do not make skillful sailors. (African proverb)

From The Motherland To The Fatherland

Ours has been an impossible journey but by grace we can make it to our
Fatherland!
A journey
    From earth to heaven:
From the dusty to the glory
    From the earthly to the heavenly
        From the children of Adam to the children of God.
From the flood to the Continent through the Americas to the New Jerusalem!
    From the old world through the new world to the real world
        From slavery through emancipation to freedom and real
    liberty
    From being a slave to being the President.
        From the slave ship to ownership
        From the fall and the struggles through redemption to restoration
        There have been struggles along the way.
We have gone:
    Through the blood
Through the storm
    Through the flood
We have seen (which we could not bear the sight of):
    Bones in the sea
Bodies in the deep (we are yet to mourn!)
    Blood trail along the way!
    Casualties:
        Destruction of economy
        Stealing of culture
        Destruction of identity
        Degradation of manhood
        Discrediting of our achievements
The Abuse: The lies - The insults & the rape - But we are survivors!
    We have not yet arrived, oh no!
    We still have a mighty long way to go, but we shall overcome someday.

Weeping may endure for the night but joy cometh in the morning. But amidst the weeping we can also admit that surely goodness and mercy have followed us all the days of our lives and soon we shall dwell in the house of the Lord forever! We may be hurt now, but we are not slain, we may be down but not out. By the word of God Africa shall rise again. God says we will:

In that day five cities in Egypt will speak the language of Canaan and swear allegiance to the LORD Almighty. One of them will be called the City of Destruction (or city of the Sun). In that day there will be an altar to the LORD in the heart of Egypt, and a monument to the LORD at its border. It will be a sign and witness to the LORD Almighty in the land of Egypt. When they cry out to the LORD because of their oppressors, he will send them a savior and defender, and he will rescue them. So the LORD will make himself known to the Egyptians, and in that day they will acknowledge the LORD. They will worship with sacrifices and grain offerings; they will make vows to the LORD and keep them. The LORD will strike Egypt with a plague; he will strike them and heal them. They will turn to the LORD, and he will respond to their pleas and heal them. In that day there will be a highway from Egypt to Assyria. The Assyrians will go to Egypt and the Egyptians to Assyria. The Egyptians and Assyrians will worship together. In that day Israel will be the *third,* along with Egypt and Assyria, a blessing on the earth. The LORD Almighty will bless them, saying, *Blessed be Egypt my people, Assyria my handiwork, and Israel my inheritance'* (Isaiah 9:18-25).[196]

In Christ, we shall rise again!

So, Rise, Africa Rise!

**Africa cast to the ground will rise (again);
Will rise, with our loved ones, we'll rise.
Will rise, with our young ones, we'll rise,
Will rise with our old ones, we'll rise,
Will rise, with our ancestors, we'll rise,
Will rise, with our Savior, we'll rise!
Arise! Mother Africa! Arise!
With Your Children Arise![197]**

---

[196] *Compton's Interactive Bible NIV.,* (SoftKey Multimedia Inc.11996).
[197] Author

POSTSCRIPT

TRIBUTE TO AFRICA

"But the stolen gold and other treasures were of no importance when compared with the mass of priceless historical materials that are scattered over Europe and Asia, some in museums, some destroyed or thrown away, all from the heartland of black civilization. Today the descendants of the robbers still smugly declare, 'The Blacks never had any worthwhile history; if so, where are their records?'"[198]

If without roots there can be no fruits, then it is an insult to the memory of (African ancestry) to despise (their successors) upon whose shoulders our modern advancement is based.

I REGISTER MY RESPECT!

I register my respect for modern technology with all its conveniences that seek to make life a little better for us today. I acknowledge the wisdom behind modern technology that seeks to help ease humanity's burden.

Moreover, I register my respect for the Egyptians whose skills predated our modern technology. I register my respect for the Medieval Arabs who kept the records of history upon which modern technology was based. My respect goes to the Arabians who stored the knowledge of the past and handed down by the Egyptians through the Greeks. I register my respect for the people behind the wisdom of our modern technology.

I register my respect for the Greeks for their stewardship of knowledge, their faithfulness in record keeping, and for preserving the knowledge they received from the Egyptians upon which our modern technology is based. Furthermore, I register my respect for the Egyptians whose discoveries were the basis of that history. I register my respect to the Egyptians for laying the foundation upon which our technology was built, for their pioneering work in science, math, and writing, for discoveries in biology, astronomy and physics, and for trailblazing in agriculture leading to irrigation, architecture, and pyramid construction which has never been surpassed by moderns with their sophisticated technology.

---

[198] Chancellor Williams, *Destruction of Black Civilization* (Chicago: Third World Press, 1956), 91.

So who were the Egyptians really? Hollywood says they were Europeans, White people caught in the African desert. The account of the Ancients say: "broad nose, thick lips, woolly hair and black." Penned for posterity in his book *Histories*, the Father of History, Herodotus, an eyewitness who visited Egypt about 457 B.C. immortalizes the description of the Ancients when he says, "The...Ethiopians and Egyptians have thick lips, broad nose, woolly hair and they are burnt of skin." If such were not Black people, then I guess we are all white people in North America.

"All honors must go to the ancient Greek and Roman historians who did not seem to know what racism was, certainly not as it developed in modern white civilization. They, in dealing with Africa, simply 'told it like it was.' Pliny, Herodotus, Diodorus, Erastosthenes, Plutarch, etc all, along with the Bible, all refute the interpretations of African history by modern Caucasians."[199]

The truth is that Egyptians and Babylonians started ancient civilizations. This was borrowed by the Greeks and handed down to the Romans who in turn revived it in Africa and transferred it to Europeans. This might be what Dr. Clarke was saying when he wrote, "The Africans have also preserved the intellectual masters of Europe, Plato, Aristotle and Socrates, as well as some of the basics of Christianity."[200] Robert Hood adds his voice: "Adolf von Harnack noted that the person who played a major role as a conduit for funneling the church's hitherto variform Greek theology into the uniformed tidiness of Roman culture was the Latinized African lawyer Tertullian (160-225)."[201] So, I say in conclusion, I respect the black Egyptians who built the foundation for the earliest civilization on which our modern civilization with all its conveniences is based!

Richard Poe, in *Black Spark White Fi re writes*, "We hear, for instance, how Herodotus, writing in the fifth century B.C., attributed to Egypt the invention of astronomy, religion, medicine, art geometry, and the making of solemn processions."[202] Let's give the descendants of Ham some respect and honor where honor is overdue as we enjoy the conveniences of our modern civilization. These conveniences are based on African achievements! I therefore, celebrate the roots which bore the fruits of our Modern advancement.

---

[199] Chancellor Williams, *Destruction of Black Civilization* (Chicago: Third World Press, 1956), 88.

[200] John Henrik Clarke, *Christopher Columbus and the African Holocaust* (Brooklyn New York: A & B Publishers Group, 1993), 14.

[201] Robert Earl Hood,. *Must God Remain Greek?: Afro Cultures and God-talk* (Minneapolis: Fortress Press, 1990), 5.

[202] Richard Poe, *Black Spark White Fire: Did African Explorers Civilize Ancient Europe?* (Lava Ridge Court, Roseville: Prima Publishing, 1999), ix.

APPENDIX

"SANKOFA" AFRICAN HERITAGE

Only When Lions Have Historians Will Hunters Cease Being Heroes! (African proverbs)

Sankofa: Going Back to Go Forward!

Akan people referring to Sankofa say, "It is not a taboo to return to take what you have left behind." There are some things we have left behind in our journey, without which we cannot go forward. We can't take someone's words for it. The time has come to go back to take what we have left behind in order to really go forward. It is a critical time in our journey. It is like saying that those who forget their past are more likely to repeat their foul-ups over and over. Therefore, Sankofa your Heritage:

To African Children, I say "Sankofa"!

"Sankofa" Symbol of Wisdom[203]

African Wisdom in Proverbs!

[Here Is an Exercise You May Find Interesting]
Assignment: Match these 2nd sets of Proverbs with Biblical Proverbs and Share Your Findings and Explanations'!

1. A child whose hand is clean may eat with the elders.
2. A fool looks for his keys where he has not lost it.

---

[203] http://www.marshall.edu/edu/akanart

3. A man does not wander far from where his corn is roasting.
4. A master drummer must have seven eyes.
5. A tiger does not have to proclaim his own Tigeritude.
6. Ashes fly back into the face of him who throws them.
7. By the time the fool has learned the game the players have gone home.
8. Do not call to a dog with a whip in your hand.
9. Do not look where you fell, but where you slipped.
10. Don't set sail on someone else's star.
11. Every time an old man dies it is as if a library has burnt down.
12. Fire and gunpowder do not sleep together.
13. He who rides the horse of greed at a gallop will pull it up at the door of shame.
14. If nothing touches the palm-branches they will not rattle.
15. If you run after two birds you end up catching none.
16. If your tongue turns into a knife, it cuts your own mouth.
17. It is the fool's sheep that break loose twice.
18. It's not what you are called, but what you answer to.
19. Looking at a king's mouth one would never think he sucked his mother's breast.
20. One goat cannot carry another goat's tail.
21. Peace is costly but it is worth the price.
22. Smooth seas do not make skillful sailors.
23. The day the monkey is destined to die, all the trees get slippery.
24. The hunter does not rub himself in oil and lie by the fire to sleep.
25. Great lion does not turn around when a little dog barks.
26. The moon moves slowly, but it crosses the town.
27. Tomorrow belongs to the people who prepare for it today.
28. Two small antelopes can beat up a big one.
29. Until Lions have their own historians, tales of the hunt will always glorify the hunter.
30. When the cock is drunk, he forgets about the hawk.
31. When you follow in the path of your father, you learn to walk like him.
32. When your neighbor's horse falls into a pit, you should not rejoice at it, for your own child may fall into it too.
33. Whoever pays respect to the great paves way for his own greatness.
34. Wood already touched by fire is not hard to set alight.
35. Words are spoken in their shells; it is the wise man's duty to find the kernel.
36. You can tell a ripe corn by its look.
37. You do not laugh at your neighbor when you see his beard on fire. Get water by yours.
38. You don't light a fire if you are supposed to be in hiding.

BIBLIOGRAPHY

Abraham, W. E. *The Mind of Africa.* Chicago: University of Chicago Press, 1962.

Achtemeier, Elizabeth. *Preaching Hard Texts of the Old Testament.* Peabody, Massachusetts: Hendrickson Publishers, 1998.

Address to the Territorial Legislature, 16 January, 1852, recorded in Wilford Woodruff s Journal, 1852.

Adelle, Banks, M. Religion News Service, 2009 (Review and Herald) 2009.

Adubofour, Nana Otamkuro. *Asante: The Making of a Nation.* Buokrom, Ghana: City Press Ltd., 2000.

Adult Sabbath School Bible Study Guide, Oct., Nov., Dec., 2003 Teachers Edition (Pacific Press 2003), 154.

Afre, S. A., *Ashanti Region of Ghana: an annotated bibliography, from earliest times to   1973.* Boston: G. K. Hall, 1975.

Aggrey, J.E.K. *Ebobo Bra Den 1.* "Bureau of Ghana Languages" Accra, Ghana: Ghana Publishing Corporation, 1992.

Anyike, C. James. *Historical Christianity African Centered.* Nashville, Tennessee: Winston-Derk Publishers Group, Inc., 1994.

Appiah-Kubi, Kofi. *Man cures, God heals: Religion and medical practice among the Akans of Ghana.* Totowa, N.J.: Allanheld, Osmun, 1981.

Asante, Emmanuel. *Toward an African Christian theology of the Kingdom of God: The kingship of Onyame.* Lewiston, N.Y.: Mellen University Press, 1995.

Barker, Kenneth, Ed. *The New International Study Bible.* Grand Rapids, Michigan: Zondervan Bible Publishers, 1985.

Bernal, Martin. *Black Athena: The Afroasiatic Roots of Classical Civilization.* New Brunswick, New Jersey: Rutgers University Press, 1999.

Bleeker, Sonia. *The Ashanti of Ghana.* New York: Morrow, 1966.

Boyd, Paul C. *The African Origin of Christianity, Volume 1* London: Karia Press, 1991.

Braffi, E. K. *The Akan Clans: Totemism and 'Nton'*. Kumasi, Ghana: University Press, 1992.

Brookes, Edgar Harry. *The city of God and the city of man in Africa*. Lexington: University of Kentucky Press, 1964.

Budge, Sir Wallis. Egyptian Religion (Bell: New York 1959), 17. Sir Wallis Budge, Egyptian Religion (Bell: New York 1959)

Busia, J. A. *The Ashanti also in African Worlds: Studies in the Cosmological Ideas and Social V alues of Af rican Pe oples*. Oxford: Oxford University Press, 1954.

Carlston, Kenneth S. *Social Theory and African Tribal Organization*. Chicago: University of Illinois Press, 1968.

Carruthers, Jacob. *Mdw Ntr: Divine Speech*. Karnak House, 1995.

Carruthers, Jacob. *Intellectual Warfare*. Chicago: Third World Press, 1996.

Christaller, J. G. *A Collection of 3,600 Tshi Proverbs*. Basel: Evangelical Missionary Society, 1933.

Christaller, J. G. *Dictionary of the Asante and F ante Language called Tshi (Chwee, Twi) Classics*, 1912.

Clarke, John Henrik. *African People in world History*. Baltimore, Maryland: Black Classic Press, 1993.

Clarke, John Henrik. *Christopher Columbus and the African Holocaust*. Brooklyn New York: A & B Publishers Group, 1993.

Compton's Interactive Bible NIV., (SoftKey Multimedia Inc. 1996).

Conrad, R. E. *In the hands of strangers: Readings on foreign and domestic slave trading and t he cri sis of t he Uni on*. University Park, Pennsylvania State University Press, 2001.

Crayner, J.B. *Yeehyiahyia oo!* "Bureau of Ghana Languages" Accra, Ghana: Walsco Printing Works, 1998.

Danquah, Joseph Boakye. *The Akan doctrine of God: A fragment of Gold Coast ethics and religion*. London: Cass, 1968.

Danquah, Joseph Boakye. Gold Coast: Akan Laws and Customs and the Akin Abuakwa Constitution. London: George Routledge & Sons, Ltd., 1928.

202

Danquah, Joseph Buakye. *The Akan Doctrine of God.* London: Frank Cass and Co. Ltd., 1968.

Darkwah, Nana Banchie. *The Africans Who Wrote The Bible.* White Plains, MD: Aduana Publishing, 2002.

Davy, Yvonne. *Going with God; on missions of mercy in Central Africa.* Washington: Review and Herald Publishing Association, 1959.

Decretals of the Lord Pope Gregory IX, (Decretales Domini Gregorii Papae IX).

Diop, Cheikh Anta. *Civilization or Barbarism: An Authentic Anthropology.* Brooklyn, New York: Lawrence Hill Books, 1991.

Diop, Cheikh Anta. *Precolonial Black Africa.* Chicago: Lawrence Hill Books, 1987.

Diop, Cheikh Anta. *The African Origin of Civilization Myth or Reality.* Chicago: Lawrence Hill Books, 1974.

Dolphyne, Florence Abena. *A Comprehensive Course in Twi (Asante) for the Non-Twi learner.* Accra: Ghana University Press, 1996.

Doukhan, B. Jacques. *Secrets of Daniel.* Hagerstown, MD: Review And Herald Publishing Association, 2000.

Drake, Melody & Richard. *God's Holidays.* 2003.

DuBois, W. E. B. *Black Reconstruction.* New York: Meridian Books,1964.

Dzobo, N. K. *Modes of Traditional Moral Education among Anfoega-Ewes.* Cape Coast, University Press, 1971.

Estrin, Jack. *World History Made Simple.* Garden City, New York: Doubleday & Company, Inc, 1968.

Evans, Williams. *How to Prepare Sermons.* Chicago: Moody Press, 1964.

Farstad, L. Arthur. *The New Open Bible Study Edition.* Nashville: Thomas Nelson Publishers 1990.

Felder, Cain Hope, Original African Heritage Study Bible, (Iowa Falls, Iowa: World Bible Publishing, 1998), 665.

Fillon, Mike. *"The Real Face of Jesus: Advances in Forensic Science reveal the most famous face in History."* Popular Mechanics, 2002.

Finley, Mark, Testimony, Northeastern Conference Commenting, 1999.

Freeman, Dr. http://www.freemaninstitute.com.

Fly, James. *Ghana Ashantis.* Afritell, 1988.

Fosu, Kwaku Amoako-Attah. *Festivals in Ghana.* Kumasi, Ghana: Amok
    Publications, 2001.

Freeman, Joel A. Ph.D. &Don B. Griffin. *Return to Glory: The Powerful Stirring of
    the Black Man.* Woodbury, NJ: Renaissance Productions, 1997.

Funk, and Wagnells. *Encyclopedia Americana. Vol. 1.* New York: Funk and
    Wagnells, 1976.

G., Ronald and Emile J. Lewis, Black Survival in Crisis: The Plight of Afrikans in the
    Globalization of Western (European) Culture, (Mpambo Multiversity
    Conference on Jinja, Uganda), June 8 - 11, 2004/
    http://www.blackherbals.com/black_survival_in_crisis.htm.

Gates, Henry Louis. *Loose Cannons: Notes on the Culture Wars.* New York: Oxford.

Godbey, Allen. The Lost Tribes a Myth (Durham, N. C.: Duke University Press,
    1930), 206. Also Windsor, 133.

Goodwin, Mary Ellen. *A Pilgrim to the Musama Disco Christo Church: An
    Independent African Christian Church. Ghana.*

Gowan, Donald E. Genesis 1-11: Eden to Babel, (Wm. B. Eerdmans), 110-15.

Green, Richard L, ed. A Salute to Historic African Kings and Queens (Chicago,
    Illinois: Empak Publishing Company, 1996), 8.

Green, Richard L. *A Salute to Historic African Kings and Queens.* Chicago, Illinois:
    EmpakPublishing Company, 1996.

Griffin, Freeman, Joel A. Ph.D., and Don B. Return to Glory: The Powerful Stirring
    of the Black Man (Woodbury, NJ: Renaissance Productions, 1997), 20.

Gyekye, Kwame. *An Essay on African Philosophical Thought: The Akan Conceptual
Sche   me.* New York: Cambridge University Press, 1987.

Haangala, Victor H., ed. David Marshall. *In the hand of God: The story of divine
    intervention in th e life o f an African family.* Grantham: Stanborough Press,
    2001.

Haddad, Yvonne Yazbeck and Wadi Zaidan Haddad. *Christian-Muslim encounters.*
    Gainesville: University Press of Florida, 1995.

Haddon, Alfred C. *Races of Man and their Distribution,* New York, 1925.

Hess, Robert L. *Ethiopia and Modernization of Autocracy.* London: Comwell University Press, 1976.

Hood, Robert Robert Earl. *Must God remain Greek?: Afro Cultures and God-talk.* Minneapolis: Fortress Press, 1990.

http://www.wikipedia.org/wiki/History_of_Africa (14 Nov 2004).

http://en.wikipedia.org/wiki/Blacks_and_the_Latter_Day_Saint_movement.

http://en.wikipedia.org/wiki/Pentecostalism#History.

http://www.extension.umn.edu/units/diversity/mlk/mlk.html.

http://www.ghanaweb.com/GhanaHomePage/history, Posted 994-2005.

http://www.marshall.edu/edu/akanart

http://www.metmuseum.org/toah/hd/ghan/hd_ghan.htm (Posted 2000 -2005.

http://www.seanet.com/~raines/discrimination.html.

http://www.worldbook.com/wc/features/aajourney/html/aa_1_songhai.shtml (Posted 2004/Quoted 4/24/2005).

http://www.xmission.com/~country/reason/black_1.htm.

Hume, David. Essays: *Mora, Political and Literary.* New York: Indianapolis Liberty Classics, 1912.

Hughes, Langston. The Collected Poems (Alfred A. Knopf, Inc.).

James, George G. M. *Stolen Legacy.* Chicago, Illinois: African American Images, 2002.

Joel A. Freeman Ph.D., and B. Griffin, Don. Return to Glory: The Powerful Stirring of the Black Man (Woodbury, NJ: Renaissance Productions, 1997)

Jehu-Appiah, M.M. *The Musama Book of Rituals.* Accra, Ghana: Fredico Printing Press, 1981.

John Henrik Clarke, Christopher Columbus and the African Holocaust (Brooklyn New York: A & B Publishers Group, 1993)

Johnson,   James   Weldon.   (1871-1938)
ttp://en.wikipedia.org/wiki/Lift_Every_Voice_and_Sing

Journal of Discourses, Vol. 7, 290-91.

Kilgo, J. *Colors of Africa.* Athens: University of Georgia Press, 2003.

Knight, Kevin, *The Catholic Encyclopedia,* Volume XI 1911, Robert Appleton
    Company Online Edition, 2002.

Kuada, John & Yao Chachah. Ghana: *Understanding the People and their Culture.*
    Accra, Ghana: Woeli Publishing Services, 1999.

Laine, Daniel. *African Kings.* Bereley, Toronto: Ten Speed Press, 1988.

    Language G uide (Fante Ver sion). Accra: Bureau of Ghana Languages,
    1986.
Latter-day Saints, Blacks and The Church of Jesus Christ of Latter-day Saints.

Lewis, Bernard. *The Middle East: A Brief History of the Last 2,000 Years.* New
    York: Simon & Schuster, 1997.

Lichtblau, George E. Jewish Roots in Africa http://www.ubalt.edu/
    kulanu/africa.html.

Loftus, Ernest. *A visual History of Africa.* London: Evans Brothers Limited, 1976.
    Logos Bible Dictionary (Digital Edition).
Luther King Jr., Martin.
    http://www.americanrhetoric.com/speeches/mlkihaveadream.htm

Mbiti, John S., *Concepts of God in Africa.* London: S.P.C.K., 1970.

Maranatha Christian News Service, @ http://www. Charismanews.com (January 5,
    2003).

Martin, Dana. The American Baptist Convention and the Civil Rights Movement:
    Rhetoric and Response, 1999

McCarthy, Virginia Quinn, Ed, *The New Book of Knowledge*, Grolier
    Publishing Company, 2003.

McCray, Walter Arthur Rev. *The black Presence in the Bible: Discovering The Black
    and Africa n identity o f Biblical persons a nd na tions.* Chicago, Illinois:
    Black Light Fellowship, 1991.

McDermott, Gerald. *Anansi the spider; a tale from the Ashanti.* New York, Holt:
    Rinehart and Winston, 1972.

McVeigh, Malcolm J., *God in Africa: Conceptions of God in African traditional religion and Christianity*. Cape Cod, Mass: C. Stark, 1974.

Mendelsohn, Jack. *God, Allah, and Ju Ju; Religion in Africa today*. New York: Nelson, 1962.

Mensa, Owusu K. *Onyamee Kwamee: The Akan God of Saturday*. Accra Ghana: The Advent Press,1990.

Muhammad, Akbar. (Slaves and Slavery in Muslim Africa, vol. I)

Musgrove, Margaret. *Ashanti to Zulu: African traditions*. New York: Dial Press, 1976.

Nelson. *God bless Africa*. Hoboken, NJ, Music Club, 2000.

NIV Study Bible, (Margin)
NIV Zondavan Bible Commenting on Genesis (Chapter 10), 22 margin

Nkansa-Kyerematen, K. *The Akans of Ghana their History & Culture*. Accra: Sebewie Publishers, 1996.

Nkansa-Kyeremateng K. *Akan Heritage*. Accra: Sebewie Publishers, 1999.

Nolan, Albert, *God in South Africa: The challenge of the gospel*. Grand Rapids, MI.: W.B. Eerdmans, 1988.

Nyimdzee Kw an. Jurong, Singapore: FEP International Private Limited 1977.

Obeng, Pashington. *Asante Catholicism: Religious and cultural reproduction among the Akan of Ghana*. Leiden, New York: E.J. Brill, 1996.

O'Connor, Daniel. *Three centuries of mission: The United Society for the Propagation of the Gospel, 1701-2000*. London; New York: Continuum, 2000.

Osei, O. Kwame. *A Discourse on Akan Perpetual Calendar for Religious Ceremonies and Festivals (1700-2200 A.D.)*. Accra, Ghana: Domak Press Ltd, 1997.

Osei, O. Kwame. *The Ancient Egyptians Are Here*. Kumasi, Ghana: Vytall Printing, 2001.

Otoo, S. K. *Prama*. Accra: Presbyterian Press, 1981.

Owens, Moore, Dr. T. The Science of Melanin: Dispelling the Myths, (Beckham

207

House Publisher, 1995).

Pearce, Justin. (BBC News website, Johannesburg) (700, 000 manuscripts found in Timbuktu and its surroundings to date, a living testimony of a highly advance civilization on the Continent of Africa. Mali's written treasures.url, Alida Jay Boye/Undesco/afrol News and News $ Notes, January 1, 2007.

Poe, Richard. Black Spark White Fire: *Did African Explorers Civilize Ancient Eur ope?* Lava Ridge Court, Roseville: Prima Publishing, 1999.

Price, Christine, *Talking drums of Africa.* New York: Scribner, 1973.

Priest, Robert J, L. Nieves, Alvaro ed., This Side of Heaven: Race, Ethnicity, and Christian Faith. (Oxford University Press, 2007)

Raboteau, Albert J. *Slave Religion: The "Invisible Institution"* in the Antebellum South. New York: Oxford University Press, 1980.

Rattray, R. S. *Ashanti Proverbs: The Primitive Ethics of a Savage People.* Oxford, 1969.

Rattray, R. S. *Ashanti.* Oxford University Press, 1956.

Rattray, R. S. *Religion and Art in Ashanti.* Oxford: University Press, 1958.

Rattray, Robert Sutherland. *Ashanti law and constitution.* New York: Negro Universities Press, 1969.

Real Face of Jesus, Popular Mechanics, December 2002.

Robinson Jr., C.A., and Williams, S.G. *The Ancient History.* New York, 1981.

Rodney, Walter. *How Europe Underdeveloped Africa.* Washington, DC: Howard University Press, 1982.

Rogers, J.A. *World's Great Men of Color,* Vol. 1. New York: A Simon & Schuster, 1996.

Royalty in Ghana, A Very Brief History of Ghana (Cinderella 2002) http://www.royalty.nu/Africa/Ghana.html,

Salmon, Jacqueline L. "Southern Baptists Diversifying to Survive: Minority Outreach seen as Keys to Crisis (Washington Post Feb. 16, 2008).

Sawyerr, Harry. *God, ancestor or creator? aspects of traditional belief in Ghana, Nigeria & Sierra Leone.* Harlow: Longmans, 1970.

208

Sertima, Ivan Van. *African Presence in Ancient America: They Came Before
Co   lumbus*. New York: Random House, 1976.

Shaw, Mark. *The kingdom of God in Africa: A short history of African Christianity.*
Grand Rapids, MI.: Baker Books, 1996.

Smith, Edwin William, *The golden stool: Some aspects of the conflict of cultures in
Africa*. London: Holborn publishing house, 1927.

Smith, William. Bible Dictionary

Smith, Edwin William. *African ideas of God: A symposium*. London: Edinburgh
House Press, 1950.

Snowden, Frank M. Jr. *Blacks in Antiquity: Ethiopians in the Greco-Roman
Experience.* Cambridge, Massachusetts: The Belknap Press of Harvard
University Press, 1970.

Stuyvesant, Carolyn. *Storytime in Africa.* Kensington, MD: Josephine Mayo, 1995.

Talmud Bavli, Sanhedrin 108.

The Advent Hymnal (Washington, DC: Review and Herald Publishing Association,
1985) Hymn

The Book of Mormons, II Nephi, Chap. 5, verses 21-23.

The Holy Bible : King James Version. Electronic ed. Bellingham WA :
Logos Research Systems, Inc., 1995, S. Jn 14:16

Talbert, David A. *Contemporary Ethiopia.* New York: Hallmark Press, 1952.

Tutu, Desmond. *The rainbow people of God: The making of a peaceful revolution.*
New York: Doubleday, 1994.

Webster's Ninth New Collegiate Dictionary (Springfield Massachusetts, 1989),
"Black."

Westermann, *Africa and Christianity.* Oxford University Press, 1937.

White, E.G. *The Great Controversy.* California: Pacific Press, 1950.
Testimonies for the Church. 9 vols. 1855-1909. Mountain View, CA: Pacific
Press Publishing Association, 1948. [1T, 2T, etc.]

White, Jon Ewbank Manchip. *The land God made in anger: Reflections on a journey
through South West Africa.* Chicago: Rand McNally, 1969.

209

White, Ellen Education. (Mountain View, CA: Pacific Press Publishing Association, 1952), 254

White, Ellen G. Testimonies for the Church vol.1 (Mountain View, CA: Pacific Press Publishing Association, 1948)

White, Ellen The Great Controversy Between Christ and Satan 1911 (Mountain View, CA: Pacific Press Publishing Association, 1911)

White, Ellen. Instruction for Men in Positions of Responsibility, Manuscript Releases Volume 14, 1903)

White, Ellen. Letter 30, 1895.

White, Ellen. Spirit of Prophecy. 3 vol. 1878.

White, Ellen. Spiritual Gift 3 vol. 1864 (Battle Creek, MI: Seventh-day Adventist Publishing Association, 1945), 33. White, Ellen. The Spirit of Prophecy. 3 vol. 1878,

Williams, Joseph John. S.J. *Hebrewisms of West Africa, from Nile to Niger with the Jews.* New York: Biblo and Tannen, 1967.

Williams, Chancellor. *Destruction of Black Civilization.* Chicago: Third World Press, 1956.

Williams, Chancellor. *The Rebirth of African Civilization.* Chicago: Third World Press, 1987.

Willis, W. Bruce. *The Adinkra dictionary: A Visual Primer on The Language of Adinkra.* Washington, DC: The Pyramid Complex, 1998.

Wilks, I., J. O. Hunwick, et al. *The cloth of many colored silks: Papers on history and society, Gh anaian and I slamic in honor o f I vor Wilks.* Evanston: Northwestern University Press, 1997.

Windsor, Rudolph R. *From Babylon to Timbuktu: A History of Ancient Black Races Including the Black Hebrews.* Chicago Illinois: Windsor's Golden Series, 1988.

Woodson, Carter G. *The Mis-Education of the Negro.* Trenton, NJ: Africa World Press, 1998.

Zion's Watch Tower, February 15, 1904: 52-53.

INDEX

TO MAKE AN APPOINTMENT OR ORDER

Contact: <u>sedy7@hotmail.com</u>, call (516) 486-6385
Send (Money Order) to Sednak Yankson
Call for Address or visit: <u>http://www.africasroots.com</u>

I have also developed presentations dealing with these various subjects. My purpose is to help our people understand the truth about our religious heritage and to dispel the old myth of African paganism, the reasons cited for the Justification of slavery. For if "they mess with your roots they will surely mess with your fruits." My interest is to share the whole truth and nothing but the truths, with the belief that all truth is God's truth and all lies come from the Devil. But they shall know the truth and it is only the truth that shall set people free!

Sankofa Heritage: Books, Videos, DVDs, CDs & Tapes:

<u>Rooted In God & Grounded In Africa/ African Heritage</u> (DVD, VHS, CD)

"The Knowledge Of The True God Embedded In The Indigenous African Culture"
Tracing Africa Biblically or Africa's Biblical Roots
Africa's Edenic Concepts or Biblical Concepts in Africa
Sanctuary – Temple Structure, Sacrificial System & Oral Traditional
Theology. Africa-Yahweh Connection - Did God Know Africa?
Africans and Hebrew Connection -- Did Africa Know God?

<u>Africans! Where Did We Come From? "From Eden To Eden"</u> (DVD, VHS)

Where Was Eden? Black People Looking For Their Lost Glory
From Noah through Africa to America -- From Mesopotamia to Mt. Zion
"I have seen Rivers" - *Langston Hughes*

<u>Unshackled! "Breaking Loose From the Last Chains of Slavery"</u> (DVD & CD)

Debunks Medieval Myth of African Paganism
Challenges European Justification for Slavery
Establishes the Real Truth about Our African Identity -- (Only The Truth Shall Set Us Free!)

214